25.

D1289686

Those Damned Black Hats!

The Iron Brigade in the Gettysburg Campaign

Lance J. Herdegen

To Si, [signed inscription: With thanks for your help on the book] —Lance J. Herdegen

SB

Savas Beatie

New York and California

Cataloging-in-Publication Data is available from the Library of Congress.

ISBN 978-1-932714-48-7

05 04 03 02 01   5 4 3 2 1
First edition, first printing

SB

Published by
Savas Beatie LLC
521 Fifth Avenue, Suite 3400
New York, NY 10175
Phone: 610-853-9131

Editorial Offices:

Savas Beatie LLC
P.O. Box 4527
El Dorado Hills, CA 95762
Phone: 916-941-6896
(E-mail) editorial@savasbeatie.com

Savas Beatie titles are available at special discounts for bulk purchases in the United States by corporations, institutions, and other organizations. For more details, please contact Special Sales, P.O. Box 4527, El Dorado Hills, CA 95762, or you may e-mail us at sales@savasbeatie.com, or visit our website at www.savasbeatie.com for additional information.

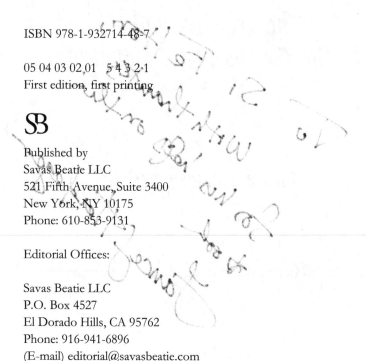

For Shirley Ann,
Bonnie, Lisa, Jill, Jennifer and Nicole

"There are them damned black hatted fellows again.
Taint no militia it's the Army of the Potomac!"

— James J. Archer's Confederates on McPherson Ridge, July 1, 1863

"O, I pitched in with them Wisconsin fellers. They fit
terribly — the Rebs couldn't make
any thing of them fellers."

—Citizen John Burns of Gettysburg

"Where has the firmness of the Iron Brigade
at Gettysburg been surpassed in history?"

— Rufus Dawes, 6th Wisconsin Infantry

Contents

Foreword   viii

Introduction and Acknowledgments   ix

Chapter 1: A Black Hat Brigade   1

Chapter 2: I Cannot Stand it to Fight   13

Chapter 3: He has Gone to Stonewall's Funeral   17

Chapter 4: Greenhorn Patriots   21

Chapter 5: To be Shot Like Sheep in a Huddle   29

Chapter 6: The Iron Brigade of the West   39

Chapter 7: Bad News About the Rebs   43

Chapter 8: A New Regiment and a Veteran Battery   51

Chapter 9: The Black Hats   57

Chapter 10: A Young Lieutenant and a Fair Maid   67

Chapter 11: King's Pet Babies   73

Chapter 12: I Will Fight Them Inch by Inch   81

Chapter 13: It's Those Damned Black Hats!   87

Chapter 14: One Sword is All I Need on This Line   101

Chapter 15: Fire by File! Fire by File!   109

Contents (continued)

Chapter 16: What Became of That Sword I Gave You?   121

Chapter 17: I Can Stand it No Longer   129

Chapter 18: Yelling Like Demons   135

Chapter 19: I Grew About a Foot and a Half   143

Chapter 20: In a Tight Place   147

Chapter 21: We Left Behind the Rebel Flag,
That Dearly Bought the Prize   155

Chapter 22: Are you Satisfied With the Twenty-fourth?   161

Chapter 23: Our Best and Bravest   167

Chapter 24: The Finger of God Paralyzed his Brain   175

Chapter 25: This Battle Will go by the Name of Gettysburg   179

Chapter 26: A Shot From a Smoothbore Gun   187

Chapter 27: The Old Army had Come to Itself Again   195

Chapter 28: They Have Played Their Hand Long Enough   201

Chapter 29: I Guess He is All Right on the Fight Question   213

Chapter 30: No Man Can Fight Surrounded by Cowards   221

Chapter 31: The Trust Imposed Upon Them   231

Contents (continued)

Chapter 32: The Chance of a Lifetime   237

Chapter 33: Glorious Remembrance   243

Epilogue: An Unknown. July 1, 1997   258

Appendices   260

Notes   273

Bibliography   302

Index   309

Maps

1. Iron Brigade Route to Gettysburg   45
2. The Iron Brigade Reaches the Field   91
3. Cutler's Brigade Against Davis' Brigade   93
4. Archer's Brigade vs. The Iron Brigade   95
5. The 6th Wisconsin Charge on the Railroad Cut   111
6. Confederate Attack on McPherson Ridge   136
7. The Last Stand on Seminary Ridge   151
8. The Culp's Hill Line   170
9. The 6th Wisconsin and 14th Brooklyn Defend Culp's Hill   184
10. The Pursuit of Lee's Army   205

Photos and Illustrations

Photos and illustrations have been placed throughout the book for the convenience of our readers.

Foreword

*A*lan Nolan's 1961 classic *The Iron Brigade* plowed the fertile ground of this remarkable Western organization, opening the door for others to step through. Lance Herdegen answered the call admirably. Numerous accounts of the battle of Gettysburg have been written, but seldom if ever has one described in such detail the personal side of the common soldier.

Those Damned Black Hats! The Iron Brigade in the Gettysburg Campaign describes the brigade's monumental days at Gettysburg in a unique way. Lance takes the reader back in time to the unassuming beginnings of many of the men who fought so courageously in this battle, marching each up to his moment of fate. He masterfully blends battles and social history in a way few others have even attempted. He introduces these soldiers as the real men they were, exploring their lives, their families, and on occasion even their loves—all as a prelude to what nearly all of them believed were the defining hours of their lives.

Now, finally, nearly five decades after Mr. Nolan introduced the reading public to the Iron Brigade of the West, we are able to identify with these men in a way that was previously impossible. The fact that the majority of these Iron Brigade men were simply hardworking individuals called upon to defend their country and protect our rights as citizens will forever be remembered and appreciated because of Lance's efforts to memorialize their deeds.

Therefore, it is with tremendous pride and honor that on behalf of my ancestors and others who fought so bravely at Gettysburg and other fields, that I fully endorse this incredible and poignant book.

Steve Victor

July 2008

Great-Great-Great Grandson of Colonel William Wallace Robinson

Great-Great Grandson of Colonel Hollon Richardson

7th Wisconsin Volunteer Infantry

Introduction

The men of the Iron Brigade of the West, famous for their black felt hats and Western origins, marched confidently to Gettysburg in 1863. The key role they played in the Union victory of July 1-3 earned them a distinguished place in American military history. Their legacy came at a high price. The bloody fighting, especially on the morning of July 1, nearly destroyed the 2nd, 6th, 7th Wisconsin, 19th Indiana, and 24th Michigan. The regiments fought on in 1864 and 1865, but were never again a major force on any battlefield.

The Iron Brigade is probably more celebrated today than it was a century and a half ago. The fighting organization was largely overlooked in public acclaim in the years immediately after the Civil War, an unfortunate circumstance due more to distance than deliberate slight. The Wisconsin, Indiana, and Michigan men were far removed from the major veteran reunions and old soldier campfires in Eastern cities. Attention centered on such fighting organizations as the Irish Brigade, Jersey Brigade, Vermont Brigade, and New York's Excelsior Brigade. It was not until 1890 that Rufus Dawes published his *Service with the Sixth Wisconsin Volunteers*. O. B. Curtis added his history of the Twenty-fourth Michigan the following year, and veterans Philip Cheek and Mair Pointon told their story of Company A of the 6th Wisconsin in 1909. Other lesser works by the Iron Brigade veterans received little attention outside of Wisconsin, Indiana, and Michigan.

Bruce Catton first brought the Black Hats to popular attention just before the Civil War centennial when he wrote extensively about the Iron Brigade in his popular *Mr. Lincoln's Army* and *Glory Road*. The brigade's compelling story and rich historical record made it a popular subject for modern writers. In 1961, Alan T. Nolan's powerful and authoritative *The Iron Brigade* expanded the outfit's reputation and solidified its place in the eyes of the public. Almost all of the accounts of Gettysburg in the 150 years since the battle (and even one recent movie) single out the Iron Brigade and called attention to the fabled black hats worn by its soldiers. As the years slid past other books appeared offering detailed and rather narrow accounts of the fighting, including my own (with William J.K. Beaudot) entitled *In the Bloody Railroad Cut at Gettysburg* (1990).

I never really gave much thought of going back to the Pennsylvania fighting since finishing that book two decades ago on the 6th Wisconsin's famous charge on the unfinished railroad cut on July 1, 1863. Much like the veterans who fought there, however, Gettysburg continued to haunt me. Every week and every month and every year, new information on the Iron Brigade at Gettysburg surfaced. Copies of letters, faded newspaper clippings, diaries, journals, and carefully preserved old photographs of the soldiers in big hats were sent to me by kinsmen and distant relatives of the men who fought there. They came not only from my native Wisconsin, but Michigan, Indiana, and other more distant states. The written accounts of Sergeant James P. Sullivan of the 6th Wisconsin and the journals of Private William Ray of the 7th Wisconsin made their way into print. Elsewhere, other authors published additional Iron Brigade material.

In this flurry of publication, however, a book-length treatment of the compelling story of the Iron Brigade of the West during the Gettysburg Campaign was somehow overlooked. Although many who read Civil War literature believed the story of the Black Hats in Pennsylvania had been covered, in fact only a very small slice of their remarkable service had been studied. Much of their story remained untold. Charles Foster, a good friend and Civil War scholar in his own right, was aware of the new material I had been gathering over the years. He admonished me to go forward: "If you don't write of the Iron Brigade at Gettysburg, so many of the men who fought there will be forgotten." He was right, of course.

And it was those men of the 2nd, 6th, 7th Wisconsin, 19th Indiana, and 24th Michigan who fought one of the most significant military actions in American history. It was there, on those Pennsylvania fields, that the Confederates called them "those damned Black Hats." It was there these Westerners knocked back the initial Confederate thrusts, held the defensive positions west of town against tremendous odds, and helped win the battle that perhaps preserved the Union. And it was there the fabled Iron Brigade of the West was wrecked beyond recognition. "Where has the firmness of the Iron Brigade at Gettysburg been surpassed in history?" asked Rufus Dawes of the 6th Wisconsin.

Here, then, is the first book-length account of the Iron Brigade in the Gettysburg Campaign. Some of the Iron Brigade's role at Gettysburg has been detailed extensively (primarily that concerning the 6th Wisconsin at the railroad cut, as noted above). This present volume includes a substantial amount of recently uncovered material gleaned from letters, diaries, journals, and newspapers. These accounts offer, for the first time, a richer and more complete portrait of the attack and defense of McPherson's Ridge, the final stand at Seminary Ridge, the occupation of Culp's Hill, the final pursuit of the Confederate Army, and the reconciliation of the 50th Anniversary Reunion.

Gettysburg appeared even closer to me when I spent most of a day with James F. Sullivan, the *son* of Sergeant James P. "Mickey" Sullivan of the 6th Wisconsin. Still spry and bright near the age of 100, J. F. (who has since passed away) was as much the poet/soldier as his father, who died in 1906 when he was five. A veteran of General Billy Mitchell's 2nd Bomb Group before World War II, J. F. had not seen his dad's Civil War writings and knew next to nothing about him. He got rather misty during his first reading of "Mickey's" experiences at Gettysburg. "Ah, Dad, I'm proud of you," he announced before looking up to catch my eye. "We did not have much time to get acquainted."

This volume is what the Black Hats did at Gettysburg, and how they remembered it.

Lance J. Herdegen
Town of Spring Prairie
Walworth County, Wisconsin

Acknowledgments

No book is ever written alone and many hands stir the kettle. The following are the kind my grandfather who worked the deep pineys as a boy lumberjack in the early 1900s would praise as good folks "to ride the river with." In no special order, and to others I might have overlooked, I offer thanks to: Si Felton, Tom Finley, Steve Victor, Kent Gramm, Sharon Vipond, Alan Nolan, Steve Acker, Scott D. Hann, Kim J. Heltemes, Lance Myers, Brian Hogan, Alan Gaff, Sharon Murphy, John Wedeward, William Washburn, William J. K. Beaudot, Daniel Joyce, John Cox, Larry Lefler, Pat and Bob Sullivan, and Howard Michael Madaus.

And finally, to Bradley M. Gottfried for his maps, and to Theodore P. Savas and his great staff at Savas Beatie LLC for publishing my work.

Chapter 1

A Black Hat Brigade

It began with the arrival of the 2nd Wisconsin Infantry in Washington, D.C. The men were answering President Abraham Lincoln's first call for 75,000 volunteers to put down the Rebellion.

The train carrying the regiment reached the nation's capital at daybreak June 25, 1861. Proud and self-conscious in their new gray militia frock coats and tall caps, the Badgers found the city humming with war excitement. The Southern states were in a state of armed insurrection, Fort Sumter in South Carolina had fallen, and an enemy army was massing just a handful of miles outside the capital. A swarm of wagons, buggies, and horses moved along muddy Washington streets fouled by unspeakable filth. Plank sidewalks were shared by citizens and soldiers, dignitaries, and footpads. Hotels were overflowing, saloons did a steady business day and night, and tents and camps littered the countryside. And everywhere a variation of the same basic question was on everyone's lips: When and where would the major battle be fought that would decide the war?

The 1,000 Wisconsin men and officers made a good first impression. Above average height with what was called "a steady prairie manner," the new soldiers were the first three-year volunteers to reach Washington. Previously raised active militia regiments mustered for just 90 days of service. Growing concerns that it might take longer than three months to put down the rebellion prompted a change to three years or the length of the war. Faced with the longer term of service, the Wisconsin men signed the

Private Frederick Lythson
2nd Wisconsin Infantry

Frederick Lythson poses in Madison wearing the Wisconsin militia gray frock coat and tall cap of the type issued to the 2nd Wisconsin in the early days of the war. He was wounded at Gettysburg and transferred to the Veteran Reserve Corps in 1864.

new papers with light hearts and hardly a second thought, for the fighting, most believed, would surely be over within a few weeks.

The regiment was held in Woodward's Block before being moved to Seventh Street Park, where the men pitched their tents in a grove. The site was named "Camp Randall" in honor of the Wisconsin governor. "Around us on all sides," one soldier wrote home, "can be seen the camping grounds of 40,000 men, all ready to fight for the good cause." Camped nearby were newly arrived volunteers from Maine, New York, Rhode Island, Connecticut, and New Hampshire. During the next few days the Wisconsin men toured the city to gawk at the large stone buildings of the Federal government and look over the dignitaries of the day—including President Abraham Lincoln. The president, wrote one Wisconsin private, was "drest in black with a white vest and turned down collar. He was tall and rather slim." Another Badger found Lincoln "rather homely, but he wears a very pleasant face, I should say, an honest one, too." Secretary of State William Seward was "a great deal shorter than I supposed," wrote another Badger, while old General Winfield Scott of Mexican War fame—"the greatest military man in the whole world"—towered "high above all the other men around him. He is also large in proportion to his height. . . . He looked precisely like the portraits of him found in stores for sale."[1]

The commander of the new makeshift Federal army was Irvin McDowell, a well-liked Regular Army officer with a reputation for congeniality, but—like so many officers gathered around the capital—little field or command experience. The 2nd Wisconsin was brigaded with the 13th New York, 69th New York, and 79th New York under the command of a new brigadier from Ohio named William Tecumseh Sherman.

Pressured by the newspapers and Lincoln, McDowell gathered his force of greenhorn patriots and marched out in hot mid-July to Manassas Junction to confront the equally green Confederates under Gen. P. G. T. Beauregard. The general consensus was that if a full-scale battle was fought, it would decide the outcome of the war. The engagement that unfolded on July 21—a long, hard-fought, and wide-ranging affair—ended in a stunning Federal defeat that shook Northern confidence to its core. As the final hours of daylight ticked away, the National soldiers ran from the field in wild disarray, with the Wisconsin men fleeing in fear and confusion with the rest. The Badgers referred to the July 21 fight in their letters and journals as "Bull's Run." The Federals had discovered just how quickly a battle could go awry. The Confederates also learned a lesson—that a victory is nearly as debilitating as a defeat. Following up a battlefield success with an immediate, vigorous, and well-ordered pursuit is often a nearly impossible task. As a result, McDowell's army escaped. Back inside the Washington defenses, the army and the government shook off the defeat and began preparing for what would come next.[2]

The soldiers were soon given a bright, new young hero named George McClellan, a West Pointer promoted to army command following a smallish victory in the mountains of what would become West Virginia. The general, in his well-fashioned uniform and riding a fancy horse, found the city and government near panic. Within hours of his arrival, however, provost squads began sweeping off-duty soldiers back to their camps. Chaos was replaced with order, and confusion with discipline. Camps were policed and sentry posts established. Drill and training schedules were drafted. The sprawling city defensive works were expanded. The young energetic general seemed to be everywhere. To his new regiments and brigades he proffered a name that has a certain ring even today—the Army of the Potomac. The newspapers dubbed McClellan "the young Napoleon"; his soldiers simply called him "Little Mac."

When the 6th Wisconsin reached Washington on August 7, 1861, it found the city on an elevated war footing. The men marched to City Hall Park and then to Meridian Hill, where the Badgers laid out company streets along Rock Creek. Defensive positions were well-established around the city and there were soldiers camped in every direction of the compass. The new Badger regiment had just settled in when the 2nd Wisconsin came swinging up the hill a few days later with the confident stride of soldiers who had been in battle and were proud of it. The new volunteers of the 6th gathered in groups to watch the arriving column, taking in the field-worn uniforms and the smooth and easy Western step. "They had been through the first battle of Bull Run," wrote one 6th Wisconsin men with a touch of envy and awe. "They had fought for their country. We looked up to them, regarded them as heroes, and they were."[3] Another Badger outfit, the 5th Wisconsin, arrived a few days later to loud "helloing" from the men of both regiments. In the ranks were friends and relatives from back home. It was a pleasant camp; three Wisconsin regiments together, the new soldiers from the far frontier shy around strangers, but laughing and talking in an easy fashion amongst themselves.

The "rattle of a large drum corps" at sundown a week later marked the arrival of the 19th Indiana. Rumors quickly spread around the coffee fires that night that the unit was "the pet" of powerful Indiana Governor Oliver Morton. The addition of the 19th Indiana completed the new brigade. If three regiments were from Wisconsin (2nd, 5th, and 6th), the fourth was acceptable. The Badgers looked them over and came away with satisfied nods. The Hoosiers were, after all, Western men.

The commander of the new brigade was Rufus King, a New York state man well known in Wisconsin, where he had served as editor of *The Milwaukee Sentinel,* helped frame the Wisconsin Constitution—he was named after his grandfather, a signer of the U.S. Constitution—and served as superintendent of Milwaukee schools. Of more importance was the degree he held: King was an 1833 graduate of the U.S. Military Academy at West Point. One of King's academy classmates was the luckless McDowell, now reduced to commanding a new division in McClellan's reorganized and revitalized army. At the outbreak of the war King was named U.S. minister to the Papal States in Rome, but he turned down the appointment to serve in the field.

King's new brigade moved across the Potomac River to Arlington Heights. The Westerners camped near the columned front door of the home of a well-known and respected Regular Army officer named Robert E. Lee, who had resigned his commission to serve his native Virginia. The Federal government had seized the mansion, which King now used as his headquarters. The home had been built by George Washington's stepson, John Parke Custis, and passed to Lee through George Washington Custis, Lee's father-in-law. It was at Arlington Heights that the new brigade suffered its first shake-up in organization when the 5th Wisconsin was unexpectedly transferred to another brigade. Upset over the loss, King demanded another Western regiment to replace it. When the 7th Wisconsin arrived in Washington on October 1, it was attached to King's brigade.

King's organization was the only all-Western unit serving in the Eastern armies. "We felt we were the test of the West," one private said, but the "test" would not be soon in coming. The weeks of late summer and fall were spent drilling and manning sentry posts, and the onset of cold weather ended any plans for active campaigning that year. It was not until early 1862 that McClellan announced his grand plan to defeat the Rebels, but weeks were consumed before the army finally moved by water to the tip of the Virginia peninsula at Fort Monroe.

The Western brigade, however, did not make the journey. As part of McDowell's First Corps, King's soldiers instead marched overland to

Charles L. Foster Collection

General John Gibbon

Born in Pennsylvania, but raised in North Carolina, this West Pointer stayed with the Union and is credited with turning frisky Western volunteers into an Iron Brigade.

Fredericksburg, Virginia, where they halted to act as a reserve for McClellan's army and as a blocking force to protect Washington. "I cannot tell you how we all felt at being left behind when the army went to the Peninsula and we were left out of the ranks of McCellan, the ideal of all the army," one officer wrote home.

While at Fredericksburg, King was promoted and Captain John Gibbon of the Regulars was named to command the brigade. Although no one knew it at the time, the promotions marked an important moment in the history of the unit. An intense professional, Gibbon previously commanded Battery B of the 4th U.S. Artillery (famous in the Old Army for its service at Buena Vista in the Mexican War), which was attached to the brigade. The new brigadier proved to be one of the few West Pointers able to adapt the rigid discipline of the Regulars to volunteers. Born in Pennsylvania in 1827, Gibbon grew up in North Carolina and was appointed to West Point from that state. He served occupation duty in Mexico and then in Florida against the Seminoles. When his promotion to brigadier of volunteers was delayed in Congress because he had no patron, Gibbon asked Major General James Wadsworth of New York, who had strong political connections, for advice. Wadsworth immediately saw that the promotion was advanced and won Gibbon's friendship and gratitude. Given Gibbon's natural ability and strong reputation, some friends believed that his Southern background (his brothers were in the Confederate service) had played a part in his snail-like advance through the ranks.

Gibbon spent the next six months turning the frisky backwoods rustics and small town boys from the frontier into an effective fighting force. Early on, Gibbon saw the merit of Frank Haskell of the 6th Wisconsin. A Dartmouth graduate who was practicing law in Madison at the start of the war, Haskell was in the habit of writing long letters to his brother back at Portage, Wisconsin. Gibbon promoted Haskell from regimental to brigade adjutant. The new general's camps of instruction, as shaped and directed by Haskell, proved a revelation to the new Wisconsin and Indiana soldiers. The general, "was a most thorough disciplinarian, and the manner in which he put the brigade through drill will never be forgotten by those who participated," recalled one volunteer. "There were early morning drills, drills before breakfast, forenoon drills, evening and night drills, besides guard mounting and dress parade. Probably no brigade commander was ever more cordially hated by his men. He was all soldier, both in looks and deeds. When Gibbon's brigade marched," he concluded, "there was no straggling."[4]

Gibbon grew to admire and respect his volunteers, whom he insisted be outfitted in a distinctive manner. The gray militia uniforms originally issued the four regiments were in sad disrepair (especially in the 2nd Wisconsin which, despite hot words and quick fists, was now called in camp "the

Brian Hogan

Private John Bissett
Co. B, 7th Wisconsin

This photograph was taken between October 1861 and March 1862 and shows the transition from Wisconsin militia gray to Federal issue. Bissett is wearing a newly issued Regular Army frock coat, but is wearing a gray state issue kepi.

ragged assed 2nd"). Colonel Lysander Cutler of the 6th Wisconsin, at the time acting brigade commander, began to replace the state uniforms with Federal equipment. One of the items issued was the famous Model 1858 dress hat of the Regulars, a tall, black felt affair with plume and brass trim. It was believed by some in ranks that the outdated felt hats were issued to the

Private Charles Keeler
Co. B, 6th Wisconsin Volunteers

A member of the Prescott Guards, Keeler is shown here with the Iron Brigade uniform of Model 1858 Hat, Regular army dress frock coat, and linen leggings. He was shot through the legs at Gettysburg on July 1, 1863.

Alan T. Nolan

Westerners because the more stylish kepis were going to Eastern regiments with more political influence.

The tall hats made a striking impression, however. Gibbon ordered his whole brigade outfitted with them once he assumed command. He also ordered all the regiments be issued the nine- button, dark blue dress frock of the Regulars, along with white linen leggings and white gloves. The latter two items caused a stir of protest in ranks. The leggings and the gloves were very uncomfortable and hard to keep clean, but were mostly disliked because the soldiers had to pay for them out of their clothing allotments. The morning after their issuance Gibbon found the legs of his pet horse "ornamented" with white leggings. Long after the war, Gibbon was stationed at Fort Snelling in Minnesota. During this time, while wearing civilian clothing and passing through Boscobel, Wisconsin, Gibbon learned of a Wisconsin reunion gathering. The old soldier walked to the door of the hall and inquired if there were any members of the old Iron Brigade present. One veteran was brought to him.

"I am looking for a man," Gibbon announced.

"What man?" asked the old Black Hat.

"Why, the man who put the leggings on my horse when we were opposite Fredericksburg in 1862."

"Geewilikins," replied the old soldier with a start, motioning to a group of veterans nearby. "Come over here, boys, quick, here's Johnny, the War Horse!"

Despite grumblings about cost and comfort, the new soldiers looked themselves over and liked what they saw. "We have a full blue suit, a fine black hat nicely trimmed with bugle and plate and ostrich feathers," one wrote home, "and you can only distinguish our boys from the Regulars by their good looks."

King's former brigade was now Gibbon's "Black Hat Brigade." The weeks of drill and training at Fredericksburg molded the Western regiments into some of the best in the army, though the men had still not engaged in any serious combat. According to Gibbon, it was during those weeks he came to believe that "mere efficiency in drill was not by any means the most important point gained. The habit of obedience and subjection to the will of another, so difficult to instill in the minds of free and independent men, became marked characteristics of the command."[5]

In August 1862, the fighting these volunteers so longed to engage in arrived in a manner that almost destroyed them. The "Black Hats," now part of the Federal Army of Virginia under Major General John Pope, participated in four sharply-waged engagements in just three weeks. Their baptism of fire erupted on August 28 during the opening phase of Second Bull Run. The Westerners were marching along the Warrenton Turnpike when Confederate Major General Thomas "Stonewall" Jackson attacked them without warning from a stretch of wooded heights near Gainesville, Virginia. Although outnumbered and caught unawares at a tactical disadvantage, the men kept their composure, swinging into line of battle to engage the enemy. Through much of the fighting the opposing lines were but 50 to 70 yards apart, killing and maiming while standing in the open on the fields of the John Brawner farm. The slugfest continued into the dusky twilight until darkness put an end to the the shooting. Two days later, the brigade served as the army's rearguard following the stunning defeat at Second Bull Run that swept the army from the field. The actions of the Westerners caught the eye of Major General Joseph Hooker, who rode up to Gibbon and praised the four regiments under his command. Two weeks later on September 14, the Black Hats fought their way up the National Road to Turner's Gap at South Mountain under the eye of General McClellan, who was once again back in command of the revitalized Army of the Potomac. Three days later on September 17, the Westerners spearheaded the opening assault of Hooker's First Corps into the bloody cornfield at Antietam.[6]

These bloody combats forged a bond and a legend that would follow the brigade off the field and into history. Following South Mountain and Antietam, soldiers outside the brigade began to speak of a brigade of "iron" men from the Western frontier. Exactly how the name was attached to Gibbon's men remains unclear. McClellan claimed after the war that he originated the famous battle name. He was watching the brigade at South Mountain, he wrote, when he asked whose troops were fighting on the pike. When he was told it was Gibbon's Western Brigade, McClellan claims he responded with no little admiration, "They must be made of iron!"[7]

New York men claimed the name was stolen. The original "Iron Brigade," they asserted, was meant for the 22nd, 24th, and 30th New York regiments, and 14th Brooklyn. When the two-year New York regiments mustered out (the 14th Brooklyn, a three-year regiment, remained), the name was "taken" by the Wisconsin and Indiana regiments. "I do not know that I can blame those western kids for taking up our name after we mustered out; but they should have added jr. making it the 'Iron Brigade, jr.'," grumbled one New Yorker after the war. According to an officer in the 24th New York on August 13, 1862, the name was first attached to his brigade following a march that covered 50 miles in two days. "Sixteen miles a day is considered good march," he wrote, "so you can see why we are sometimes called the 'Cast Iron Brigade.'" General Marsena Patrick also was cited as the originator of the name for telling a New York officer, "Your men must be made of iron to make such marches."[8]

Wisconsin and Indiana men never believed there was any confusion with the New York brigade, and that it was McClellan—the hero of the Army—who singled them out as not a two-year "Cast Iron Brigade," but as the "Iron Brigade of the West." From the very beginning they were careful to include the reference to their "Western" roots, and said it was a name won not by long marches, but by hard fighting. Jerome Watrous of the 6th Wisconsin claimed the name was first publicly attached to the Westerners by a correspondent for a Cincinnati newspaper who was at McClellan's headquarters during the fighting for South Mountain. "The last terrible battle has reduced this brigade to a mere skeleton; there being scarcely enough members to form half a regiment," the reporter wrote in a dispatch printed on September 22, 1862, five days after the bloodletting at Antietam. "The 2nd Wisconsin, which but a few weeks since, numbered over nine hundred men, can now muster but fifty-nine. This brigade has done some of the hardest and best fighting in the service. It has been justly termed the Iron Brigade of the West."[9]

The reputation came at terrible cost. "General McClellan calls us the Iron Brigade," a 7th Wisconsin man wrote a friend. "By gaining this name, we have lost from the brigade seventeen hundred and fifty men. We have never turned our backs to enemy in any engagement, although they have outnumbered us every fight we have had."[10]

The men had no way of knowing that the long road of civil war was about to get much longer and much harder.

John Gibbon was promoted after Antietam and he took Haskell with him. The general would be missed by his men but always remembered, explained one of his citizen-officers, because Gibbon possessed

> superior qualities as a brigade commander. Thoroughly educated in the military profession, he had also high personal qualifications to exercise command. He was anxious that his brigade should excel in every way and while he was an exacting disciplinarian he had the good sense to recognize merit where it existed. His administration of the command left a lasting impression for good upon the character and military tone of the brigade, and his splendid personal bravery upon the field of battle was an inspiration.[11]

In Gibbon's place as commander of the Black Hats, and over his concerns and objections, the army appointed and promoted Colonel Sol Meredith of the 19th Indiana, who was long active in petitioning his political cronies for the post. In addition to a new commander, just ahead for the Western men waited a bleak winter, bright hopes dashed by the Union defeat at Chancellorsville in early May 1863, and finally the troubling execution of a simple-minded soldier of their own brigade.

Chapter 2

I Cannot Stand it to Fight

They shot the poor fellow in an open field alongside the Virginia road carrying them to Pennsylvania. His name was James Woods, a private in the 19th Indiana Volunteer Infantry. Woods was a good soldier in every way except for the one that mattered most—he was unable to face battle. The young Hoosier walked away from his regiment before the fighting at Fredericksburg in December 1862, and then again in May 1863 before Chancellorsville. Now, faced with another pending fight, Woods acquired a gray uniform and tried passing himself off as a captured Confederate. But his luck was no better and a clerk from his own regiment recognized him in a group of prisoners and alerted the guard.

"I did not want to go in a fight," he told those overseeing his court-martial. "I can't fight. I cannot stand it to fight. I am ashamed to make the statement, but . . . I never could stand a fight." He begged for one more chance. However, it was a hard time just then in the Army of the Potomac, and getting harder. In the midst of a critical campaign, the officers were of the mind that the men in ranks might need a lesson on what happens to a soldier who fails his duty. Their verdict was swift and grim: death by firing squad.[1]

Woods' fear of battle was especially troubling to his officers because he belonged to a veteran regiment in a tough fighting outfit. If a volunteer in an "Iron Brigade" could falter, army authorities wondered, where would it all lead?

Within the week a call went to the five regiments to select "two lieutenants and twenty wholly reliable men" to report to First Division Provost Marshal Clayton Rogers of the 6th Wisconsin. The young lieutenant was one of those steady and competent men found on the Wisconsin frontier and now he faced a duty he found unsettling. After two years of hard service, much of it as a line officer of his own company, he was preparing to shoot "a simple-minded soldier without any force of decision or character" who might have been influenced by antiwar sentiments being voiced by the folks back home. In many ways Woods was the very type of volunteer Rogers trained and stood beside in battle. He prepared for the execution with little enthusiasm.

The date was set for a Friday, June 12, 1863. Marching orders, however, reached the division the night before and the regiments were on the road before daylight. Handcuffed and shackled, Woods rode along in an ambulance sitting on the wooden coffin that would be his final resting place. In ranks, some of the marching soldiers speculated that the Indiana boy was trying to take advantage of a proposal to permit rebel deserters who swore an oath to be released and "remain unmolested so far as demanding of any military service." Others were of the opinion there would be a last minute reprieve for the doomed man. They recalled and talked about old camp stories of a New Jersey soldier or a New York soldier or a Maine soldier saved at the last minute by a pardon from President Lincoln. One officer explained later that condemned men "were shot as we marched so that the sentences of the court-martial could not be mitigated by telegrams from Washington. . . . Desertions had become so frequent that only the extreme penalty of death would put a stop to them."[2]

The brigade was 20 miles into the first day's march when it halted to eat and rest. The regiments were deployed "in sort of a hollow square with one side open" around a freshly dug grave. The coffin was pulled from the ambulance and the prisoner brought forward and seated on the edge of the open box. The assembled soldiers watched in hushed silence. General James Wadsworth, the division commander, rode to the doomed man and turned to face the lines. His short speech warned common soldiers to do their duty, but the simple lesson was beyond the hearing of most of the assembled ranks. The general moved away and a line of guards filed before the 12 men of the firing squad. The two ranks faced each other. One by one, Rogers took the musket of a guard, inspected it, and then handed it to a member of the detail. The 12-man firing party was then marched single file in front of the prisoner, where one watching soldier said they showed "more uneasiness than the criminal."

A chaplain stepped forward. "Some moments [were] spent in solemn conversation and prayer, both kneeling," a soldier wrote home, "the very air still with the hush of death's angel and each heartbeat of the thousands standing around them seemed . . . measured by minutes, [then] they [rose] to their feet." The clergyman turned away. All the muskets carried by the detail were loaded and only one carried a blank. However, the musket with a blank was not reassuring. The veterans would know by the kick if their weapon fired the heavy bullet. The Provost Marshal moved forward with a blindfold. Woods shook his head against it, but the officer insisted. After tying it around his eyes, Rogers pulled open the condemned man's shirt and stepped back.

"Attention!" he ordered. "Come to the Ready!"

The sharp command caused a stirring in the ranks of the watching soldiers. Rogers lifted his hat as Woods waited quietly. The hat swept down and the detail fired a ragged volley. Woods toppled backward into his coffin, his feet kicking. Only four of the bullets found their mark. Rogers and a reserve member of the detail stepped forward and the fatal ball was fired. One witness remembered that the single shot seemed louder than the volley.

Once the limbs were tucked into the coffin and the lid nailed shut, the brigade band struck up a military quickstep and the columns filed back onto the road. That night, a Michigan man explained in a letter home that Woods had "cravenly deserted them in an hour of danger and had now paid the penalty." It was sad, he wrote, to watch a fellow volunteer die at the hands of comrades the very death he feared to "meet in the ranks of patriotism."

The veterans of the bloody fields of Gainesville, Second Bull Run, South Mountain, Antietam, Fredericksburg, and Chancellorsville fully understood that the execution of Woods was more than just the final punishment for a soldier who failed his duty or even as a warning for the men still in ranks—it was a purging of the weak and useless. They recognized safety in battle was had by "steadiness, persistence in firing, and most of all by holding together. . . ." Men like Wood weakened every battle line into which they were forced. "No man can fight when surrounded by cowards, who are easily panic-stricken, and who are unrestrained by any consideration of pride from ignominiously running way to save their lives," one soldier said.[3]

For the veterans, the quick execution in an open field was just one more stopping point on the long dark road of civil war started in 1861. Still, the incident haunted those who witnessed it. One soldier writing two decades later understood what had happened that June day in 1863 in Virginia. "I can still see that poor trembling, moaning fellow drop back into the coffin," he recalled. "It seemed hard, but it was just."[4]

And so the Iron Brigade finished its unpleasant business and marched away. Just a few miles ahead on the road they were taking was a sprawling farm and rising ridge owned by a man named McPherson west of a small town called Gettysburg, Pennsylvania. And it was going to be a place where a soldier would need to rely on the fellows around him.

Chapter 3

He has Gone to Stonewall's Funeral

With the deserter in his grave, the men of the Iron Brigade trudged north during the long hot days of June 1863. Many were troubled by the direction of their march. Why were they following a victorious Confederate army toward loyal Pennsylvania instead of chasing it south into rebellious Virginia? How could the situation have changed so quickly?

Just a few weeks earlier the talk was that the turning point was just ahead. After two bloody years trying to suppress the rebellion of the Southern states, it seemed the armed forces of the National government were now on the move. In the West, the soldiers of the Confederacy were being driven deeper into the South. Union men and gunboats were threatening the last two strongholds on the Mississippi River at Vicksburg and Port Hudson. In the East, despite a string of Confederate victories in 1862 that sapped Northern morale, the veteran soldiers of the star-crossed Union Army of the Potomac were in decent spirits and poised to meet their nemesis in battle yet again.

Gone was the unlucky Ambrose Burnside with his straw hat and bushy whiskers, his disastrous failure at Fredericksburg, and his disastrous "Mud March" of January 1863. Named in his place was the colorful and outspoken Joseph Hooker, who used his weeks in Washington recovering from his minor wound at Antietam to plot with the powerful and influential to gain promotion to army commander. In the newspapers he was always "Fighting Joe" (a name given him because of a pressman's error and which he disliked as unseemly) and he was written up as a general of stout reputation as the commander of the First Corps. Hooker's promotion to command the Army of the Potomac was generally well-received in ranks. The announcement brought to a close the dismal winter of 1862-1863, which Rufus Dawes of the 6th Wisconsin labeled the "darkest hour of our struggle." The young officer, insightful and intelligent, wrote home that the "Apollo-like presence of General Hooker . . . his self-confident, even vain glorious manner, his haughty criticism of others and his sublime courage at the battle front have combined to make his impressions upon the public judgment that obscure his most valuable traits of character and his best qualities as commander. With indefatigable zeal he addressed himself to the task of re-organization, and if I may so express it, re-inspiration."[1]

Hooker was the fifth or sixth major commander of the Union forces in the East, depending on where he was counted. The first was unlucky Irvin McDowell, who failed at First Bull Run. He was followed by the beloved "Little Mac"—George B. McClellan—who formally organized the Army of the Potomac and then stalled in early 1862 in his grand offensive against the Confederate capital at Richmond, Virginia. John Pope, following limited success along the Mississippi River in the Western Theater, was brought to Washington only to be soundly defeated by Robert E. Lee and Thomas "Stonewall" Jackson at Second Bull Run. In the subsequent emergency, McClellan was restored to command as the Confederate army moved north into Maryland. The fighting there on September 17 at Antietam was tactically a draw but strategically a significant success for President Lincoln and the Union that ended General Lee's raid north of the Potomac. An anemic effort to follow after the defeated Southern army and thus capitalize on that repulse resulted in McClellan's removal two months later. His friend, Ambrose Burnside, replaced him. Burnside quickly provided that amiability and honesty were no substitutes for military acumen. He, too, was sacked after a disastrous series of hopeless attacks in December 1862 at Fredericksburg, Virginia, followed by the disastrous "Mud March" a few weeks later. Waiting in the wings was Joe Hooker, who finally realized his ambition and was named commander of the Army of the Potomac.

Despite what some regarded as an unsavory personal reputation, the new general commanding proved surprisingly apt when it came to running an army. Rations improved. New equipment arrived. Long overdue furloughs were granted. The army was reorganized and camps of instruction resumed. Competent officers were promoted. Recognizing the merit of unit identity and pride, Hooker also assigned a woolen badge of various shape to each corps to be affixed to the hat or cap. Divisions within a corps were designated by color and the First Division of the First Corps was marked with a red sphere or circle. Hooker understood "the True Napoleonic idea of the power of an *Esprit de Corps*," explained one Wisconsin officer, and the red badges became the "almost worshiped symbols of a glorious service." Most important to the men in ranks was the arrival of paymasters to pay up arrearages. "Nothing is more disheartening and demoralizing to the soldier than to feel that his family is suffering at home for want of his small and richly earned wages," was how one volunteer put it. For the first time since the days of McClellan, the men in the ranks felt confident in their commander. When they marched out in early May 1863 to steal a march on the Army of Northern Virginia, most men felt certain they would avenge the Union setbacks of the previous year.[2]

The early moves began so well for Union arms. Holding and thrusting opposite Fredericksburg to confuse his enemy as to where the real blow would fall, Hooker quickly pushed a larger column—roughly one-third of his 134,000 available men—westward in a wide turning movement. His goal was to cross the Rapidan River and turn the army of Robert E. Lee out of its position or crush it where it stood. Alerted by his cavalry that the Union army was advancing to strike him in the left flank or rear, Lee refused to act as Hooker anticipated. Instead of withdrawing, Lee divided his much smaller command. Leaving behind a small force opposite Fredericksburg, he moved quickly with the balance westward to meet the surprised Hooker. The move prompted Hooker—who had indeed stolen the march on Lee and so held the initiative—to stop his advance and prepare for an attack.

On the night of May 1, 1863, Lee and his chief lieutenant, Thomas "Stonewall" Jackson, fixed on a plan for a 16-mile march across backwoods roads to strike Hooker's exposed right flank. Leaving Lee with only 16,000 men, Jackson led 26,000 Confederates in a bold maneuver and a late afternoon attack on May 2 that smashed the Federal right and tumbled it backward in confusion. By the morning of May 3 Hooker, unsure of his position or how to defeat Lee, pulled back into a powerful defensive position. A cannon shot that exploded nearby stunned and confused him, which only seemed to accelerate the stalled fortunes of the Northern army. Hooker ended his offensive on May 6 by withdrawing his army. The Army of the Potomac had suffered yet another stunning reverse at the hands of the Army of Northern Virginia.

Despite high hopes, good marching, hours of desperate fighting, and the loss of 17,000 Union men, Chancellorsville was one of the army's most humiliating defeats. Only the fatal wounding of Stonewall Jackson on the night of May 2 at the hands of his own soldiers dimmed the Confederate victory. The Federal brigades tramped back to their old camps. No one, from Joe Hooker to the lowest private, was able to fully explain how they had been whipped.

The unexpected defeat shook the resolve of the officers and men and confidence of the nation. "Never an army had such confidence as we when we gave battle," one officer wrote. "In no single instance were we outfought, but we gained nothing, and in a great degree lost our confidence in the head of affairs." Hooker returned to his camps not because his army lacked ability to fight on, another officer explained, but "because he was outgeneraled and defeated—a humiliating confession, I own, but I believe true."[3]

The Federal soldiers spent the waning days of May as they had the previous six months—waiting to see what was going to happen next. There was speculation Lee and his battalions would head north again, as he had in September 1862, to feed and supply his soldiers and lure the Federals into a decisive battle on Union soil. Unanswered, however, were the questions of when and where. Union officers spent the long days readying their companies and regiments for the fight certain to come.

The soldiers themselves were uneasy about any coming campaign and now were unsure of Hooker who had somehow, they believed, cheated them out of even a chance for victory at Chancellorsville. The army had fought well despite the defeat, and would do so again if only given the chance to *win*. The soldiers understood the coming summer campaign was especially important, and there was a growing grim determination that it must be a victory. "To speak it plainly the Army of the Potomac was mad clear through; every man's pride was touched," one soldier said. "There had been successive changes in the general command, and a heap of marching, with defeat after defeat emblazoned on our banners; the few victories were either not appreciated by those high in authority, or passed over so lightly as to be the subject of little or no concern."

"Where is Hooker now?" Rebel sentries catcalled across the Rappahannock River, adding to the Union soldiers' misery. "I haven't seen him for some time!" The response of the Federal pickets was quick, but not as satisfying: "Oh, he's gone to Jackson's funeral!"[4]

Chapter 4

Greenhorn Patriots

Chancellorsville may have dashed hopes in the North, but its negative impact on morale in the Iron Brigade was fleeting. The Black Hats, veterans of some of the hardest fighting of the war, were convinced their brigade had accomplished one of the battle's most stunning feats of soldiering: crossing a river under fire in wooden pontoon boats against an entrenched and strongly posted enemy. Private James Sullivan and his 6th Wisconsin were in the thick of contested crossing. Writing about the experience after the war, with the retrospect of a four-year veteran who suffered five wounds, Sullivan labeled the water-borne attack at Fredericksburg as his grandest fifteen minutes of war service. To make such a charge, he observed, was "worth a man's life."

Back home, friends and family called him "J.P.", but in his army days he was "Mickey, of Company K"—a bright, fox squirrel of a man with the brash attitude of a "thorough going soldier." Sullivan reached American shores from Ireland when he was three. In 1861, when Fort Sumter was fired upon, he was out on his own and working as a hired man in Wonewoc, Juneau County, Wisconsin. Sullivan soon added his name as a volunteer to defend the Union. A slight boy of average height with few prospects beyond his quick intelligence and Irish wit, he signed the roll, he later explained, because "[I] wanted to do what I could for my country." His new company included "hardy lumbermen, rugged farmer boys and sturdy mechanics" from Mauston, New Lisbon, Necedah, and surrounding farms and villages.

Elected captain of the volunteers was Rufus Dawes, an Ohio boy just then living with his father in Juneau County. The new volunteers called themselves the "Lemonweir Minute Men" after the river flowing through the valley where they worked and lived, and to honor the heroes of 1776.

Pat and Robert Sullivan

Private James P. Sullivan
Co. K, 6th Wisconsin Volunteers

Served in the Lemonweir Minute Men and was the only man in the 6th Wisconsin to formally sign a muster roll three times. He was shot in the shoulder in the railroad cut at Gettysburg July 1, 1863.

The name would remind them of home, one said. Formally, they were known as Company K of Wisconsin's new 6th Regiment.[1]

By June 1863, Sullivan was already missing a middle toe taken by a rebel ball during the fighting at South Mountain. The Maryland combat for the high ground was his third battle. He was wounded on a skirmish line, his cheeks wrapped with a silk handkerchief to ease a bad case of mumps. The ball to his foot and loss of a toe put him out of the war as wounded and disabled. Being home, however, bored the young warrior. The women complained about high prices, he said, the men growled over tight money, and the only young men in evidence were "banged-up soldiers or those dodging the war." Uneasy and restless, Sullivan made his way to Madison to see if a fellow missing a middle toe could again join the army. "Anyone owning a name can enlist," a recruiting sergeant told him, and Mickey was once again on his way to the front. It was the second of what would be three times that he would formally sign a 6th Wisconsin muster roll.

The returning young Irishman was greeted with shouts of welcome. His first commander remembered the private's "unconquerable good humor and genuine wit" and said he never saw his equal for "genuine sallies of humor at unexpected time." Another friend who thought highly of the Irishman wrote, "A hundred men wore the star of generals who did not dare or do as much in the war as J.P. Sullivan." A photograph of the young soldier from 1862, captured when he was home in Wisconsin, shows him in the knee-length blue wool army frock coat. His dark hair is carefully combed and the face full of stiff resolve, the shoulders squared so he might look taller for the camera.[2] He was one of the "greenhorn patriots," he explained, and he served in a company of "gay, fun-loving boys" who faced hardship and death in a "cool and unconcerned manner."[3]

It was equally fitting that Rufus Dawes was elected captain of the "Minute Men," given his family's long record of service to the new Republic. Several of his kinsmen served in the Revolutionary Army and his great-grandfather was Charles Dawes, who rode with Paul Revere on the night before Lexington. Rufus was born in Ohio in 1838. His parents were separated at the time of his graduation from college in Ohio in 1860, and he joined his father in Wisconsin.

Most of the letters he penned during the weeks before Gettysburg in 1863 were to Mary Beman Gates of Marietta, Ohio. The two had met the year before at her home, and the introduction provoked a surprisingly

Dawes Arboretum Collection

Captain Rufus Dawes
Co. K, 6th Wisconsin

The youthful Rufus Dawes was still a captain of Co. K, the Lemonweir Minute Men, 6th Wisconsin, when this photograph was taken early in the war.

heated discussion on the generalship of George McClellan. Those differences were resolved, however. The young lady was "twenty years of age and of her charming qualities of mind and person it is not for my partial pen to write," teased the officer. He was attracted from the introduction and his attention was returned, and soon Mary Beman Gates found herself caught up in the war. A daughter said later that she "could seldom bring herself to speak of those months when she waited and watched for news from the front."

Tall and slight, Dawes from his childhood set an impossible standard for himself. He was a good student first at the University of Wisconsin in Madison and then Marietta College in Ohio. He turned to soldering with the same careful dedication and became one of the best of the volunteer officers produced in the war. He was first elected captain, then major, and finally lieutenant colonel, and singled out in the reports for his steady leadership (although others would receive credit for what he was about to accomplish at Gettysburg). Dawes survived the war to serve one term in Congress from Ohio. One of his four sons, Charles C. Dawes (named for Mary's brother), became vice president of the United States. Rufus would not live to see it.

In June 1863, Rufus wrote to Mary on the march to Gettysburg that his 6th Wisconsin was "strong in health and cheerful in spirit, and determined always to sustain its glorious history. It has been my ardent ambition to lead it through one campaign. . . . If I do anything glorious I shall expect you to be proud of me."[4]

General Wadsworth's Oxen

General James Wadsworth had oxen brought to his camps because he thought they performed better than the mules supplied by the army. His soldiers watched the old general work his animals and called it "Old Waddy whispering to his calves." This drawing is by H. J. Brown of the 24th Michigan. *History of the Twenty-four Michigan of the Iron Brigade*

The 6th Wisconsin in May 1863 was in the First Division of the First Army Corps of the Army of the Potomac. The division, led by a New York state farmer-turned-soldier named James Wadsworth, contained just two brigades, but they were among the best in the army, the soldiers mostly veterans and first-rate. The old general, who dabbled in army politics more than he should have, was generally regarded as a man of "strong character," an "intensely practical commander, indefatigable as a worker, and looking closely after details." No other commander, wrote one officer, "could do more for the personal comfort of his men." Wadsworth was one of the richest men in New York, but the lower ranks liked the old general despite his wealth (it was widely rumored that he served without pay), and his off-hand down home manner and bushy white side-whiskers struck the right chord. The soldiers found it "a rare treat" to watch the old gentleman farmer overseeing the several oxen he brought to the army when mud hampered the movement of army mules. The general, often as not bespattered and standing ankle deep in mud and manure, would "Gee" and "Haw" the heavy animals as they pulled at the baggage wagons. The boys in ranks called the performance Wadsworth "whispering to his calves."[5]

As part of Wadsworth's division, the First Brigade was one of the most celebrated fighting organizations in either army—the famous "Iron Brigade of the West." It included the 2nd, 6th and 7th Wisconsin, 19th Indiana, and the recently added 24th Michigan, just arrived from Detroit and Wayne County. The brigade commander was the outspoken and ambitious Solomon Meredith of Indiana, a citizen-soldier with rock solid political connections but questionable military abilities. Meredith— President Lincoln liked to point him out as his "only Quaker general"—was an Indiana county clerk in 1861 at the time of Fort Sumter and a crony of powerful Governor Oliver Morton. He entered the war as a colonel of the 19th Indiana. An imposing figure with the loud and forceful voice of a stump speaker, he was remembered for his colorful use of the English language and for his height, which at 6-foot-7 made him one of the tallest men in the army. "[A] specimen of the genuine Hoosier," a Wisconsin man wrote home of the Indiana colonel. "Puts on no airs and frequently talks to the private soldiers and is therefore very popular with the men but is not much of a military man." Upon his appointment as commander of the 19th, a bitter political critic unkindly suggested "Long Sol" be cut in two so his "lower and better half" could be appointed lieutenant colonel of the regiment."[6]

Indiana State Library

General Solomon Meredith

He came into the war as colonel of the 19th Indiana and was promoted to command of the Iron Brigade over the objections of John Gibbon. One of the tallest men in the brigade, "Long Sol" was wounded by a shell at Gettysburg.

The Second Brigade of Wadsworth's Division included the 56th Pennsylvania, 7th Indiana, 76th New York, 95th New York, 147th New York, and the famous 84th New York (known more for its pre-war militia designation and bright uniforms as the 14th Brooklyn). In a sometimes confusing arrangement, the brigade commander was crusty Lysander Cutler of Milwaukee, a native of Massachusetts and one-time militia officer who, after a pre-war failure in business, traveled west to Wisconsin seeking opportunity. Cutler was 53 years old at his appointment to colonel of the 6th Wisconsin, but ability and common sense soon won him promotion to command the Second Brigade. One soldier described Cutler as "stern, rugged, determined" with a "kindly face, which, when a smile found place there, was rarely attractive . . ." He was "spare of frame" and walked an "uneven step" due to the severe wound received in 1862 at Gainesville.

All these men and many others had a role to play in the coming days. Glorious deeds awaited.

Chapter 5

To be Shot Like Sheep in a Huddle

The Iron Brigade's part in the Chancellorsville campaign became known as "FitzHugh's Crossing." It was part of the Union effort to hold Confederate forces in a defensive position at Fredericksburg as the rest of the army undertook its sweeping turning movement. To mask the main Federal operation, Brigadier General John Reynolds with his First Corps would threaten Fredericksburg. Major General Dan Sickles Third Corps was held in reserve with elements of Major General John Sedgwick's Sixth Corps to carry Franklin's Crossing on the Rappahannock River below the city while units of the First Corps hit Fitzhugh's Crossing opposite a local landmark known as the Smithfield House.

The Black Hats broke camp in late April for Fredericksburg, "only halting on the way to surround a New York regiment and force them to take back their arms." It was not much of an affair. The mutineers were "only a few men of the 24th New York," recalled a Wisconsin officer, and they had thrown down their muskets and refused to pick them up, claiming their enlistments had expired. James Wadsworth ordered the 6th Wisconsin to load muskets and surround the troublemakers. "A few pointed remarks by Wadsworth, rendered pungent by the presence of our regiment with loaded muskets," continued the officer, "brought them to their senses and they quietly fell in."

The brigade reached the Rappahannock River below Fredericksburg at midnight on April 29, 1863. The men were ordered to a ditched fence to wait for army engineers to lay a pontoon bridge. The plan was simple but tactically complicated, for it called for the movement of thousands of men and mule-drawn pontoon wagons to water's edge. The idea was to cross one brigade on boats under cover of darkness while engineers constructed a bridge with the pontoons. The boats were late, however, and were just reaching the river about dawn. Despite a heavy fog, the Confederates on the opposite bank more than 100 yards away opened with muskets and field pieces. The explosions panicked the Federal mule train hauling the pontoons and some of the animals bolted in a "grand skedaddle" for the rear, carrying off pontoon boats and extra duty men. The watching infantry scattered in front of this "frantic and ludicrous flight" and were jeered with some laughter and catcalls.[1]

When engineers trying to get the boats into the river were driven back by enemy fire, men from the 6th Wisconsin, 24th Michigan, and 14th Brooklyn were sent to the water's edge to return fire. The bank on the Union side of the river, however, sloped gradually down to the water and there was little cover there, while the Confederates on the higher opposite bank were in "a thriving growth of young timber down the side of the hill to the water. The copse was full of rifle pits, arranged for sharp-shooters." Beyond the bluff was "an elaborate system of breastworks." The Rebels were "entirely concealed and all we could see was puffs of smoke, and our fire and a heavy cannonade had no effect on them."[2]

In that flurry of shooting, one of the Lemonweir Minute Men, Billy Hancock of Clifton, suffered bad luck—or, depending upon how one looks at it, good luck. Always a great company favorite, the young private was considered to be extra careful with his equipment and accouterments in order to escape the unnecessary cost of replacing them out of his pay. Hancock was wearing his dress frock coat to avoid carrying it and had outfitted himself with his best "big hat and an enormous black feather." As a flurry of bullets fell upon the Union position, explained Private James Sullivan, a ball cut "a gash in his [Hancock's] scalp and knocking the top out of his hat, splitting down the side, in army parlance, 'completely demoralizing it.'" Hancock picked up the black hat and examined the damage, a "look of distress on his face," and then blurted, "Gaul darn their ugly picture. They've split my new hat." His words triggered an eruption of laughter that ended when the firing resumed.[3]

For thirty minutes both sides fired on each other and it was apparent to General Reynolds that something else had to be done. He withdrew the men along the river. Already hours late in his assignment of making a crossing, the general decided to storm the far bank. Selected to spearhead the assault in boats ("clumsy, flat bottomed, square-bowed institutions, about 25 feet long, 4 feet wide and 3 feet deep," recalled one soldier) were the veterans of the 6th Wisconsin and the new men of the 24th Michigan along with three companies of the 2nd Wisconsin. The other regiments of the brigade, joined by the 14th Brooklyn, were tasked with delivering a covering fire. The 2nd Wisconsin men, using ropes attached to the pontoons, were the first out, pulling the boats to the river. One company was assigned to each boat with four of the men to man the oars. It was a bold and daunting situation, and the practical men of the frontier could see immediately that several things might go wrong. "I confess," admitted one officer, "that a shrinking from the proffered glory came over us to be shot like sheep in a huddle and drowned in the Rappahannock appeared to be the certain fate of all if we failed and of some if we succeeded."[4]

Colonel Edward Bragg carried news of the planned assault to his 6th Wisconsin. Slight and always sharp-spoken, he bluntly laid out the situation in his usual bitten-off manner. Knapsacks, haversacks, canteens, and other equipment were to be left behind. The boys should mind their "western breeding and . . . skill as oarsmen . . . rush down to the river and each company take two boats and launch them and paddle and pole over as fast as possible."

The Black Hats stripped away excess gear. One, in a joking, loud voice, exclaimed, "good-bye, vain world, farewell, knapsack, haversack and canteen!" Some took letters many times read and tore them and scattered the pieces. Photos were tucked into inside pockets. Only their weapons and cartridge boxes remained, and one Badger remembered how his comrades "seized the muskets with a firm grip and with teeth set as firm." The colonel ordered the percussion caps removed from the muskets to prevent accidental firing. "We looked over the river with thoughts of what will be the destiny of the Sixth in the next half hour," one soldier remembered.[5]

As his regiment was formed by fours, Bragg moved to the front to look over the situation, saying later that he expected half of his men would be killed in the crossing. An aide from Wadsworth rode up to present the general's compliments. "You are slow, Sir," was the message. Giving the rider a hard look and pulling down his hat a little firmer, the little colonel looked around, then said, "Come on boys." That was "all the orders we got" said one Wisconsin soldier, and the regiment broke for the river on the run.

Behind them, another officer called out, "Keep your heads down, boys!" It was just after 9:00 a.m.[6]

Ahead of 6th, the 2nd Wisconsin men on the ropes dragging the pontoons were yelling as "only soldiers can." When the soldiers cleared a rise approaching the river they were "met by a volley from the rifle pits on the opposite bank; but the balls mostly passed over our heads, lodging in and making the splinters fly most beautifully from the pontoons we were hauling," wrote one Badger. The regiments left behind were firing frantically and "woe to the gray back that showed his head long enough for an Austrian rifle to be trained him. The boats reached the river—were shoved in; some of them were so riddled as to be rendered useless; but others were soon filled with the boys."[7]

The running men of the 6th Wisconsin passed Bragg, "who being small and short-legged, and having an immense pair of military boots and spurs on, was not able to keep ahead." The colonel and his men reached the river together where all was a jumble—officers and men trying to manhandle the heavy boats into the water and climb aboard. Behind them, the 2nd Wisconsin men began pulling more boats to the water. Soldiers of the 6th Wisconsin climbed into one boat only to find the oars were still in the bottom of the pontoon. There was a mad scramble to pull them up and the men were shouting, "Shove her off!" again and again. One private called out, "The first man up the bank shall be a general!" and another shouted back something about showing "the Army why the old 6th was chosen to lead them."

This boat was finally loaded in a shower of bullets that ripped the river bank and knocked giant splinters from the boat. "It was no time to quail or flinch, one halt or waver was destruction," reported Rufus Dawes, who climbed to the bow of his boat swinging his sword in one hand and cheering the oarsmen, while holding his pistol in the other to shoot them if they wavered. Nearby, Captain Thomas Kerr of Milwaukee pressed the barrel of a revolver against the head of one frightened Badger to force him to advance and climb into a boat.

The pontoon carrying Sullivan was the second of the Company K boats. "The Johnnies opened on us a deadly fire," he recalled years later. "Hoel Trumbull was one of our company who assisted in pushing our boat off, and he waded into the water and made a spring to get in, and some of us were assenting him when a bullet hit him the head and he let go his hold and sank, and I was watching to see if he could come up until we were more than half

FitzHugh Crossing 1863
Fredericksburg, Virginia

This drawing by H.J. Brown of the 24th Michigan shows his regiment and the 6th Wisconsin crossing the Rappahannock River at Fredericksburg and carrying the opposite heights during the Chancellorsville Campaign in May 1863. *History of the Twenty-fourth Michigan of the Iron Brigade*

way across; and then, being on the upper side of the boat, I commenced firing on the rebels. . . . [T]he water fairly boiled [from the striking Confederate bullets]. . . and it is a mystery to me now how our boat escaped being sunk." The men were piled three deep in some boats. "The scene of wild excitement which then ran high is indescribable," said one Wisconsin soldier. "Whiz-whiz-spat-spat, their bullets struck around us. Our men rose in the boat and fired." One of the Sauk County boys in the 6th Wisconsin stood at the edge of his nearby boat, shouting at the top of his voice. "I half expected to see him fall into the river and drown," said a friend, but the young private escaped the day without injury.[8]

The Confederate fire was heavy now, the bullets splashing alongside the boats and pinning down the oarsmen. "The balls from the rebels came skipping over the water and occasionally crashing through the boat amongst the men's legs and musket stocks," recalled a Wisconsin officer, "while the regiments in the rear were firing over our heads at the rebels in the work beyond the river had good effect in keeping the Johnnies down." According to Dawes, fifteen of his men were shot before they even reached the boats.

Colonel Henry Morrow of the 24th Michigan was also in one of the first boats to cross. A watching soldier described him as "so impatient . . . [he] could hardly keep himself in the boat." Ahead of the small fleet of boats, amid the shouting and paddling, the Black Hats could see "shaggy-backed butternuts began to climb for the top of the rugged bank" only to be hit and tumble back down again. A Michigan man wrote home that his regiment crossed under "a heavy fire, but we came at them like so many wild men. They were scared and left their holes in a hurry as soon as we struck the shore."[9]

The first boats drew near the bank. "We tumbled into the mud or water, waist deep, wade ashore, crawled and scrambled up the bank," remembered Dawes. "Nobody could say who was first." Bayonets which had been kept sheathed on the crossing were fixed, and then, said one soldier, with a yell and very little shooting it was "every man for himself—and a Rebel." Officers got the men together to form a line and then pushed quickly up the rough slope.[10]

When they reached the top of the bluff, they could see the enemy fleeing over the open field beyond. Bragg described the moment:

> The 24th Michigan were ordered across the same time & did their duty nobly, but the 6th were in for a fight, and they led the run, and flung out their flag, first on the enemies [sic] shore, and then, such cheering & shouting that you never heard—Everybody was crazy—we had been ordered to do it—had done it in the face of the enemy & gallantly—that old soldiers "behaved foolishly in the exhibitions of joy."[11]

The boat carrying the Anderson Guards, Company I under Lieutenant Earl Rogers, claimed to be the first to reach shore. "The men were quickly on land and without waiting for any formation, as quickly rushed up the tangled slope, through grape vines and brush on to the works," said Rogers, "when the rebels ran in great confusion, our men shooting and in such great excitement were as unmanageable as wild men, made so by the complete victory under such disadvantage." Corporal Gabriel Ruby of De Soto fell dead at the works, the victim of friendly fire from across the river. When Private Charles Conklin of Viroqua was mortally wounded by a Rebel in front of him, "Private Sam Waller's shot killed the rebel," remembered Rogers. Private Levi Stedman of Brookville, "a big, overgrown boy of 17, standing on the right of the company and 6-feet-6" dislocated his knee jumping out of the boat and was "left sitting in the mud with his feet in the water, and crying because he could not go on with his company."[12]

Men of the 7th Wisconsin landed on the left. As they were getting organized, a volley slammed into them, knocking down Captain Alexander Gordon, Jr., and killing Lieutenant William O. Topping. "Boys, I am struck," said Gordon, who pulled opened his accouterment belt and sat down with a surprised look on his face. One of his privates told the officer that he appeared to be hit in the arm, but Gordon said he could feel the bullet in his chest. He was taken to the rear where it was discovered the bullet had entered his arm and passed into his body. The wound was mortal and his death a short time later was especially troubling. Gordon was much admired, and his marriage to his childhood sweetheart while the regiment mustered at Madison was a great celebration with the men of new company. His burial in Beloit drew a mournful assembly larger than the First Congregational Church could accommodate.[13]

The 6th Wisconsin men quickly moved right and left of the Smithfield House, a strong point soon cleared of the enemy. There was some laughter and excitement when one of the Sauk County "little fellows," Charles Kellogg of Baraboo, "brought in a large, burly fellow about twice his own size," and Private William Palmer of Leicester chased down a Rebel, gaining on him at every step until he finally caught him. (Palmer was known in camp as "Nosey" Palmer because of an incident before Antietam, when he pressed a $5 bill into the hands of a passing staff officer. "When I left Wisconsin," Palmer explained, "I said that the first galoot I met with a longer nose than mine had to have a fiver—so here 'tis.")[14]

When the first boats returned to pick up more Federals to secure the beachhead, General Wadsworth, caught up in the excitement of the moment, yelled out, "Hold on!" to the men of one boat. The general tossed the reins of his horse over the animal's head and jumped into the stern of the boat, pulling at his horse as the boat pushed off. But the horse balked. The general called to a nearby officer, "Push him in lieutenant!" With the horse in the water and swimming, the boat moved across the water under a hail of bullets. Wadsworth struck a pose not unlike that imagination suggests George Washington affected while crossing the Delaware. Reaching the bank, he jumped into the shallow water and made his way up the bluff where he went from "company to company, thanking the men for their brave assault." The old general's cap showed two new bullet holes.[15]

Library of Congress

General James Wadsworth

The wealthy New York State farmer commanded the First Division of the First Corps at Gettysburg. Men in the Iron Brigade believed he served without pay and called him "Old Daddy Wadsworth." He was mortally wounded at the Wilderness in May 1864.

By 10:30 a.m., the pontoon bridges were in place and the rest of the First Division moved across the river to secure the bridgehead. "Without discredit to any regiment, I have the honor to report, without the fear of contradiction, that the 6th Wisconsin Volunteers first scaled the bank and their colors first caught the breeze on the southern bank of the Rappahannock on the morning of April 29," Colonel Bragg wrote in his official report. Colonel Morrow disagreed, claiming it was his 24th Michigan "in the lead, its flag landing first . . . " According to the historian of the Wolverines, however, it mattered not in the least which regiment touched the enemy shore first. "It was a neck and neck race, between two friendly regiments of the Iron Brigade . . . and there were bullets and glory enough for both."

The Michigan regiment led the casualty list with twenty-one killed and wounded. The 6th Wisconsin claimed sixteen casualties while the 7th Wisconsin lost nine from all causes and the 2nd Wisconsin six. Southern losses are more difficult to determine with any precision. Nearly 100 Confederates were captured during the intense affair, and between two and three dozen were killed.

According to Private Sullivan, it took only fifteen minutes from the time his company ran toward the river until the bluff was seized, but it was the "grandest fifteen minutes of our lives!"[16]

Grand it might have been for Sullivan and his comrades, but the river assault had little consequence on the course of the unfolding combat. On May 2, the division withdrew and the First Corps started for the field at Chancellorsville, where it was placed in reserve. By May 6, the Army of the Potomac was withdrawing over the river crossings, another defeat tucked firmly under its belt.

Chapter 6

The Iron Brigade of the West

In early June 1863, Lee's Army of Northern Virginia left its camps and began moving west toward the Shenandoah Valley and then north toward the Potomac River. The Confederates marched with the confident step of veterans accustomed to victory. The Army of the Potomac, still stung by the defeat at Chancellorsville, cautiously followed, shielding Washington and Baltimore while trying to divine Lee's intentions. The Southern commander wanted to seize the initiative and take the war out of his native Virginia with hopes of providing his soldiers with fresh sources of forage, horses and other supplies. He was also convinced the recent Federal reverses dampened the war spirit of the North, and that a decisive Confederate victory on Northern soil might bring about a political end to the war. If successful, Lee believed, the Republicans supporting the war would suffer defeats at the ballot box and enemies of the war would "become so strong that the next administration will go in on that basis."[1]

John Reynolds' First Corps and the Iron Brigade led the advance as Union forces tracked and shadowed the Confederates. The twisting columns flowed slowly northward over the dusty roads in a dull tangle amid the din of shuffling feet, rolling wheels, creaking harness, animal cries and, as usual, cursing and shouting. Men and beasts alike were out of sorts over the column's fitful lurching, but overall the army was moving rather quickly. The marching men were jolly in rainy weather and sullen when the sun beat down upon them. When temperatures reached uncomfortable levels, large numbers of men dropped out of the moving columns; some collapsed of sunstroke. Some officers carried the muskets and knapsacks of used-up men. The straggling thinned the regiments as they tramped on, churning up muddy roads or stirring up immense clouds of dust on dry thoroughfares. Dead men and those unable to keep up were left by the roadside. "[We were] tired, sore, sleepy, hungry, dusty and dirty as pigs," a Wisconsin man wrote home. "Our army is in a great hurry for something."

People who saw the Iron Brigade during those days in late June recognized that the men of the far-off frontier were somehow different, that they moved with a certain dash and sense of themselves as they marched along roads with a quick stride, eyes bright under their big hats. The open land, deep woods, and good water of Wisconsin, Michigan, and Indiana attracted ambitious and active men interested in making a name and a future. It was not a place for the weak. Those who made it that far north and west were the hardy sons of New England and Pennsylvania and Ohio and New York, as well as steady fellows from Germany, Ireland, and Norway. "They were young men and youths in their very prime," explained one observer, "a sturdy, stalwart, self reliant element such as push out to develop a new country, their superiority was noticeable." Whenever a Western regiment appeared, the "fine physique, the self-reliant carriage of its men at once challenged attention." One Badger put it plain: "We would have died rather than have dishonored the West. We felt that the eyes of the East were upon us."[2]

Here and there in the faraway states were also settlements of free blacks, runaway slaves, and larger camps of Ojibwa, Oneida, Potawatomi, Menominee, and other Indian tribes. It was not a place of strict class lines, refinement of culture, or even formal government. Individuals were judged for their ability to wield an axe, a saw, or a plow. Family connections, money, and color of skin played a role, but more important was the strength of heart needed to tame a wilderness and wait out the harsh winters.

Among those who ventured to the frontier were Clayton and Earl Rogers. Pennsylvania natives, they traveled west to open a saw mill on a river in the Wisconsin Territory that was, one friend said, "10 miles from the nearest white woman." Rufus Dawes of Ohio arrived with his father to make a future on the open land. Poor boy Sol Meredith walked out of North Carolina to Indiana. Educated and cultured Henry Morrow of Virginia arrived in Detroit seeking advancement and to make a name for himself. Even Abe Lincoln, born in Kentucky and late of Indiana, ventured to

Springfield, Illinois, where he married well and became a lawyer of some reputation.

In many ways, these frontier settlers were a new kind of American, with only a limited kinship to the folks who pushed into the Ohio River Valley and Kentucky in earlier times. These new Americans were better educated and were riding the wave of an industrial revolution. They had a sense of place and section fed by the growth of newspapers, railroads, highways, canals, and the telegraph. They counted among their frontier friends men who were white, black, and red.

But "Iron Men of the West" were expected to march farther, shoot straighter, and stand firm in a battle line when other men just as brave give way. It was a fact recognized by the members of the 24th Michigan when they joined the brigade after Antietam in late 1862. "They knew the record [that] the balance of our brigade had made," explained one Badger, "and realized that if they were to rank with their brethren from Wisconsin and Indiana, no time must be lost in preparing for the serious work ahead." The rebuke of the veterans came when the new regiment was drawn up to be introduced. The Michiganders wore new uniforms; those adorning the men from Wisconsin and Indiana were "army-worn." The Michigan unit fielded nearly as many men as the four veteran regiments combined. When the four regiments were asked to lift a cheer of welcome for

Unidentified Corporal
Co. B, 19th Indiana Infantry

This unidentified soldier of the 19th Indiana proudly displays his Model 1858 hat with an embroidered "B" to mark his company, the Richmond City Greys, and a First Brigade, First Division, First Corps badge on the side.

Carroll College Institute for Civil War Studies

the Michigan men, the call was met with silence. "A pretty cool reception, we thought," grumbled a Wolverine. "We had come to reinforce them and supposed they would be glad to see us."[3]

There was also another development: a reorganization of the Army of the Potomac following Chancellorsville. The shuffling of units touched the proud "Old First Corps," which dated existence to 1861 when McClellan was creating his army to put down the rebellion. General Irvin McDowell first led the corps, followed by Joe Hooker who carried it onto the field at Antietam early on the morning of September 17, 1862. The famous unit was now under West Pointer John Reynolds, an officer with a solid reputation. The corps entered into its third summer of war reduced by hard service and the mustering out of the two-year New York regiments and the brigade of nine-month New Jersey volunteers that had temporarily replaced them. As a result, two of the three divisions of the First Corps marched north that June with two infantry brigades in their ranks instead of the usual four.

As far as the Western men were concerned, the most important decision of Hooker's reorganization was that the Wisconsin, Indiana, and Michigan men formally became the *First* Brigade of the *First* Division of the *First* Army Corps. The news triggered a wave of loud and harmless boasting. An example of all this was found in an officer's letter to his best girl. His 6th Wisconsin, he told her, was now, "by designation, the first regiment in the volunteer army of the United States. As a brigade, we are one of the oldest in the army and deserve the title"[4]

If Robert Lee and the Confederate army would only give us a "good opportunity," another soldier in the Iron Brigade exclaimed, the Black Hats were ready to "pitch into him."[5]

Chapter 7

Bad News About the Rebs

The Iron Brigade regiments marched twenty miles on the first day of the pursuit of the Confederate army, twelve miles the second, and thirty miles on the third. The march to Leesburg, Virginia, on June 17, 1863, was especially severe with little water and "heat like a furnace." The "sun poured down," a Wisconsin soldier said, and along the road "you could see the boys laying, given out. Perhaps one fainting, a sun struck man and others you would see pouring water on their heads. . . . The heat and dust is awful." A Michigan man agreed the march was a hard one, writing home, "I hardly think I shall ever again think water too muddy to drink—not in the Army at least." Another soldier recalled that the dust was a "foot deep" in some places, and when "the wind blows the dust flies so that it is impossible to see the sky." At Centerville, Virginia, the First Division halted to rest. Fresh newspapers reached the column with "bad news about the rebs in Maryland & Penn. Some . . . within 16 miles of Harrisburg [Pennsylvania]." Sketchy reports claimed the enemy was spread out, threatening not only Harrisburg but Philadelphia and Baltimore. The enemy, the papers duly noted, was gathering up anything that could be used or carried off, including wagons, fodder, horses, mules, and various foodstuffs both on the hoof and off.[1]

A few bright moments punctuated the otherwise difficult march. As the Iron Brigade approached the Maryland-Pennsylvania line, Lieutenant Loyd Harris, commanding a company in the 6th Wisconsin, looked ahead to see a "beautiful girl, scarcely twenty" at the gate of her home, waving a large American flag. Mounted officers doffed hats and bowed in the saddle, but

Lieutenant Loyd Harris
Co. C, 6th Wisconsin Volunteers

Enlisted from Prairie du Chien and was one of the regimental singers. He saluted a pretty girl on the march to Gettysburg, where he commanded the Iron Brigade Guard in the charge on the railroad cut.

Wisconsin Historical

Society WHI 10699

the men in ranks were smitten to silence. "Every last man seemed ready to give his life if necessary for that fair patriot, yet did not seem to know just what to do," he wrote. Taking matters in his own hand, Harris ordered his men take up the step and bring rifle-muskets to "Right shoulder, shift." The boys "caught the idea, every head was up; the fours perfectly aligned—then as we just opposite the maiden, I commanded, 'Carry arms!' Down came the very bright shining muskets. The next company did the same and all the companies . . . gave her a salute as if she were general of the army."[2]

When the long blue columns pushed into areas untouched by war, foraging became a problem—especially the capture of plump Union chickens from nearby farms by the always hungry soldier boys. A circular from headquarters established a camp guard. On June 22, General Sol Meredith issued an order forming a "Brigade Guard" to be "mounted at the same hour each day when circumstances will permit until further orders." The detail, about 100 men under the command of two officers selected from the regiments, was comprised of privates and noncommissioned officers from each of the five regiments. Meredith's order also contained this curious directive: From the detail would be selected "each day one Sergeant, three corporals and fourteen privates for special guard duty at HeadQrs"; the soldiers were to be picked "with special reference to cleanliness and soldierly bearing," and were to be brought to the guard formation about 9 a.m. with the brigade "band playing." No reason was given for the special headquarters detail.[3]

The commander of the First Division, James Wadsworth, appeared to be everywhere those days, trying to lift the burden of the marching soldiers.

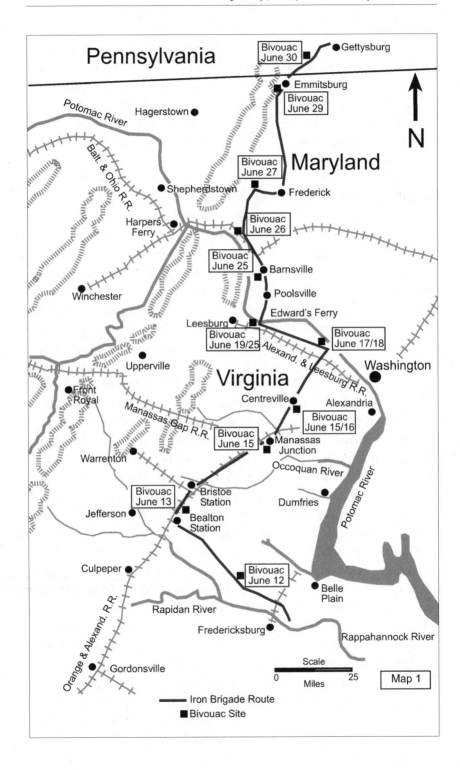

Pennsylvania

Bivouac
June 30

Gettysburg

Emmitsburg

Bivouac
June 29

Potomac River

Hagerstown

N

Bivouac
June 27

Maryland

Balt. & Ohio R.R.

Shepherdstown

Frederick

Harpers
Ferry

Bivouac
June 26

Bivouac
June 25

Barnsville

Poolsville

Winchester

Edward's Ferry

Leesburg

Bivouac
June 19/25

Bivouac
June 17/18

Alexand. & Leesburg R.R.

Washington

Upperville

Virginia

Front
Royal

Centreville

Alexandria

Manassas Gap R.R.

Bivouac
June 15/16

Bivouac
June 15

Manassas
Junction

Warrenton

Occoquan River

Bivouac
June 13

Bristoe
Station

Dumfries

Jefferson

Bealton
Station

Potomac River

Culpeper

Bivouac
June 12

Belle
Plain

Rapidan River

Orange & Alexand. R.R.

Fredericksburg

Rappahannock River

Scale

0   25
Miles

Map 1

Gordonsville

—— Iron Brigade Route
■ Bivouac Site

At one point he reached into his own pocket to buy fence rails to build roadside fires so his men could heat coffee; at another, he secured straw from a farmer to make beds, and at a third place, the 55-year-old Wadsworth ordered the valises of the officers on his staff thrown from an ambulance so the vehicle could be filled with the knapsacks and muskets of his exhausted men. It was a kind gesture by the old gentleman and hailed as such by his grateful soldiers. Many of the men must have enjoyed a hearty chuckle when it was discovered that the division headquarters papers, as well as the general's own valise, had been tossed overboard and had to be recovered.

When Wadsworth and his staff passed a large flour mill, the general noticed the owner and his employees sitting on the front step watching the tramping column. The general rode over to greet the men and ask whether they knew of any source of footwear for his soldiers. The proprietor was "surly and ungracious," reported one of the staff officers, and his attitude aroused the general's temper. "You have a good pair of boots on your feet, give them to one of my soldiers," Wadsworth ordered. When the surprised miller sputtered a refusal, the general instructed an orderly to dismount and take possession of the footwear. "It was quickly done," said one of Wadsworth's staff. The soldiers loved "Old Daddy Wadsworth." According to Private James Sullivan, "[If] there was a patriot in the army it was him."[4]

Another sign of the hard marching manifested itself at Broad Run, Virginia. Lieutenant Harris was finishing breakfast when one of his 6th Wisconsin men, worn out by the long miles and lack of water, was brought in under armed guard. The arrested private was Dick Marston, a farmer boy from Seneca in Crawford County found sleeping on a guard post. Marston was known within the ranks as a man of such "phlegmatic nature" that he was known as "Sleepy Dick." Harris knew full well that sleeping on a picket post "in the face of Lee's Army, meant a drum head court-martial and death; for the discipline of the army was being enforced in a most vigorous manner." But he was convinced it would be "like murder to have this young man, only twenty-one years of age, shot like a deserter or a traitor." Harris approached the commander of the regiment, but Rufus Dawes refused to simply release Marston with a warning for such a serious infraction. Harris "stormed considerable; then begged," and finally Dawes agreed to go to brigade headquarters to see what could be done.

A short time later, "Sleepy Dick" walked into camp without guards, released from arrest. He had heard it all, he told his friends—how Dawes had enlisted General Meredith, how the two went to headquarters to see

Wadsworth ("Three warm hearts," Harris said later of the officers), and how Wadsworth ("glorious old man that he was") ordered the young soldier be given a stern warning and released. When he finished his story, Marston could only shake his head in thanks as the "tears started in his eyes, and his voice failed him; but we all felt happy that he was with us, safe and sound," wrote on his his comrades. That night, in a letter to his sweetheart in Ohio, Dawes commented on the clemency, noting, "I had a chance to do a good thing this morning and it gave me pleasure . . . "[5]

On June 25 at Poolsville, Maryland, a group of school children stood solemnly by the roadside watching the Western regiments pass by. The youngsters were a "most beautiful sight," wrote a Michigan man, who said the reminder of home "brought tears to many an eye."[6] By the 27th of June, the advance column was at Middletown, Maryland, not far from the field at Antietam. That evening, Dawes and Meredith guided their horses across the old battlefield. "The grass has grown green over the graves of our brave boys, who lie buried there," Dawes wrote. "The inscriptions on the head boards are already scarcely legible and with their destruction seems to go the last poor chance that our sacrifice these men have made for their country shall be recognized and commemorated."

As the dusty columns passed Emmitsburg, students of St. Joseph's Catholic College pushed their way outside to welcome the Black Hats "with great enthusiasm and several of them marched along with us beyond the town," remembered Dawes in his postwar memoirs. "They were much interested in watching the movements of our advance guard and flanker, the feelers of the army. They wanted to see us 'flush the enemy'."[7]

The next day, General George Gordon Meade of the Fifth Corps was named to succeed Joseph Hooker as commander of the Army of the Potomac. The surprise news of Hooker's removal and Meade's elevation coursed through the ranks. The Western men chewed on the news a short time before deciding they did not like it. Like Meade, John Reynolds—their First Corps commander—was a Pennsylvania man. As far as they were concerned, Reynolds should have gotten the post. "Meade lacked the martial bearing and presence of Hooker," one officer claimed. "Few of our men knew him by sight. He was sometimes seen riding by the marching columns of troops at a fast trot, his hat brim turned down and a poncho over his shoulders. The only sign of rank was a gold cord on his hat." Meade added to their unease by getting off on a clumsy note in his first official communication to the army. After reminding the soldiers that the "whole country looks anxiously to this army to deliver it from the presence of the foe," he announced the following: "Corps and other commanders are authorized to order the instant death of any soldier who fails to do his duty at this hour." A disgusted Michigan man noted that a simple appeal to the honor of the men in ranks "would have sufficed." After the 6th Wisconsin mustered for pay on June 30, Dawes read Meade's address to the regiment without comment. At the top of his letter to his sweetheart that night he wrote: "Bivouac in Pennsylvania, On Marsh Creek, near Gettysburg."[8]

The five-mile march on June 30 from Emmitsburg, Maryland, into Pennsylvania was an easy one. The Iron Brigade led the way, and the 6th Wisconsin was the first to cross into the Keystone State. When the column stopped at midday at Marsh Creek, the Second Brigade camped in a cultivated field south of the sluggish stream while the Western regiments erected their small shelter halves along its north bank. The 19th Indiana drew picket duty. The Hoosiers pushed north on the road until four of the companies stopped just south of the small but thriving crossroads town of Gettysburg. Exactly where the Confederates were was a subject open for debate, but reports put them somewhere in the same general vicinity.

The Marsh Creek bivouac was a pleasant one. The soldiers used the afternoon to wash clothes or get rid of the dust and dirt with a swim in a nearby millpond. It was also an opportunity to gather in a decent meal. Farmers brought in chicken, fresh bread, and pies for the soldiers, and a Michigan soldier said foragers who slipped through the picket line brought in an "abundance of chicken, geese, pigs, mutton, milk, butter, honey." Private Sullivan filled his canteen with milk given him by a Dutch farmer, while Charles Walker of the 7th Wisconsin, assigned to the Brigade Guard, stretched out for a well-earned rested in a barn. Another member of the detail, Private William Ray of the 7th Wisconsin was tasked with guarding a farmhouse, where he got "a good supper & some milk for which we paid 25 cts a piece." Lieutenant Amos Rood, also of the 7th Wisconsin, rode about until he found a tavern. "I went in and said, 'Boss, fill my three canteens for the General.' I got the stuff. Kept one for myself and distributed the others to brother officers and men." A satisfied Rood rode back to Emmitsburg to find a home in which he could complete his monthly company returns.[9]

Others soldiers were less fortunate. A Wisconsin man attached to Battery B, 4th U.S. Artillery, scuffled with a farmer who demanded too much for his milk. Shrugging off the protests, the soldier milked the cow. The farmer demanded the officer in charge punish him for theft. A career officer in command of the battery, Lt. James Stewart regarded the private as a good soldier. If he did not punish him, Stewart concluded, the farmer would take his complaint elsewhere and the punishment might be worse. The Regular Army man ordered the citizen-soldier lashed spread-eagle on the extra wheel of an artillery caisson. The private's friends gathered around to grumble against the punishment. One called the farmer an "Adams County Copperhead" out to cheat a poor soldier. Stewart ordered the sullen soldiers to leave, but they stood their ground. For few moments it looked as though might be trouble. When the lieutenant, this time with more force, ordered them away a second time, they wisely heeded him and dispersed.[10]

Punishments of a different variety also disappointed. The Union soldiers expected to be welcomed as "deliverers of the country from a hated foe, to live on the fat of the land, milk, chickens, honey, eggs, butter and potatoes in profusion, without much money, and not at very high price," one officer explained. "Butter was the disappointment and sour the buttermilk doled out at 25 cents a glass, and other things in proportion."[11]

That night south of Gettysburg, Loyd Harris entertained his tent mate, Orrin Chapman, with music from a harmonica he bought in Frederick, Maryland. His last song before they turned in was "Home, Sweet Home."[12]

Not every soldier ended relatively quiet his day along Marsh Creek enjoying music and peaceful thoughts. In the mail sacks that reached the army was a letter for Ordnance Sergeant Jerome Watrous of the 6th Wisconsin. The news was not good: Jerome's brother Henry had been killed by an artillery shell on May 23 while serving with the 4th Wisconsin at Port Hudson, Louisiana. The news was especially hard to bear because the brothers were so close. Back in Wisconsin before the war, they joined the new Republican Party together and, along with a collection of abolitionists, Free Soilers, Whigs, Know Nothings, and disillusioned Democrats, worked to create a new political force. The brothers marched in Appleton's "Wide-Awake Company" for Abraham Lincoln of Illinois in the 1860 presidential campaign. The firing on Fort Sumter and the call for volunteers convinced Jerome to enlist in an Appleton contingent that joined with volunteers from nearby Fond du Lac to form a company in the 6th Wisconsin Volunteer Infantry. His brother Henry cast his lot with the 4th Wisconsin.

One of the last times the brothers were together was a few weeks after their regiments reached Washington in 1861. Jerome secured a pass and picked up his brother from the nearby 4th Wisconsin camp. While touring the city, the pair walked to the White House "hoping that our candidate of the year before would appear." As they watched a regiment tramp past on Pennsylvania Avenue, the two brothers realized that President Lincoln was standing behind them. "My boys, I see by your uniforms that you have come to help save the Union, to be my partners in the enterprise," said the president, shaking each man's hand and expressing that he "hoped that our lives would be spared, and that we would never regret the partnership."

Now, two years later, with Independence Day just four days distant, Watrous recalled the patriotic holiday of 1850 when the two brothers and four neighbor boys fought make-believe battles over a homemade fort in the woods. All six, including the lone black boy with them that day, ended up in real uniforms a dozen years later. One had already been killed at Vicksburg, Mississippi. Now, Henry was dead, killed by a cannon ball at Port Hudson. Every one of the six, Jerome later recalled with pride, won promotion, the lowest rank attained a sergeant, and the highest a major.[13] But as the last day of June 1863 drew toward its close, one of the "Lincoln partners" stood next to an army wagon south of Gettysburg with a letter announcing his brother's death. His was a long night of memories.[14]

About sunrise on July 1 a few miles south of Marsh Creek, Colonel Charles Wainwright, the First Corps Artillery Brigade commander, eased himself awake and threw down a quick breakfast. The men assigned to his batteries had mustered for pay the previous day, and he began his morning working on his June returns. Around him, the makeshift camps were stirring as soldiers built fires to roast coffee. Before Wainwright was able to complete his paperwork, a staff officer rode up with orders to move immediately up the road to the town of Gettysburg. Wainwright issued the appropriate orders and rode ahead to find General John Reynolds, who was in command of the three army corps leading the advance of the army.

The general was in no great hurry, Wainwright discovered. When he asked about the prospects of a fight that day, Reynolds waved it off. The army was moving up to be within supporting distance of General John Buford and his cavalry, who was pushing his cavalry brigades to Gettysburg and beyond to scout for the elusive Confederates. Reynolds mounted up and headed up the road to Marsh Creek where his First Division was camped. Behind him, Wainwright watched the various units form slowly "without dreaming of a fight, and fully expecting to be comfortably in camp by noon."[15]

Chapter 8

A New Regiment and a Veteran Battery

The soldiers of the 24th Michigan Volunteer Infantry always said the regiment owed its existence to the quiet words of the wife of Michigan Governor Austin Blair, which were more powerful than the howling of a mob.

The idea for a Detroit or Wayne County regiment was born in the wave of patriotic meetings organized after Southern sympathizers, draft resisters, and hooligans disrupted a mass war rally in Detroit's downtown. The rally was arranged following President Abraham Lincoln's June 28, 1862, call for 300,000 additional Union volunteers. Michigan had already raised seventeen regiments; the new quota called for six more. The patriotic speeches had just gotten underway when angry shouts from protesters turned the crowd into a crazed mob. Organizers and city officials scattered for safety. Over the next few days, amid gloomy newspaper accounts of the shameful incident, consensus was reached that the best way to prove the city's loyalty would be the creation of a new regiment—above the quota Washington requested—of men from Detroit and Wayne counties.

A delegation was sent to the governor for his permission. Blair, faced with the seemingly insurmountable task of raising six additional regiments, stubbornly refused. When his wife observed that the war news was anything but good, and that in her opinion the Republic needed every regiment it could get, her governor-husband consented. Another rally was called and organized at the very same place the mob had broken up the earlier meeting.

The crowd swelled to proportions "to cause every patriot to rejoice," said one witness, and included "determined and enthusiastic patriots," some armed with clubs for "any secesh rowdies who would open their blatant mouths." The two men proposed to lead the new regiment were citizens of importance and promise. Henry A. Morrow, the first judge of Recorder's Court, was tapped as the new outfit's colonel. A native of Virginia and veteran of the Mexican War, Morrow arrived in Detroit in 1853 on the urging of his friend and mentor, Senator Lewis Cass, and his abilities were quickly recognized. The man who became lieutenant colonel stood out in any crowd—6-foot 4-inch Wayne County Sheriff Mark Flannigan. The meeting kicked off a frenzy of recruiting. By August 11, 1862, the regiment was filled.[1]

The attachment of Battery B of the 4th U.S. Artillery to the Western organization was a different story. The Iron Brigade and the battery were together from the first days of the war until the May 1863 reorganization of the artillery in the Army of the Potomac. At that time, individual batteries attached to units were assigned to the various army corps. Battery B was shuffled to Colonel Charles Wainwright's First Corps Artillery Brigade. The order also directed the complement be raised to150 enlisted men for six-gun batteries. The artillerymen needed were raised from the volunteer regiments.[2]

Of the First Corps artillery units, Battery B was one of the most famous. It was one of 36 artillery companies (the "companies" officially became "batteries" in 1861) created in the artillery reorganization of 1821. Battery men fought as dragoons during the Seminole War and served with distinction as artillery at Monterrey and Buena Vista during the War with Mexico. When John Gibbon was promoted to infantry command, Lieutenant James Stewart, who joined the unit as an enlisted man at Fort Brown, Texas, assumed command of the guns. Born in Edinburgh, Scotland, Stewart immigrated to the United States in 1844. Little is known of his time in America before his enlistment as a private in1851. His ability quickly became apparent, and Stewart was promoted to first sergeant. At the start of the war in 1861, Battery B was stationed at Camp Floyd, Utah, for the Mormon Uprising and serving as cavalry escorts to guard the Pony Express route. In fact, it was a Pony Express rider who brought Stewart and others word of the firing on Fort Sumter. The battery was ordered to move overland to Fort Leavenworth in Kansas, from which point it traveled by rail to Washington.

Major James Stewart
Battery B, 4th U.S. Artillery

Stewart was still a lieutenant when he commanded Battery B at Gettysburg. This rare post war photograph shows him as a major. His battery men called him "Old Jack," and said he could drink more than any man in the army and still be ready for duty.

The December 1861 roll showed Battery B with three lieutenants and forty-seven enlisted men. It was at this time that Gibbon, already a familiar figure to the volunteers of the 2nd, 6th, 7th Wisconsin and 19th Indiana, looked to the regiments to fill his ranks. In the 6th Wisconsin, he had trouble convincing the soldiers to join his battery, partly because of the distrust volunteers held for West Pointers. Only one man stepped forward after Gibbon concluded his opening appeal. A tad exasperated, Colonel Lysander Cutler stepped forward to explain to the men what Gibbon wanted, and why. Cutler's words did the trick, and a "large number stepped forward." A pleased Cutler cautioned, "There, there, that will do—you needn't all come out—they don't want the whole regiment for the battery."[3] A Michigan volunteer called Battery B one of the best in service, and "one that had made more than one Rebel bite the dust." He wrote home that he was glad he made the transfer. "I pity the poor infantry when they move, for they have got to carry five days' rations in their knapsacks and three days in their haversacks, besides their clothing and blanket, while we have only got a canteen of water to carry," he continued. "When we get tired of walking we can ride. I never have been better suited than I am at present."[4]

Gibbon's promotion to brigade command moved Stewart to an officer's slot within the battery, and while Gibbon rejoiced in the promotion of his friend, he stubbornly resisted resigning his hard won and coveted Regular Army captain's billet, effectively blocking the promotion of anyone else—including Stewart.

The new lieutenant of artillery proved an able officer. Stewart, described a friend, was a "handsome man, of fine, soldierly presence, rather grave and taciturn in manner; fond of 'creature comforts,' [who] sometimes indulged in them quite as much as was good for him. But he always realized when it was 'time to quit,' and . . . was always on hand in the morning when duty called." The lieutenant was called "Old Jack" behind his back and one infantry volunteer said while Stewart was very strict with the rest of the battery, he would at the same time "drink more than any one else."[5]

Despite Battery B's splendid record and cadre of colorful officers and men ("No battery in the field ran it's nose up, under, and into the enemy so often, and so successfully as old Battery B. with her Napoleon guns," claimed one Wisconsin officer), it was most famous in the army for a horse named "Tartar," a team bay wounded at Second Bull Run by a solid shot that cut off the animal's tail and "removed a dozen pounds of flesh." Tartar was four-years-old when he entered the service at Fort Leavenworth,

Kansas, in 1847, just before Battery B started on the Utah expedition. Abandoned when taken sick with distemper, Tartar showed up again the next spring when two Indians brought him in to sell. After being injured at Second Bull Run, the unfortunate animal was once again left behind in a small pasture, only to be found again the next morning with the battery horses after jumping the fence. The animal was wounded again at Fredericksburg and once again abandoned, only to show up on a Federal cavalry picket line a month later. Tartar's bob-tailed condition was even the cause of a presidential joke. When he spotted the horse as the battery passed a reviewing stand, President Lincoln slyly remarked to the generals around him, "This reminds me of a tale."[6]

Chapter 9

The Black Hats

The Wisconsin, Indiana, and Michigan soldiers moving up the Emmitsburg Road toward Gettysburg had marched a good many miles since being called to Washington in 1861. It was a sight no one of them would ever see again—the Black Hat brigade swinging along with an easy stride, the famous headgear now more serviceable instead of showy. One who saw them said they "looked like giants with their tall black hats," and recalled they moved with a "steady step" and filled the "entire roadway, their big black hats and feathers conspicuous . . ."[1]

Two years of service had left its mark on the men in the original four regiments. Their letters, journals, and diaries, which once brimmed with the bright hopes of quick victory 1861, no longer evidenced such naiveté. The survivors gathered in close, tight messes to share food, drawing upon each other for support. While they marched and died, enduring unspeakable hardship, the home folk "growled" about high prices, short money, and hard times. The army tossed out the used-up soldier and the "patriotic" speculators fleeced them of their pay. The men fought well, but were denied victory by incompetent generals and a strong, resilient enemy. Officers used their rank to get through sentry posts to forage and their authority to execute weak men unable to stand the travails of combat.

By June 1863, only about one of three soldiers was still in ranks from the regiments formed in 1861. The others were dead from battle or illness or even homesickness. Scores more had been sent home sick and disabled.

Lance J. Herdegen

Unidentified
6th Wisconsin Volunteers

This unidentified soldier from the 6th Wisconsin is wearing the Black Hat and issue nine-button blue frock coat. He is wearing a non-commissioned officer eagle belt plate. His hat is marked only with a brass "6" indicating this could be a mid-war image.

Others had simply melted away, gone only God knows where or why. The survivors owed their allegiance first to the men around their campfires, then to the small companies, and finally to their regiments. They were isolated from the folks back home, misused by their generals and the country's leaders, cheated by sutlers, and snubbed by the Easterners because of their Western origins. They trusted only their comrades and the few officers who had proved to be skillful and brave. They were a hard lot, these Westerners, good soldiers deeply proud of their reputations.

Only the men of the 24th Michigan, even after ten months in service, marched toward Gettysburg feeling they still had something to prove. The Michigan regiment and its famous brigade had seen only limited service at Fredericksburg, where the Wolverines first experienced enemy fire. When the combat began, their colonel had yelled out, "Steady, men, those Wisconsin men are watching you!" The Michigan regiment joined the 6th Wisconsin in the spirited river crossing during the Chancellorsville Campaign, but it was not the kind of heavy, terrible fighting their comrades had endured at Second Bull Run, South Mountain, and Antietam. It was only after Chancellorsville the Michigan regiment's coveted black hats arrived. "They made our appearance like the name of the brigade, quite unique," recalled one Wolverine with pride.

The five regiments were also marked by what John Gibbon later called "the habit of obedience and subjection to the will of another, so difficult to instill in the minds of free and independent men."[2] The "men who carried the knapsacks," a Wisconsin officer said, "never failed to place an officer just where he belonged, as to his intelligence and bravery. Even if they said nothing yet their instinctive and unconscious action in battle, placed upon the officer the unavoidable brand of approval or disapproval. For no regiment acted well its part under fire and great danger, without the officers had the confidence of the rank and file."[3] To veteran soldiers, said one officer, battle is an "awful experience" and they had not the "headlong recklessness of new men, who start it, acting as though they would rather be shot than not, and then lose their organization and scatter like sheep." They understood from "much experience in fighting that safety is best had by steadiness, persistence in firing, and most of all by holding together."[4]

The fight these Western men were unknowingly marching toward that morning of July 1, 1863—one many would come to regard as the turning point of the conflict—was in many ways the last great fight for the "Boys of '61," those bright volunteers who flocked to the National flag in a swell of patriotism after Fort Sumter. The army itself was changing into something that, two years earlier, would have been unrecognizable. By the summer of 1863, the veterans were unsettled by recruits who enlisted to collect

Private Peter L Foust
19th Indiana Infantry

Foust is pictured with the Iron Brigade uniform about the time of Gettysburg. His linen leggings are long gone and his Black Hat is untrimmed. Faust was mortally wounded on July 1, 1863.

John Wedeward Collection

Private Oliver Fletcher
Co. K, 6th Wisconsin Infantry

He joined the Lemonweir Minute men in May 1861. Fletcher won promotion to corporal, but was captured in June 22, 1864. This photograph was taken in 1862 while the 6th Wisconsin was at Fredericksburg, Virginia.

---

bounties and newspapers reporting lack of support for the war back home. After the first three days of July 1863, it would all be different, partly because of a change in the way the war was fought, and partly because of the men brought in fill the battle-depleted regiments. However, late in the war and afterward, at the old soldier campfires and reunions, even those bounty and drafted men would be accepted. Why? Because they had been *there;* They had *shared* the hardship the stay-at-homes had not. But the aftermath of the greatest combat in the Western hemisphere and its aftermath was still ahead of them.

*   *   *

General John Reynolds caught up with the marching column of the First Division just after it left Marsh Creek. The general had spent the night of June 30-July 1 at Mortiz Tavern six miles south of Gettysburg. That evening, he was joined by Major General Oliver O. Howard, commander of the Eleventh Corps. The two officers examined the latest reports and Reynolds showed Howard "a bundle of dispatches—the information brought to him during the day—with evidence of the proximity, nearness and designs of the enemy." Reynolds, remembered Howard, "impressed me as unusually sad; perhaps more so than any clear-headed officer would be on the eve of an important battle." The report from cavalryman John Buford, who was already at Gettysburg with his troopers, was that one Confederate infantry command, perhaps as much as one-third of the Rebel army, was massed near Cashtown to the northwest. Another Confederate body was near Carlisle, Pennsylvania, and a third was close to Chambersburg, west of Cashtown. This information was deemed reliable and Reynolds understood the gravity of the situation. Howard left about 11:00 p.m. to return to his corps. Just a handful of miles distant, General Robert E. Lee was operating without any clear picture of the Federal Army's whereabouts or intelligence of its intention to concentrate near Gettysburg.[5]

Reynolds was up at 4:00 a.m. the next day. His first order was to Wadsworth of the First Division: push your men ahead to Gettysburg. General Abner Doubleday with the rest of the First Corps would follow Wadsworth. Other riders sought out Third Corps commander Dan Sickles near Emmitsburg, Maryland, with instructions to also move toward Gettysburg. Howard and the Eleventh Corps were ordered to follow the First Corps. Reynolds, meanwhile, rode ahead to briefly confer with Wadsworth before pushing his black horse "Fancy" up the Emmitsburg Road toward Gettysburg. It was early Wednesday morning, July 1, 1863.

The soldiers of the Iron Brigade finished a "hearty breakfast of coffee and hardtack" just as the sun was rising above the horizon. "The Pennsylvania line had been reached and the forces of the enemy must be met very soon," a Michigan man predicted, "though none suspected that the foe was within a few hours march." Union cavalry moving up the road the previous day—Thomas Devin's brigade of John Buford's cavalry division—leaned from their saddles to warn the infantrymen they had run into Johnnies just ahead near Gettysburg—and a lot of them. Lee's whole army was gathering up there, one officer cautioned them. Despite the ominous news, no sense of urgency rippled through the marching column. Men atop ordnance wagons parked nearby, however, began passing out the required fresh "60 rounds of ammunition in the boxes and upon the person." An awkward moment transpired within the ranks of the 24th Michigan as the men drew cartridges while the chaplain tried to complete a morning prayer. The Black Hats shoved two packets of 10 cartridges each in the tin containers of their cartridge boxes, then broke open two more and put the individual paper cartridges in readiness at the top of the tins. The paper twists with percussion caps were opened and the caps added to the small leather boxes looped to their waist belts. The remaining two packets of cartridges boxes were stuffed in haversacks and pockets. It went unrecorded how much of the chaplain's prayer was heard.[6]

The Iron Brigade was equipped with a variety of weapons ranging from imported Model 1854 Austrian Lorenz rifles to the Springfield pattern rifle-muskets. There was a minor supply problem as the 2nd Wisconsin carried Austrian Lorenz rifles in their original .54-caliber, while the shoulder arms of the other regiments were in .58-caliber.

The Lorenz was the second most common imported firearm in the Civil War and the Badgers, who were used to handling firearms, generally liked them. The 2nd Wisconsin was first issued "sheet metal" smoothbore .69-caliber Harpers Ferry muskets that had been altered from flintlock to percussion. "Is there any wonder, then that we should weep for joy rather than for sorrow," a Badger wrote home when the new rifles were issued in January 1862, "when we exchanged them [muskets] for true and trusty rifles that will bite as well as bark and kick. We now have the best guns in the Brigade, and I think they are in the hands of men who know how to use them." A week later, following a firing drill, the correspondent seemed to agree with that assessment when he concluded, "the results proved highly satisfactory. They are a splendid piece, rough as they look; and in the hands of the Second will do good execution when the opportunity for their use occurs."[7]

Kim J. Heltemes Collection

Unidentified (Wisconsin)
1st Sergeant, Iron Brigade

This soldier is outfitted as First Sergeant with non-commissioned officer sword. The backdrop is typical of Iron Brigade photographs in the May-August 1862 period when the unit was stationed at Fredericksburg, Virginia.

The 6th Wisconsin, 19th Indiana, and 24th Michigan generally carried the model 1861 .58-caliber Springfield pattern rifle-muskets and found them superior to the Austrian variety. One of the backwoods boys, Private

James Patrick Sullivan of the 6th Wisconsin, knew how to hit a mark as well as any man. He mounted his rifle-musket with "some silver ornaments and fixed the screw in a stock against the dog [sear] so it [trigger pull] worked almost as easy as a squirrel gun, and felt very proud of it." The fix involved placing a screw next to the trigger guard extending into the works of the lock. During an inspection one day, when General Wadsworth asked the private about the screw in the gunstock, Sullivan wrote, "I told him so that I could hit a canteen at one hundred yards and he asked me no more questions."[8]

The 7th Wisconsin was also issued Model 1854 Austrian Lorenz rifles in February 1862, but unlike the smaller caliber given to the 2nd Wisconsin, they were re-rifled or reamed up to .58-caliber—the standard being adopted by the army. One soldier said the new rifles were "colored black except for the lock guard and rammer, which are bright." The rifles were four inches shorter than the old musket and half a pound heavier, he said, but "they carry very nice and much easier than the musket. So we are ready for the secesh now." A few weeks later the beechwood stocks of the 7th Wisconsin rifles were bleached almost yellow by the elements and it was ordered they be "varnished" with a dark stain at a cost of ten cents to each soldier. The extra cost was met in ranks with "strong opposition."[9]

In appearance, the Western men carried knapsacks (or an occasional bedroll), and common to all was the famous big black felt hats marked by the red wool badges of the First Corps. Most of the men wore the dark blue four-button sack coats, but the Regular Army nine-button blue frocks were still plentiful—especially in the 6th Wisconsin where they were favored. Over the shoulder each soldier carried a haversack and canteen and in each knapsack a rubber or woolen blanket (in addition to personal items). On the top straps of the knapsack, soldiers tied a shelter half where overcoats usually were carried. Two soldiers would combine shelter halves and button them together to form a common tent and share their woolen and rubber blankets.[10]

As the men began forming their companies, some observed Lysander Cutler's Second Brigade already on the road. The soldiers also saw Reynolds conferring with Wadsworth.[11] James Hall's 2nd Maine Battery followed Cutler's brigade and the Second Brigade's 7th Indiana was left behind to guard the division wagons. Sol Meredith was slow getting his men in formation and Cutler's brigade pushed off and was well ahead—almost a full mile—before Wadsworth sent a rider galloping with orders to "close up." The 2nd Wisconsin led the way, followed by the 7th Wisconsin. A short distance ahead, the soldiers of the 19th Indiana, which had been on sentry duty, waited to file in behind the 7th. The 24th Michigan closed up behind the Hoosiers. The 6th Wisconsin was last in line, followed by the Brigade Guard of 100 men and two officers.[12]

The weather was warm but pleasant, and the Western men, well-rested and looking forward to a friendly reception in the town just ahead, moved with an easy route step. They were in "high spirits," remembered one man, and a Milwaukee company in the 6th Wisconsin lifted up a "soul stirring song as only the Germans can sing." The regiment took up the step of the music and when the Milwaukeeans finished, three rousing cheers were offered on their behalf. Then the Juneau County company ("with about as much melody as a government mule") began a song about "a heifer wild" that stole cabbage "in the moonlight mild" and that everyone knew she should be "killed and quartered and issued out for beef."

And so it went, verse after verse, with the whole column joining the chorus, "On the distant prairie, Hoop de dooden doo," until the song broke down in laughter. Another soldier began the scandalous "Paddy's Wedding," and another recalled he found it "odd for men to march toward their death singing, shouting and laughing as if it were parade or holiday." Finally, the men settled down and the column "plodded along" in a march of "unusual quietude." The peaceful moment was broken when cavalry clattered up the roadway, scattering the infantry left and right. An Irish soldier in a Wisconsin regiment raised a fist and called after them, "May the devil fly away with the roofs of your jackets; yez going now to get us into a scrape and thin walk off and let us fight it out like you always do!"

He had no idea how accurate his prediction would prove to be.[13]

Chapter 10

A Young Lieutenant and a Fair Maid

Lieutenant Hollon Richardson of the 7thWisconsin was already in the saddle when the Iron Brigade regiments moved onto the roadway from the Marsh Creek camp. Always open and full of energy, he was looking forward to a friendly welcome by the loyal citizens of Gettysburg. As usual, however, the young officer attached to Sol Meredith's staff rode along the column careful to avoid his new father-in-law—Colonel William Robinson of his own regiment. The two men were at irreconcilable differences over an age-old dilemma—a young man seeking the hand of a fair maiden over the strong objections of her father. The war romance was a source of great amusement and interest to the officers and soldiers of the 7th Wisconsin, and the interest spilled into the other regiments as well.

The romance began during the winter of 1861-62, when the brigade was quartered on the grounds of the Arlington House opposite Washington, D.C. It was a pleasant location, and Robinson was one of several officers who had wives and families visit. His pretty young daughter Leonora, "was soon a favorite" of not only the young officers, but the men in ranks. "Lieutenant Richardson was particularly well pleased with her," a friend remembered. "Indeed, he soon learned to love her, and loved her very ardently, and her heart warmed, toward him as thoroughly as his did toward her." Her father, the colonel, a native of Vermont and a veteran of the Mexican War, liked the handsome 25-year-old Richardson as an officer and man well enough, but "would not consent to his daughter marrying a man who might be felled with windows made by rebel bullets the day after he became his son-in-law. He was emphatic in the matter and was not at all backward in making known his opposition to the proposed union."

Robinson's objections were puzzling, for Richardson was a promising suitor. A native of Poland, Ohio, and the son of a construction contractor, Richardson passed the bar in 1857 and moved to Chippewa Falls, Wisconsin, where he practiced law. He was elected prosecuting attorney of Chippewa County and—with the coming of the war—closed his office and at his own expense enlisted about thirty men and started with them to Madison on an open flatboat. Richardson declined a captain's commission, and it was only after the urgent solicitation of his friends that he accepted a commission as first lieutenant of the Lodi Guards, which became Company A of the 7th regiment. He was soon regarded as a capable officer and won attention during a Fourth of July celebration in summer of 1862 at Fredericksburg where, during a series of foot races, Richardson proved the fastest man in the brigade. Although cash prizes were offered, he turned them away with a quick smile, saying he ran for the "fun of it" to see if he had "lost speed any since coming to the army." Despite Richardson's merit and promise, however, and despite the efforts of the young man and young woman to win his approval, Robinson continued to oppose the match.

There were two family stories about how the marriage came to happen outside the colonel's influence. In the first, the lieutenant and Miss Robinson "met in Washington by accident—such as an accident, as they had carefully planned to bring about—and were married." In the second, told by a Richardson descendant, the two were traveling by carriage together to Washington on May 9, 1862, to stand up at the wedding of another young couple. Sometime during the carriage ride, the young lieutenant (who was "a good talker," explained a relative) convinced her to join him in a double wedding.

It was "some months" before the colonel discovered he had a new son-in-law and the length of the deception made it all the worse. When Robinson discovered "the true state of affairs he was unwise enough to let his angry passions come to the surface." In one report, the colonel went looking for Richardson with his revolver, unaware that his wife had emptied the chambers of bullets. In any case, the two officers were not on speaking terms as the army tramped its way toward Gettysburg. In fact, it would be well into 1864, an officer wrote, "that the sun shone, the ice broke and melted away and they became warm friends." In the meantime, however, the

Howard Michael Madaus Collection

General John Reynolds
First Corps, Army of the Potomac

Was killed in the opening infantry fighting at Gettysburg July 1, 1863, as he directed the 2nd Wisconsin into the woods on McPherson's Ridge. One Confederate claimed the general was mortally wounded in a volley fired by the 2nd Mississippi across the Chambersburg Pike.

colonel and the young lieutenant suffered through a stiff and formal relationship watched with dismay by many in the brigade because Richardson was a great favorite, and his father-in-law well respected. Now, riding toward Gettysburg with one eye out for Colonel Robinson and the other out for rebels, young Richardson was about to face a trying day on two fronts.[1]

One of the men the young lieutenant passed that morning was General John Reynolds, who was about to make a decision that could determine the course of the war in the Eastern Theater. As a Pennsylvanian, Reynolds faced an enemy army on his native soil with his family less than a day's hard ride away. He was born on September 21, 1820, in Lancaster, where his father John Reynolds, Sr., published the Democratic newspaper *The Lancaster Journal.* A friend of the family and business associate was soon-to-be-president James Buchanan. It was Buchanan, as a U.S. Senator, who appointed the younger Reynolds to the Military Academy at West Point, New York. He graduated in 1841 and saw service in Florida, on the frontier, and during the Mexican War in which he was twice cited for bravery. When the Confederates fired on Fort Sumter, Reynolds was commandant of the cadet corps at West Point. Unable to stand by with his country at war, he immediately sought a Regular Army position before being offered (partly due to the efforts of his friend George McClellan) the First Brigade of the Pennsylvania Reserve Division. He showed ability and was soon advanced to command of the First Corps, succeeding Joseph Hooker.

In June 1863, while visiting Washington, Reynolds was offered command of the Army of the Potomac, but he refused the post when operatives of President Lincoln, with political cronies whispering about Reynolds' connections to the Democratic Party, were unable to assure him a free hand. One who saw him about that time described the general as "tall, dark, and slender" with "a wild look a rolling eye. Very nervous to all appearance."

When his rival, George Gordon Meade, was named instead to command the army, Reynolds put on his best uniform and offered his congratulations. To Colonel Charles Wainwright of his Artillery Brigade, however, Reynolds confided that he had refused the army command because he was "unwilling to take Burnside and Hooker's leavings." Wainwright wrote in his journal: "For my part, I think we have got the best man [Meade] of the two, much as I think of Reynolds. He will do better at carrying out plans than devising them, I think."[2]

To the men in the ranks of the Iron Brigade, the general was a distant and formal Old Army Regular, respected for his ability and "common sense" but not a great favorite. Few were willing to forget how Reynolds had been ready to abandon the 19th Indiana in the retreat from Fredericksburg. The Hoosiers were manning an advance picket line when the withdrawal began and Reynolds, to avoid alerting the rebels, was prepared to leave them behind. Only the intervention of Colonel Lysander Cutler and the efforts of his staff officer, Clayton Rogers, who made a successful attempt to bring off the pickets, saved the outfit from potentially significant losses.[3]

In manner, Reynolds was a tough disciplinarian with a hands-on manner of command (one artillery officer complained the general sometimes got caught up in the minor details of running an army corps) and not the officer of the colorful uniform or quick remark. He lacked colorful personality, dress, and nickname, and there were few camp stories about "that dark, silent, alert man," as one Wisconsin soldier described him. Instead, he was remarked on for his striking military appearance and steady professionalism. Accoring to one private, on days of hard marching the general would send an aide with word whether there was time to boil coffee. "If we did not receive that order no man started a fire and during the whole march there was never a fire lighted in vain."[4]

A fellow officer described the general as a "superb-looking man, dark-complexioned, wearing full black whiskers." He sat his horse, he continued, "like a Centaur, tall, straight and graceful, the ideal soldier." A member of the 24th Michigan admitted that "perhaps few knew him intimately, for he was a strangely reticent man. . . .[But] his opponents recognized his ability and his soldiers know that he held in reserve a latent force of clear and coolheadedness that could always be relied upon. They trusted him implicitly."

As an officer, Reynolds had not been particularly lucky during the war's first two years. He led his Pennsylvania brigade with promise during the Seven Days' fighting of 1862 only to be captured one night when his horse became mired in mud. His division won praise at Second Bull Run, but it was lost in the sour wrangling following the defeat. Reynolds missed South Mountain and Antietam on a political assignment in Pennsylvania that did not advance his career or his reputation. He commanded the First Corps during the Fredericksburg Campaign in December 1862, but it was his rival Meade who won attention on the field of battle. At Chancellorsville the following spring, Hooker gave him an assignment that kept his men in reserve and thus out of advancement's limelight. His atrocious string of ill-luck continued when Lincoln offered him command of the army at a time when the president and the administration were unable to give the assurances the general believed he needed to accept such an honor.

Now, as Reynolds moved toward Gettysburg with the command of three army corps in hand, he was being handed a chance to play a significant role in what would almost certainly be a major battle on his native soil. A 2nd Wisconsin soldier spotted the general that morning. He looked "careworn, sad and stern," he remembered, "but the high purpose of his patriotic spirit was stamped upon every lineament."[5]

Chapter 11

King's Pet Babies

The oldest and most famous of the five regiments, the 2nd Wisconsin, marched in the lead as the Iron Brigade moved toward Gettysburg. It was one of the first three-year organizations (the 1st Wisconsin was mustered for three months) to reach Washington in 1861. When the men were called to Madison to form a regiment, the eager volunteers learned no more 90-day men were being accepted, and that they would have to enlist for three years or until the war ended. After a bit of discussion, all but one of the ten original companies accepted the new term and another was called to fill the vacancy.

The regiment enjoyed a reputation for hard fighting even though it was an organization with a troubled record of leadership and marked earlier at times by a wont of discipline. In the Washington camps of 1861, the grey militia uniforms—especially the trousers—were "sadly depleted" to the point where, as one 6th Wisconsin man said, there was nothing quite like "a view of their rear ranks when they attempted a dress parade." Other soldiers, with cruel smiles and sharp tongues, began launching hard soldier references to a "ragged assed" regiment. Later, in more polite times and so as not to offend the folks back home, the 2nd Wisconsin's name was softened to "ragged backed 2nd."

Part of the reason for the verbal sparring was that during the first days of the war there was a great rivalry among the regiments, and it was those Bull Run veterans of the 2nd Wisconsin who made much of the fact they

Carroll College Institute for Civil War Studies

Unidentified

2nd Wisconsin

This photo shows an unidentified enlisted man of the 2nd Wisconsin. He is wearing a Model 1858 dress hat and the nine-button blue regular army frock coat.

faced real rebel bullets and the men of the other three regiments had not. The 2nd quickly forged an alliance with the 7th Wisconsin and boys of both regiments singled out the prideful 6th Wisconsin for special abuse, referring to them as "the Calico Boys" (for the colorful homemade shirts worn by the volunteers from the backwoods areas) or as brigade commander Rufus "King's pet babies." (There was a story attached to the latter name: The wife of a visiting Badger Congressman asked about a passing regiment. "The Baby 6th, M'am," she was told by a nearby lieutenant. The woman

Co. K. 7th Wisconsin. A company photo of Company K, 7th Wisconsin, taken between May and August 1862 while the brigade was stationed at Fredericksburg, Virginia. The town is in the background. *Beloit Historical Society*

indignantly replied, "Sir! I am from Wisconsin, and allow me to inform you, that we send no infant to war from there.")

If it was the "Ragged Assed 2nd" and "Calico 6th," the 7th Wisconsin became the "Huckleberries." One officer recalled that they were always talking about "pies and things to eat," while the "lean, lank" men of the 19th Indiana were simply "old Posey County" or "Swamp Hogs, Number 19" and "every man of them did not care a goll darn how we was dressed, but was all hell for a fight." In the army lore of those days, the infantry volunteers and regulars serving with of Battery B of the 4th U.S. Artillery became the "One hundred and forty thieves" for their admired ability to carry foraged goods on their limbers and caissons. When the 24th Michigan was added to the Western Brigade in 1862, the Wolverines became "the featherbeds" because they were slow to enlist and brought so many creature comforts from back home.

One 2nd Wisconsin soldier wrote that his regiment was "probably the hardest set of boys, but good natured and easy to get along with. They wear an air of fearless carelessness wherever found. The 6th is more stately, and distant, and march to slower music than we do. The 7th puts on the least style and crow the least . . . and is well drilled. . . . The 19th Indiana is an indifferent, don't care regiment," he continued. "They pride themselves on their fighting pluck—which is undoubtedly good—more than their drill. As a brigade we get along finely together."[1]

If the relationship of the four original regiments was good, the men of the 24th Michigan Infantry marched to Pennsylvania in brand new black hats still feeling much the outsiders.

The survivors of Gettysburg left no record of haste or concern during those first miles from the Marsh Creek bivouac toward the Pennsylvania crossroads town. Just ahead and out of sight, Cutler's brigade halted to rest near an orchard. Bringing up the rear of the Iron Brigade column was the 6th Wisconsin. Lieutenant Colonel Rufus R. Dawes commanded the 6th that morning for Colonel Edward Bragg was away at Washington recovering from a kick from Major John Hauser's horse. Enjoying "a beautiful morning," the young Dawes decided "to make a show in the streets of Gettysburg."[2]

Orders were given to close up the regiment and the hood was pulled off the National flag.[3] The silk banner, complete with its gold fringe and bullet-rips, was bright in the morning sun. Sergeant Thomas Polleys of Company H, a farmer from Trempealeau, carried it proudly. The flag had been sent to the regiment by Governor Alexander Randall those first weeks after the 6th Wisconsin reached Washington. The regiment carried only one flag, for the state blue colors was so damaged it was returned to Wisconsin to be replaced. The flag was accompanied with a proud letter that included these words: "History will tell how Wisconsin honor has been vindicated by her soldiers, and what lessons in Northern courage they have given Southern chivalry. If the past gives an earnest of the future, the 'Iron Brigade' will not be forgotten when Wisconsin makes up its jewels . . . ."

The flags from the very first were as much a part of the Civil War organizations as the soldiers themselves. "We are the color company of the 6th Wisconsin regiment, and carry the regimental colors," W. H. Druen of Rockville wrote home August 1, 1861, "and I feel safe in saying . . . the splendid flag entrusted to our care, shall not be dishonored by any act of ours. We shall bright it back unsullied by traitor's hands."

The bright regimental flags—one National, the other state—came to represent home, duty, and cause to the Union volunteers. At the presentation of a flag to the 5th Wisconsin, it was not considered unusual that an officer "commanded all his men to kneel down and swear to fight for the flag as long as a drop of blood remained in their veins . . . " A witness said the action was "enthusiastically complied with."

The flags were always with the men—on the drill field, on the march, and always in battle. The colors were carried in the center of the regiment in line of battle. It was their movement more than the shouted commands of the officers (which were usually lost in the din of battle and went unheard by most of the men) that directed the soldiers. The banners served to lead a charge or rally a broken regiment. It was not by chance that soldiers often singled out enemy color bearers for careful aim. If the flags advanced, so did the battle line; if the flags fell back, so did the men.

The color bearer of a regiment's national flag was usually a hand-picked sergeant. A corporal was assigned to carry the state flag. The sole responsibility of the color party—usually a detail of six or eight corporals—was to protect the unit's flags and color-bearers. The flags and color parties marched in the center of the line of battle. It was the most perilous kind of duty, and it was not surprising, given the sentimentalism of those days, that a popular war song called Union men to "Rally around the flag, boys, rally once again."[4]

So when the hood was pulled from the 6th Wisconsin National flag outside Gettysburg, and the drummers and fifers moved to the head of the regiment, the moment was a stirring one for all who witnessed it. With the sharp command of Drum Major R. N. Smith, the musicians struck up the fierce rallying song of the clans, "The Campbells are Coming." According to Dawes, he selected the song "through a fancy that the people would infer that the 'rebels are running,' or would run very soon after so fine a body of soldiers as the 6th Wisconsin then was, confronted them."

Only a few moments after the flag was unfurled, a distant "boom . . . boom . . . boom" from northwest of town descended over the shrill fifes and rumbling drums. The veterans recognized the distant thunder for what it was—artillery fire. "But for some reason," Dawes later recalled, "the sound was very dull, and did not attract our attention as indicating any serious engagement." Lieutenant Loyd Harris with the Brigade Guard behind the 6th Wisconsin broke a grin and leaned over to Levi Showalter of the 2nd Wisconsin: "The Pennsylvanians have made a mistake and are celebrating the 4th [of July] three days ahead of time." From the front of the column came word that Buford's cavalry had "found the Johnnies over at York or Harrisburg."[5]

A mounted staff officer caused a stir that moved the men more than the sound of artillery fire when he rode along the column swinging his hat and shouting over and over, "Boys, Little Mac is in command of the Army of the Potomac!" In an instant, the uncertainty in the ranks over Joe Hooker's resignation and the promotion of George Meade gave way to joyous shouts. The talk just the day before was that McClellan was marching from Harrisburg with a force of Pennsylvania militia and when he reached his old army he would again assume command. "Our fellows cheered like mad," one private remembered, "glad to be rid of such vainglorious fools as hind-quarters in the saddle [John Pope] and old stick-n-the-mud [Ambrose Burnside], to say nothing about drunken Joe, who had Lee where he would have to fight him on his own ground or seek safety in inglorious flight. Our fellows thought Hooker did the inglorious part to perfection on that occasion . . . ." Major Cornelius Otis of the 2nd Wisconsin said the announcement created the "greatest enthusiasm" because Little Mac was the "idol" of the army and "one in whom our confidence remained unshaken."

Of course, the news was not true. McClellan was not returning to the army. Later, some in the ranks grumbled it was nothing more than a calculated ploy to boost the fighting spirit of the soldiers. A 2nd Wisconsin officer called it "a rumor," but admitted the men had "a lighter and more elastic step. Our hearts were full of gratitude." Thousands of the marching soldiers fought the opening of the battle of Gettysburg believing McClellan was in command of the army.[6]

This loyalty to "Little Mac" with his dapper kepi and smart uniforms and fancy horses never faded for the "Boys of '61," those first volunteers to answer President Lincoln's call. Perhaps it was simply the innocent emotion of young men filled with their great cause and caught in the strong bond of soldiering. To them, McClellan looked the grand general, acted the great soldier, and in the final result, made the volunteers feel they were real soldiers. The little general, in his own unique way, stamped the Army of the Potomac with a certain dash and identity that carried it through wet camps and over hard roads. It was McClellan who "blended the untutored enthusiasm of a nation unused to war," explained one of his soldiers. Even if the general himself was not at hand this July morning in Pennsylvania, it was McClellan's drill and discipline that would be needed by the army as it moved toward Gettysburg.[7]

Even before the Little Mac cheers faded, a new sound reached the ears of the marching men. Between the distant fitful booms of artillery fire came the lighter staccato sound of small arms fire. The town of Gettysburg was approaching, one private wrote, and "our fellows straightened up to pass through it in good style." Alongside the roadway, the brigade band halted to play "Red, White and Blue" when "all at once, hell broke loose . . . in front."[8]

Chapter 12

I Will Fight Them Inch by Inch

James Wadsworth's Second Brigade was well ahead of the Iron Brigade as it moved toward the sounds of the nascent battle. Lysander Cutler's men, followed by James Hall's 2nd Maine Battery, stepped off promptly that morning and Cutler's brigade was resting near an orchard when its members heard gunfire in the distance. Without waiting for orders, old Cutler directed his brigade back on the road at a quick pace. John Reynolds rode up and ordered Wadsworth to hurry forward his division forward.[1]

The Confederates spotted the day before by Buford's troopers belonged to the Brigadier General James J. Pettigrew Brigade, part of Major General Henry Heth's Division, A. P. Hill's Third Corps. Heth believed there were shoes in Gettysburg (although that seemed unlikely because other Confederates had been in the town a few days earlier) and the previous day ordered Pettigrew to get them. Pettigrew, inexperienced at brigade command and not a professional soldier, returned to claim he could not enter Gettysburg because it was occupied by Federal cavalry. He added that some of his officers heard drums beating on the far side of the town, which indicated the presence of infantry. About this time, General Hill rode up and, being told of the developments, replied: "The only force at Gettysburg is cavalry, probably a detachment on observation. I am just from General Lee, and the information he has from his scouts corroborates what I have received from mine—that is, the enemy are still at Middleburg, and have not yet struck their tents." If there were no objection, Heth replied, he would take his division to Gettysburg. "None in the world," answered Hill.[2]

Heth, called "Harry" by his friends, was well-liked in the army. His cousin, George Pickett, commanded a division under James Longstreet in the First Corps. Heth served as a quartermaster for Lee in the Virginia Provisional Army early in the war and was one of the few soldiers in the army Lee continued to call by his first name. Heth was remembered in the Old Army for getting stabbed in the leg with a bayonet at West Point—and the fact that he finished at the bottom of the class of 1846.

At 5:00 a.m., July 1, Heth's division moved east from Cashtown on the Chambersburg Pike. By about 9:00 a.m., his men reached a high ridge about one mile northwest of Gettysburg. He was under orders not to bring on a general engagement, so he halted and shelled woods to the right and left of the Chambersburg Pike. No reply was forthcoming, and no enemy spotted. Heth deployed two of his infantry brigades, one north and one south of the pike and pushed forward. He was quickly engaged by Buford's Federal cavalry fighting dismounted. Although the horsemen were outnumbered, they were using their fast breech-loading carbines to advantage.[3] The weight of the advance was with the infantry, however, and Buford's line was rolled back until Gettysburg was directly behind them. The cavalry held a good position in the undulating fields west of Seminary Ridge, and fought to the best of their limited resources. How the fighting would develop from that pivotal point now rested on the shoulders of the man who commanded the men on that part of the field: John Reynolds. Should he fight or fall back?

It was now about 10:00 a.m. Wadsworth's two infantry brigades were near at hand, but his next closest division was still an hour away. Advance elements of O. O. Howard's Eleventh Corps could not arrive until noon or later, and the Third Corps under Dan Sickles was miles away at Emmitsburg, Maryland. But the rolling ground around Gettysburg was a good position, as Buford pointed out to Reynolds, where a defense could be mounted in depth. The town could also be used to advantage if the Union soldiers were forced to retreat. High ground south of Gettysburg also appeared promising. It was later said that Reynolds had already made up his mind to fight at Gettysburg because he believed an engagement might force decisive action from Meade, whom he regarded as being hesitant and slow in gaining control of his new army. It was also whispered that Reynolds acted simply because he was a Pennsylvania man facing an invading army with his home and family only fifty miles distant. Here, then, was the First Corps commander's chance to strike a blow and win glory.[4]

Whatever his reasons, or however he made his decision, Reynolds told Buford to hang on and ordered Wadsworth's division to come on the run. Riders were sent to the other divisions of the First Corps as well as the Eleventh and Third corps: Come quick as you can! Another galloper was dispatched to Meade: "Tell him the enemy are advancing in strong force and that I fear they will get to the heights beyond the town before I can. I will fight them inch by inch and if driven back into town, I will barricade the streets and hold them back as long as possible."[5]

As a result of the marching order, Wadsworth's division would be the first Union infantry on the field. Also by chance, his command included two of the best brigades in the army. The First Division led the march the previous day and ordinarily would have brought up the rear in the regular marching order. It was Reynolds who ordered the division to again take the lead because it was closest to Gettysburg. From near the Lutheran Seminary building, Reynolds rode back into the town, where he got lost briefly on a back street. (Citizen John Burns said afterward he helped the general get to the Emmitsburg Road.) The general found his infantry column near the Codori Farm south of town. The general ordered fences knocked down so Wadsworth's men could march across the fields northwest directly toward the fighting. He waited until the First Brigade reached the turnoff point, waving them to follow the Second Brigade, and then rode ahead a second time.

Cutler's brigade moved over the low ridge marked by the large stone Lutheran Theological Seminary toward a second parallel ridge to the west. Just behind the rise, Reynolds placed three of Cutler's regiments north of the Chambersburg Pike and two others south of it. The left flank of the brigade's line rested against a knot of timber on what was known as McPherson's Ridge. After directing Hall's Battery to unlimber on the road, Reynolds told a staff officer he would hold the Chambersburg Pike and that Abner Doubleday, who was bringing up the rest of the First Corps, should extend the line southward to prevent a possible enemy flanking maneuver.

It was about this time when Reynolds spotted Confederate infantry in the form of a heavy line of skirmishers moving forward followed by at least a brigade across an open field to the woods on McPherson's Ridge. If the Confederate line gained the crest and seized the wood lot, Reynolds realized, it could threaten the entire Union defensive position. Looking back, the

Wisconsin Historical Society 25110

Cornelius Wheeler
2nd Wisconsin Infantry

A sergeant, Wheeler watched as General John Reynolds fell from the saddle and was with the 2nd Wisconsin as it charged on McPherson's Ridge. This image shows him with leggings and the early issue dark blue Regular Army trousers given only to the 2nd Wisconsin in 1862. Light blue trousers later became the regular issue.

general could see the regiments of the Iron Brigade, marching en echelon, in lines of battle, crossing through the swale to McPherson Ridge at the double-quick.

It was going to be very close.

As luck would have it, the 2nd Wisconsin was at the head of the Iron Brigade as it plunged into the fighting at Gettysburg. Just before the regiment surged forward, Cornelius Wheeler recalled how George Legate of Mineral Point came to him in distress earlier in the morning: "Corny, we are going to have a fight today, and I will not come out alive." Wheeler laughed off the premonition, telling Legate that he was the "second man" who had come to him that day and that such feelings were "all nonsense." Sergeant Joseph Williams of Dodgeville also complained earlier that he did not feel quite right and that he would not get through the day. Wheeler brushed Williams off as well with a quick remark. Now he told Legate the same thing, adding with a smile that Legate could easily get out going into the battle. The sergeant major shook his head. "No, I will stay with the regiment whatever happens."[6]

The 2nd Wisconsin was just nearing Gettysburg when the sound of gunfire brought up the heads of the marching soldiers. The talking gave way to an uneasy quiet marked only by the shuffling of feet and noise of equipment. The Badgers came upon Reynolds sitting his horse along the side of the Emmitsburg Road near a farm house. The general waved the head of the column through an opening knocked in a roadside fence. Once the men were pouring through the gap and crossing the fields, the general rode off toward the sound of battle and was soon lost to sight.

No sooner was the turn made than scattered artillery shells clattered through the treetops above the marching column, knocking down leaves and branches. The fighting was closer than anyone expected. Colonel Lucius Fairchild slid from his horse, shouting, "Non-combatants to the rear!" Extra baggage was tossed along the roadside and officers dismounted and sent their horses to the rear. In the ranks, the men started snapping percussion caps—without orders—to clear firing vents of moisture and then began loading their short Austrian rifles. Bayonets were snapped and locked into place as the column pressed forward toward to the seminary, a large building with a tall cupola on the ridge just ahead. Later remembered was the sharp manner in which Fairchild handled the regiment that morning. His days as a soldier were about to end as he led the 2nd Wisconsin toward McPherson's Ridge west of Gettysburg.[7]

Chapter 13

It's Those Damned Black Hats!

*L*ucius Fairchild came into the war with a reputation. Back home he was just "Lush" (pronounced "Loosh") and remembered for his winning smile and frisky energy. The Fairchilds arrived in Wisconsin in 1846, and his early education was marked by escapades and disciplinary scrapes. As he approached eighteen and as many young men in the same circumstances did, he set off for the gold fields of California to seek his fortune.[1]

Unlike so many others, however, Fairchild returned home in 1855 with a modest nest egg (he was always secretive about the amount) that many believed he acquired more by merchandising and selecting good business partners than actual gold mining. He worked for a time for the Madison and Watertown Railroad, in which his father owned an interest, and engaged in an active social life that included several romances that made him the subject of town gossip. In 1859, he was elected clerk of Dane County at Madison and in the next year was admitted to the bar.

At the start of the war Fairchild was captain of the Governor's Guard, a prominent city militia company he took into the 1st Wisconsin, a 90-day active militia regiment. The regiment was sent to protect Washington D. C., and saw action at Falling Waters in Maryland in an engagement remembered only because Thomas Jackson, a few weeks away from winning his famous "Stonewall" nickname, and a young cavalry officer named James Ewell Brown (Jeb) Stuart fought on the Confederate side. When the 1st Wisconsin returned home, Fairchild obtained a commission as lieutenant in the Regular

Lucius Fairchild
2nd Wisconsin Infantry

Fairchild, shown here in a pre-Gettysburg photo, came to the 2nd Wisconsin after First Bull Run and commanded the regiment at Gettysburg, where he was wounded and lost an arm during the charge on McPherson's Ridge, July 1, 1863. Fairchild became active in the veteran movement after the war and was a prominent three-term Wisconsin governor.

Army. He was subsequently named a major of volunteers and then lieutenant colonel of the 2nd Wisconsin, joining the regiment at Washington. Many men remembered him in those innocent early days of the war for his special attachment to the regimental pet, a large half-bulldog named "McClellan." The dog—white with yellow spots (the men in ranks said those cowardly yellow spots were stolen from the Confederates)—would carefully watch the regimental drills and sometimes, with great dignity, parade with the band alongside the lieutenant colonel.[2]

Fairchild took full command of the 2nd Wisconsin in late 1862 after Colonel Edgar O'Connor was killed at Gainesville, Virginia. He proved to be an effective commander and was well-respected by his soldiers. Now, on the morning of July 1, 1863, the former California gold camp boy turned militia officer turned volunteer and his small regiment were running toward a fold in the Pennsylvania land whose name they did not yet know, deploying for the opening phase of what would explode into the largest battle of the American Civil War. What was about to happen would make Fairchild and his regiment famous forever, and mark the beginning of his long and storied political career.

The line of Confederate infantry approaching McPherson's Ridge was a brigade of Alabama and Tennessee troops under Brigadier General James J. Archer. The rebels were moving with a steady swaying step. They were not in any particular hurry, and in fact were rather careless with their approach. Their leisurely advance was the result of the mistaken assumption that they were dealing with only Federal cavalry and some Pennsylvania militia thrown in. As Archer's men reached the western base of McPherson Ridge, they came upon a sluggish creek called Willoughby Run. They splashed across the shallow stream with a yell and a shout to clear the wooded ridge looming just ahead and above them. The stand of timber—known locally as Herbst Woods—was used as a pasture and was fairly open due to the grazing of farm animals. The Confederates pushed on quickly now. Ahead they could see only a scattering of Union soldiers confronting them.[3]

North of the Chambersburg Pike, meanwhile, three regiments in Brigadier General Joseph Davis' Brigade—the 2nd and 42nd Mississippi and 55th North Carolina—advanced more quickly than their comrades to the south. Their fortunate timing put them on the ridge crest just as Cutler's New Yorkers and Pennsylvanians were sorting themselves into lines of battle. Joe Davis—the likeable but wholly inexperienced nephew of Southern President Jefferson Davis—was still new to brigade command. He

General Lysander Cutler
Second Brigade, First Division

A New Englander, Cutler came into the war as colonel of the 6th Wisconsin, but was commanding the Second Brigade at Gettysburg. He probably opened the infantry fighting on July 1. Cutler was hobbled by a wound suffered at Gainesville, Virginia, on August 28, 1862.

Howard Michael Madaus Collection

was practicing law at the start of the war in 1861 and became a captain in the 10th Mississippi Infantry. After a promotion to colonel, he became an aide-de-camp to his uncle. When he was nominated to be a brigadier general, however, the commission was delayed in Congress by charges of nepotism from his uncle's political opponents.

The 56th Pennsylvania was forming when Colonel John W. Hofmann spotted Davis' approaching line of battle. He was unable to determine the color of the uniforms. "Is that the enemy?" Hofmann called to General Lysander Cutler. The general lifted a pair of field glasses. "Yes," he said. Hofmann shouted orders to his small regiment: "Ready—Right Oblique, Aim! Fire!" To the right of the Pennsylvanians, the 76th New York also let loose a ragged volley. The Confederates returned the volleys, hitting the Union line with what one soldier described as a "shower of bullets." Although it was later disputed by some Wisconsin men, this was the first exchange of infantry fire at Gettysburg.[4]

About the same time, the 2nd Wisconsin was trotting up the east slope of McPherson's Ridge. Archer's Confederates were drawing near the crest from the west as Union cavalry skirmishers pulled out on the jump. In ranks, Private Elisha R. Reed of Evansville, Wisconsin, remembered a "feeling of dread came over me—of horrors undefined. I now began to wish that I had never been born, or, having been born, and had died in infancy. I could

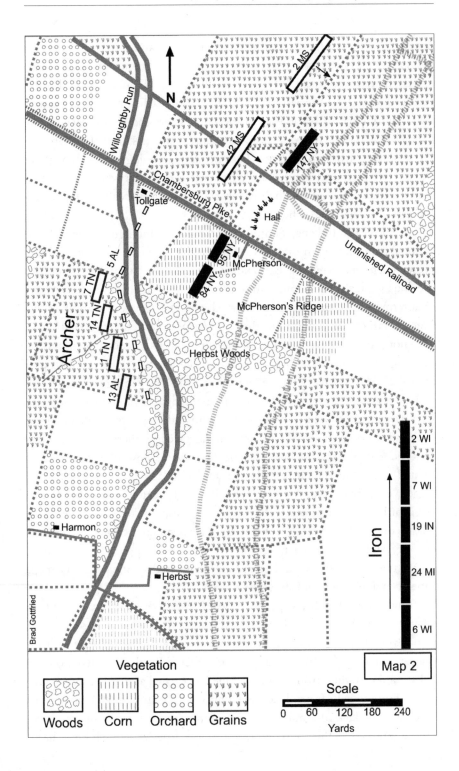

Vegetation

Woods   Corn   Orchard   Grains

Scale

0   60   120   180   240
Yards

Map 2

distinctly feel the blood receding from my face, and I know I must be looking very white. I was so sure that my face would betray my cowardice I dared not raise my head." Then came the order "Double quick, Load!" followed with "By the left flank, double quick, Charge!" The regiment swung into a line of battle toward the ridge where the Union cavalry was falling back amid scattered firing. The trailing regiments of the Iron Brigade began shifting from column into lines of battle, moving en echelon to the left and behind the advancing 2nd Wisconsin. (Long afterward, a Wisconsin man carefully stepped off the distances. It was 500 paces from Seminary Ridge to the edge of McPherson's Woods.)[5]

In the 19th Indiana, Sergeant Burlington Cunningham carried the national colors and Corporal David Phillips the state flag. The national flag presented to the regiment back home in 1861 had been sent home the previous winter and Cunningham carried a banner requisitioned from the Quartermaster Department, but marked with the regiment's number and state. A staff officer riding along the line, fearful of attracting fire, cautioned, "Do not unfurl the flag," but Cunningham, who had been singled out for rescuing his regiment's colors at Antietam, called to A. J. Buckles, "Abe, pull the shuck." He swung open the flag with a series of swirling motions as he and the regiment pushed off. Just ahead on the right, Union cavalry soldiers were clearing off to let the infantry move forward, the horse soldiers yelling to the advancing infantry, "They are coming, give it to them!"[6]

The 2nd Wisconsin line was the first to crest McPherson's Ridge. Behind what one veteran called "the unadorned, long-drawn-out line of ragged, dirty blue" was General John Reynolds seated on his big horse. "Forward men!" he shouted. "Forward for God's sake, and drive those fellows out of those woods!" When the Wisconsin line reached the crest, a line of Archers' Confederates on the other side poured in "a most murderous volley" that made "great gaps" in the Badger line.[7] "Charge men, I mean charge!" Fairchild shouted.

Private Reed barely escaped a serious wound in the first flurry of bullets when the ball hitting Virgil Helmes of Madison in front of Reed passed through his body and lodged in Helmes' knapsack. The unlucky Helmes staggered out of line. "By this time," remembered Reed, "the men began to fall around us rather promiscuously. One ball carried away my cap box and glanced on my belt. It produced a sensation in my abdominal regions very much like the kick of a mule and I was uncertain for a moment whether I was summoned to the courts above or only a little frightened; but a hasty

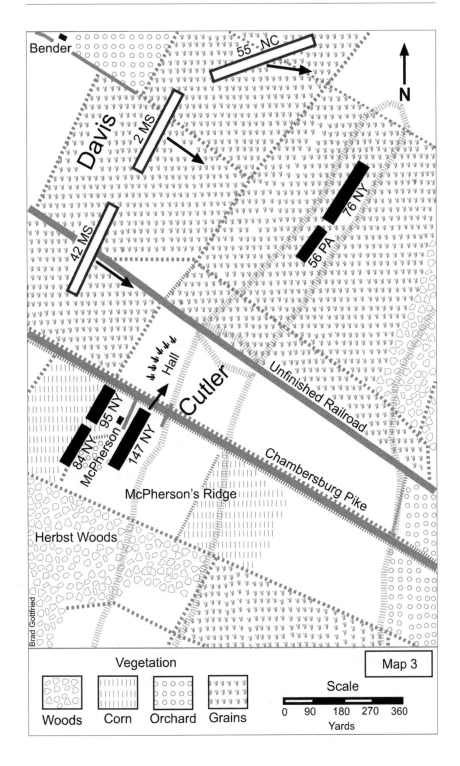

Bender

55 NC

N

Davis

2 MS

76 NY

42 MS

56 PA

Hall

Cutler

Unfinished Railroad

84 NY

95 NY

McPherson

147 NY

Chambersburg Pike

McPherson's Ridge

Herbst Woods

Brad Gottfried

Vegetation

Woods   Corn   Orchard   Grains

Map 3

Scale

0   90   180   270   360
Yards

examination disclosed the fact that I was in a pretty good state of preservation yet and I resumed my place in line."[8]

The volley was indeed "murderous," knocking one of every three Badgers out of the ranks. Somehow the line of Black Hats shook off the vicious firing and plunged forward with a yell. "We held our fire until within 10 yards of Archer's line and then gave them a volley that counted," one Badger recalled with pride. The Confederates, disorganized and surprised at the sudden appearance of a heavy line of veteran infantry, were swept down the slope through the trees as they tried to reload. "There are them damned black hatted fellows again," one rebel called out. "Taint no militia, it's the Army of the Potomac!" Another Confederate shouted, "Hell! Those are the big hat devils of the Army of the Potomac."[9]

Behind the 2nd Wisconsin, just as the two lines crashed together, Reynolds toppled from his saddle. A bullet that "entered the back of the neck, just below the coat collar, and passed downward" had killed him. His aides believed he was looking backward when struck. The very earliest speculation was that the bullet that killed the general was fired by a Confederate sharpshooter in the woods and that it was, somehow, an unfair and cowardly act.

Corporal W. B. Murphy of the 2nd Mississippi of Davis' Brigade north of the Chambersburg Pike later claimed the fatal bullet might have been fired by a company of his 2nd Mississippi. Cutler's brigade was retreating at the time, he explained, when "Genl. Reynold [sic] and staff rode up in about 100 yards to our right just over the hill in some timber to our right and our Reg. 2nd Miss, gave him one volley with our rifles, and I was told Genl. Reynold was killed and near all of his staff were killed or wounded."

Sergeant Wheeler of the 2nd Wisconsin said the general was apparently "struck by a stray ball" immediately after the volley his regiment received as it "charged over the top of the ridge." Left unspoken was the grim possibility that the fatal shot could have been fired by a federal infantryman or retreating cavalryman behind the general.[10]

As Reynolds' corpse lay on the ground, in the woods on McPherson's Ridge Archer's men fell back under the Wisconsin attack. To the left of the emerging Union line, the 7th Wisconsin reached the ridge and Colonel William Robinson halted to allow the Indiana and Michigan regiments to come up on his left. The colonel saw Confederate flags in the smoke and ordered his regiment to charge. The line pushed into the ravine with a shout. "Our skirmishers began to fire [on seeing the Confederates]," Private

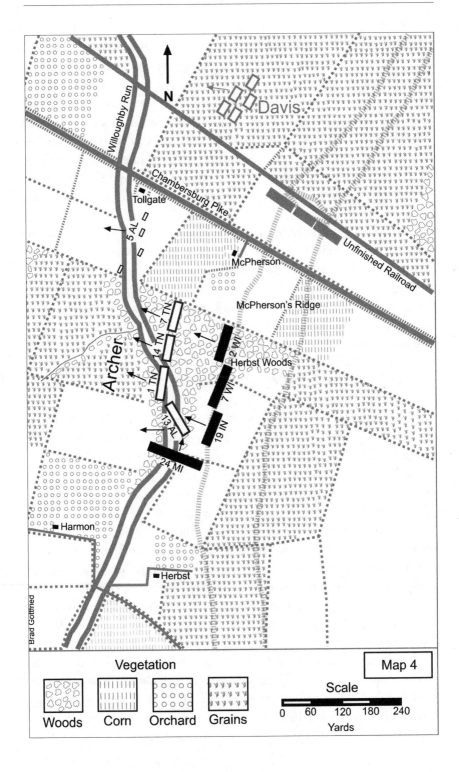

Vegetation

Woods   Corn   Orchard   Grains

Map 4

Scale

0   60   120   180   240

Yards

William Ray of Cassville later wrote in his journal. "Soon we see the top of a rebel flag. We still advance. As soon as a man sees a reb he shoots. We fix Bayonet still going on. Pass right over their dead and wounded . . . " Lieutenant Amos Rood remembered the "cusses skedaddled, or tried to under the 'roaring volleys" fired by his 7th Wisconsin. Private Alexander Hughes, one of the regiment's boy soldiers (he was fourteen when he enlisted from Columbia County), suffered his third battle wound of the war when a bullet hit his cartridge box and passed into his side. Slowed for just an instant by the "painful, but not serious wound," he ran ahead to catch up to his company.[11]

Archer's men were hit by a series of blows. First the 2nd Wisconsin, which took the brunt of their opening volley, and then the 7th Wisconsin, 19th Indiana, and finally the 24th Michigan, which swung around to overlap the ragged and exposed Confederate right flank. In the smoke and confusion, it seemed to the surprised Confederates the Black Hats were everywhere to their front and around their flank. The series of shocks tumbled them down the slope all the way to the creek and crowded them to the northwest. "It seemed to me there were 20,000 Yanks down in among us hallooing surrender," one Confederate recalled, "and of course I had to surrender."

The firing in the smoky woods was furious and sustained. Color Sergeant Abel G. Peck of the 24th Michigan was killed and Lieutenant Colonel Mark Flanigan wounded. Corporal Andrew Wood of the 19th Indiana was engulfed in a whoosh of smoke as a ball struck his cartridge box and hit a twist of percussion caps, igniting his cartridges. Lieutenant William Macy stripped off Wood's equipment and patted out the burning uniform before ordering him to the rear. The first volley to hit the advancing 19th Indiana also wounded Color Sergeant Burlington Cunningham. Corporal Abe Buckles was ordered to "take the flag" and push on. The flurry of fighting, so important to the early course of the battle, was over in just a few minutes. According to Colonel Robinson, "the enemy—what was left of them able to walk—threw down their arms" and fled toward the safety of Herr Ridge to the west.[12]

Lieutenant Colonel John Callis of the 7th Wisconsin, on foot in the powder smoke after his horse was struck and already wounded with buckshot on his side and hip, was confronted by a wild-eyed Confederate officer running toward him shouting, "I surrender!" while pointing his drawn sword at him. "That is no way to surrender," said Callis, knocking the sword away from the rebel's hand with his own sword. The Wisconsin officer took a swipe at the Confederate's neck, but missed. The two were now face-to-face. "If you surrender," said Callis, "order your men to cease firing, pick up your saber and order your men to go to the rear as prisoners." The officer did as he was told. "[W]e had more prisoners than men of our own," Callis later reported.

Callis had only moved a few yards ahead when he spotted an escaping Confederate in the woods trying to wrap a flag around its staff. Callis called out to Private Dick Huftill of Ellenboro, a boy in his old Grant County company, to shoot the rebel. Huftill stepped forward, steadied his rifle-musket on the shoulder of his friend, Private Webster Cook, and squeezed the trigger. His "unerring aim" brought down the man with the colors. The private ran ahead, picked up the flag, and handed it to Callis. Nearby, Abe Buckles of the 19th Indiana was so far ahead of his line—well beyond Willoughby Run—that Lieutenant Colonel William Dudley called out, "Come back with that flag!"[13]

The 2nd Wisconsin, knocked to the right by the first storm of bullets, also crossed Willoughby Run in pursuit of Archer's fleeing Confederates. The 2nd's flag, a hand-made National color sewn by Mrs. R. C. Powers of Madison and presented to the regiment at Camp Randall was well to the front even though the regiment's two original color bearers were down. Sergeant Philander Wright entered the woods carrying the hand-made National flag. The regimental flag of blue silk was commercially made and featured a painted representation of the Great Seal of the United States on one side and the 1851 version of the Wisconsin seal on the other. It was forwarded to the 2nd Wisconsin in late 1861 and at Gettysburg was carried by an unidentified corporal. Only two corporals were detailed to the 2nd Wisconsin color party.[14]

As the regiment ran forward down the slope, a bullet punched through Wright's black hat; another quickly followed the first. He ran forward toward a Confederate flag bearer just fifty yards ahead of him. A third bullet splintered the flagstaff, almost knocking it from his hand. The fourth bullet found him, slamming into his left leg and knocking him over. "When I looked for the guards—not one was there—all shot. I guess—sure not a man would lag at such a time—I know I wondered where one might be—I might have know each had been halted leaving me alone."[15]

Not far away, Lucius Fairchild was also down. He left a full account in his report of the action:

"My regiment . . . became hotly engaged the moment they passed the [Hall's] battery. We pushed forward slowly, loading and firing as we went, down a slight incline which was thickly studded with trees of a large growth, toward the enemy who seemed to be posted at the foot of the incline behind a small stream [Willoughby Run]. My officers and men fell, killed or wounded, with terrible rapidity—from the instant they arrived at and passed the highest point of the ridge. We had gone but a short distance after becoming engaged when I was struck by a rifle ball which struck my left arm and made amputation necessary.

Sergeant Wright watched as the first of the Confederate prisoners were herded passed him to the rear, and then Corporal Rasselas Davison of Spring Green came and collected the colors, passing one to Corporal Paul V. Brisbois of Portage. The two pushed off after the regiment. The action surprised some of the Wisconsin men. Davison, a veteran of several battles, was earlier outspoken and "sworn that he would never go into another fight if he could find any honorable way of dodging it." Now he rushed forward to carry the regimental flag and kept ten to fifteen yards in front of the 2nd Wisconsin line all the way through the woods, shouting for the Badgers to follow him. "That struck me as being a very singular way to dodge a fight," chided a friend, "but it shows how little a man knows of how he is going to act when he goes into the fight. . . . He continued to carry those colors through to the end and brought them home . . . He seemed to have borne a charmed life."[16]

With an eye on his own wounded left leg, Wright crawled over to his friend Daniel Burton of his own Company C. Burton was propped up nearby against a tree bleeding from a fatal wound. Despite Wright's attempt to assist him, Burton was dead. Nearby Wright found Otto W. Ludwig, "sweating and swearing in a spluttering yell" and still wearing his glasses. "Without specs at fifty feet he couldn't tell a man from a stump," said Wright. Ludwig was also beyond help and soon died.[17] Wright himself—"blood smeared, dust stained" and "feeling dizzily like"—began the long crawl back to the town and safety. When the regiment reformed a short time later, it was discovered that Wright was one of 116 of the 302 men the 2nd Wisconsin carried into the fight who had been killed or wounded during its opening minutes.[18]

Private Reed was still with the 2nd Wisconsin line halted in the ravine. After his cap box was shot off his belt at the top of the hill, Sergeant

Alexander Lee of Janesville gave him a handful of caps from his own supply and he joined the line again, only to be hit by a partially spent ball on his left hip. The lead slug made a terrible bruise, but no bones were broken. Reed again limped after the line as it moved through the woods firing. At the bottom of the ravine he was struck on the ankle by another spent ball. "The line now halted and I came up into my place," wrote Reed. "After halting, with no rebel in sight anywhere, a stray shot came from somewhere, and struck Jonathan Brian [Jonathan Bryan of Lodi] in the breast and he fell dead, being killed almost instantly."

Reed took in the ground around him. "We had killed and wounded many rebels, taken a great many prisoners . . . and had driven the rest from the woods," he recalled. "We now about faced and moved back into the woods and reformed our line. It was with difficulty that I executed this movement with my lame ankle. . . . We were ordered to lie down. Our orderly sergeant here took an inventory of stock and found that Company H had ten left. We struck that charge with thirty-three men." Of the survivors, he observed, "many of those left were more or less battered or bruised. . . . The rest of the brigade lost as heavily as we did."

The loquacious Confederate prisoners told the Black Hats they were part of A. P. Hill's Third Corps and that Lee's army "was close by, massed to overwhelm us before our entire army could get together."[19]

Chapter 14

One Sword is All I Need on This Line

*C*onfederate General James Archer advanced with his brigade on foot that morning. The ridge to his front was wooded with Willoughby Run along the western slope. Thick brush and clumps of willow trees grew along the rocky bank and it was not easy for a mounted man to make his way. He had little anticipation of a strong enemy force, and Archer, who was slight and prone to dysentery, carelessly pushed his regiments forward. He was well-regarded in the Confederate Army and much admired. A graduate of Princeton (where his friends called him "Sally"), he practiced law after graduation in 1834 and served in the Mexican War where he was cited for gallantry. One of his Old Army friends was Thomas Jackson. It was Jackson who served as his second in a duel with another officer in Mexico that left Archer slightly wounded.

His brigade that morning was small, just under 1,000 men comprised of three regiments and part of another. The opening fire came as the brigade attempted to carry the ridge and drive off skirmishers.[1] The surprise collision between the advancing 2nd Wisconsin and Archer's 7th and 14th Tennessee regiments tangled and opened Archer's line just as the three other Iron Brigade regiments moved up to slam into it. Expecting only militia or some cavalry, the Confederates were confused by the weight of the Union attacks from their front and right. They "slowly and stubbornly" retreated back into the dense clouds of powder smoke that filled the low area around Willoughby Run. Without a horse to help him control the situation, Archer and some soldiers from the 1st Tennessee and 13th

Alabama, firing as they moved, slipped into the cover of trees along the north base of the ridge or moved into the open ground leading back to Herr Ridge. About thirty yards west of the run, Archer was pushing his way through a tangle of weeds and willow trees when Private Patrick Maloney of the 2nd Wisconsin ran out of the smoke and grabbed the general. The exhausted Archer struggled in a vain effort to escape. Robert Beecham and Charles Dow of the 2nd Wisconsin came upon Maloney struggling with the diminutive general. Seeing Dow, Archer tried to offer his sword in surrender, but Dow refused it: "Keep your sword, General, and go to the rear; one sword is all I need on this line." Within a few minutes Archer was soon on his way to the rear with hundreds of his captured soldiers. Just ahead of the group of officers Sergeant Jonathan Bryan of the 2nd Wisconsin, waving his hat and cheering on his regiment, was shot through the heart. He was the only man in the regiment killed west of Willoughby Run. Maloney would not enjoy his brief celebrity as Archer's jailer, for he was killed later in the day.

James Archer was the first general officer captured since Robert E. Lee took command of the Army of Northern Virginia in 1862. On the way to the rear Archer—"a trim, neat looking man" remembered one Wisconsin soldier—met his old Army friend General Abner Doubleday.

"Good morning, Archer! How are you? I am glad to see you!"

Archer glowered, "Well, I am not glad to see you by a damn sight."[2]

As the fighting died away and Archer walked to the rear under guard he was confronted by Lieutenant Dennis Dailey of the 2nd Wisconsin, who was on the brigade staff. Excited and caught up in the fighting, Dailey approached Archer. "I will relieve you of that sword," he told him. The general protested, saying a Wisconsin officer allowed him to retain it. But Dailey insisted and finally Archer reluctantly turned over the blade. The Wisconsin officer, seeing the Confederate's sword was "much lighter" than the one he was carrying, dropped his own and buckled on the captured one.[3] The sword incident caused a minor stir. Beecham said much later the captured sword went to "the man who had no right to receive it. It is not always that the man on the outmost line received the reward which his due."[4]

The last Black Hat regiment to reach the field was the 6th Wisconsin followed by the Brigade Guard of 100 men. They passed over the ridge south of the Lutheran Theological Seminary. Ahead of them, the four Iron Brigade regiments were advancing toward a wooded ridge several hundred

Lt. Col. Rufus R. Dawes
6th Wisconsin Volunteers

A veteran officer by 1863, he commanded the 6th Wisconsin at Gettysburg and led the charge on the unfinished railroad cut. He was one of the best citizen-soldiers produced by the war although other officers received more attention.

Service With The

Sixth Wisconsin Volunteers

yards ahead. Dismounted Union cavalry were running out of the tree line, and Archer's men were yet invisible on the far side. To the right, across a road—the Chambersburg or Cashtown Pike with a "stake and rider" fence—were growing clouds of power smoke and the sound of heavy fighting. Hall's 2nd Maine was thumping away from a position near the road.

As the 6th Wisconsin moved forward an aide from Brigade Commander Sol Meredith rode up to Rufus Dawes: "Colonel, form your line, and prepare for action." Dawes swung his horse around and looked to the woods line where he saw "a line of rebel skirmishers, running back from my own front." He gave a series of orders. "By Companies into line!" "Forward into Line! By Companies, left half wheel, double quick, March!" Schooled for hours on the drill fields of a dozen camps, the regiment ("that unequaled body of skilled veterans," boasted Dawes) made the "intricate evolution" into a line of battle. The soldiers struggled to keep their alignment as they loaded the rifle-muskets while moving. Before the 6th Wisconsin could advance far enough to join the right flank of the Iron Brigade, another rider brought orders for Dawes to halt and wait as a reserve. The running soldiers pulled up in some disorder, but quickly dressed the line.[5]

The regiment was down in the swale between the two ridges, southwest of the seminary building with its left stretching almost to the Fairfield Road. A crash of musketry exploded ahead as the 2nd and then 7th Wisconsin plunged headlong into the woods. Loyd Harris of the 6th Wisconsin, commandeering the 100 men of the Brigade Guard, came up for orders. Divide the guard into two companies of fifty-men each, Dawes instructed him, and place one on each flank of the regiment. Harris ran back to the guard's other officer, Lieutenant Levi Showalter of 2nd Wisconsin. Harris took the left company and Showalter the right. In that moment before he moved his detachment up—the soldiers still trying to catch their breath after the hard half-mile run in knapsacks—Harris turned to his small command, admitting he was "feeling keenly my situation," commanding veterans who "no doubt felt a novel sensation in fighting under a strange officer, and away from their companies and regiments." He stepped in front of the makeshift company. "I know how much you would like to be with your own commands, and I am just as anxious to join company C over there on the right of the 6th, but it cannot be so," he said. "Do the best you can and I will do my duty toward you." The company moved forward to the left of the 6th Wisconsin.[6]

Just then, a rider from Meredith brought word to move forward again. Before Dawes could executive the order, a "very boyish looking staff officer" came up on the gallop. It was Lieutenant Benjamin T. Marten of General Abner Doubleday's staff. "Colonel," he said with a salute to the mounted Dawes, "General Doubleday is now in command of the First Corps, and he directs that you halt your regiment." Dawes ordered his men down and the Badgers flopped into the grass in a tangle of equipment and arms. One of the Fond du Lac County farmer boys remembered the field was planted with "fast ripening wheat." Private Frank King of Fond du Lac turned to his friend, Lyman White of Appleton. "Lime, this finishes my fighting," said King. White made light of the remark. To the regiment's right front, the other regiments of the Iron Brigade were exchanging long rips of musketry and the wounded men were already beginning to trickle back.[7]

Staff Officer Marten returned and pointed to the Chambersburg Pike: "General Doubleday directs that you move your regiment at once to the right." Dawes complied, ordering his regiment to its feet and to face right, forming a column of fours. "Double-quick, March!" Dawes shouted.

Ahead the "musketry fighting along the whole front of the division was very sharp." Only the 6th Wisconsin was apparently unengaged. As his regiment moved along the swale, James Wood of Meredith's staff rode alongside Dawes and the moving column. The fighting north of the pike had gone badly, Wood said, and Cutler's Brigade was in trouble. Finally, Wood pulled off to the side shouting, "Go like hell! It looks as though they are driving Cutler." In the ranks, Earl Rogers, commanding Company I, saw his brother Clayton, an officer on Wadsworth's staff, talking with Dawes. The orders were the same—help Cutler and stem the breach in the division's line north of the roadway.[8] It was the first time Dawes commanded the 6th Wisconsin on a campaign, although he had fought it with skill at Antietam after Colonel Edward Bragg was wounded.

As the 6th Wisconsin moved in columns of four toward the Chambersburg Pike, Dawes could see Hall's Battery "driving to the rear" and the men of Cutler's brigade "falling back toward town." Harris on the left with the Brigade Guard said the Confederate line was in "hot pursuit." The Federal infantry, said another Badger, "not enough to make a heavy skirmish line . . . flying before the enemy" and "scattering like sheep, leaving the . . . artillery . . . and outrunning the enemy." It was an unfair remark. The New Yorkers had been given an order to retreat with the rest of Cutler's brigade, but the commanding officer was wounded and the order was not carried out. The regiment was assailed on its front and right (bullets "flying thick and fast," remembered an officer) but hung on until a rider from Wadsworth rode "through the leaden hail like a whirlwind across the old railroad cut" with orders to retreat. The New Yorkers "ran, pursued pell-mell by the enemy" to the safety of Seminary Ridge. They later sharply denied any claim they had to be "rescued" by the charging 6th Wisconsin or any other regiment.[9]

As they moved toward the fence, men from the 6th Wisconsin watched Federal soldiers carrying an officer in a blanket. The corpse was that of John Reynolds.[10] In the days after Gettysburg, it was said Reynolds made his stand northwest of town—even though his main infantry force was not on the field—because he saw an opportunity to save the deep defensive positions he saw earlier south of town. Other officers said Reynolds was the victim of his own rashness, that he heedlessly and impetuously engaged a superior force of the enemy when he should have fallen back to a more defensive position. It was also remarked in some tents that the general exceeded his authority and it was the faulty decision of a Pennsylvania man fighting on home soil. But the whispers were lost in the eulogies for the fallen general. Officers killed at the front of their troops, even rash ones,

History of the Sauk County Rifles

Private Mair Pointon
Co. A, 6th Wisconsin Volunteers

A native of Baraboo, Wisconsin, he joined the Sauk County Riflemen in 1861. He and his friend, Phil Cheek, wrote a history of their company after the war.

even generals, escape the double-sided political questions of Congressional committeemen, the sharp pens of newspaper editors, and the side remarks of jealous officers. In the end, Reynolds, who several weeks earlier turned down an offer to command the Army of the Potomac, would not have to answer for opening the fighting at Gettysburg. Now, however, it was up to the men of the Wadsworth's division to make the general's decision the right one.[11]

The 6th Wisconsin and the Brigade Guard column ran in formation toward the Chambersburg Pike through the smoke, noise, scattered bullets and wounded soldiers filtering out of the woods where the four regiments of the Iron Brigade were fighting with Archer's Brigade. To their left front, two Union formations were slowly falling back—men of the 14th Brooklyn and 95th New York of Cutler's Brigade. Ahead across the road, a heavy Confederate line of battle rolled past with yells, chasing a broken line of Cutler's men running for the cover of a stand of trees on Seminary Ridge.

The Confederate line pushing Cutler included the 2nd and 42nd Mississippi and 55th North Carolina—Joe Davis' three regiments. The 147th New York was north of the pike when Davis' Brigade swept down on them. After a gallant but brief stand, the Union soldiers had to run for it to escape capture. The 76th New York and 56th Pennsylvania were caught just as they formed battle lines. But the rebel line extended well past the exposed right of the brigade and the converging fire from front and flank was too much for any soldiers. Finally, they had been ordered to retreat with Davis' men surging in pursuit, but the Confederate line was piling up and the officers were quickly losing control of the situation.

It was Doubleday, now in command of the field after Reynolds' death, who called this the "critical" moment of the opening infantry fight. The four regiments of the Iron Brigade were driving Archer, but three regiments of Cutler's brigade were on the run with two others in retreat. Davis' Brigade was slowly reaching a place from which it could pour volleys into the exposed right and rear of the make-shift Union line on the McPherson property. According to Doubleday, he ordered the 6th Wisconsin ("a gallant body of men, whom I know could be relied upon") to the right to prevent "the defeat, perhaps the utter rout of our forces."[12]

The 6th Wisconsin was approaching the rail fence lining the south side of the Chambersburg Pike. Looking ahead, Dawes made out "a long line of yelling rebels" coming over the ridge beyond what he later discovered was a deep and unfinished railroad cut. The ridge was gouged for the track, but no rails were laid and the bed was strewn with boulders and piles of dirt and stone. It was almost impossible to see the cut from the Union position. The Confederate line was moving past his approaching column and slowly drifting right. The young officer realized an opportunity to hit their flank. "File right, March!" he ordered. His column swung to move alongside the flank of the rebels pursing the retreating Federal soldiers of Cutler's brigade. Dawes ordered his men to move "By the left flank!" This order, he explained, "threw my line parallel to the turnpike and the R.R. cut, and almost directly upon the flank of the enemy"[13]

Confederates saw the approaching line and began firing toward the Wisconsin soldiers, who bowed into "the leaden storm and dashed forward."[14] Dawes had just turned his horse to the fence when the mare was "struck in the breast" and began rearing and plunging. The bullet struck the shoulder bone and careened around it before stopping fourteen inches from the entry wound. Dawes, unaware of the injury, savagely spurred the animal until it fell heavily on her haunches, tumbling him to the ground just as his advancing line swept past him in the double-quick."[15]

"I am all right boys!" the young officer called in a loud voice as his men swept past him. The soldiers responded with a friendly yell just as they reached the rail fence. Behind them, Dawes was shouting "Fire by file, fire by file!" "I could see the enemy coming over the hill now by the railroad cut in a heavy line," remembered Dawes. "I looked back and saw that my gallant old mare was on her feet and was hobbling sturdily to the rear on three legs." (The horse was found later among the brigade's wagons.) The 6th Wisconsin men, their rifle-muskets resting on the fence rails, fired by file from right to left and the ripple of shots from "our carefully aimed muskets" checked the rebels in pursuit of Cutler's men. Exposed to this grueling fire, Davis' Confederates began seeking cover in the unfinished railroad cut. Not far away, an officer of the 147th New York saw the 6th Wisconsin and Brigade Guard—only "a little band," but, he said, every "man of that band was a host in himself. Steady, swiftly and furiously they charged upon the enemy's flank."[16]

Chapter 15

Fire by File! Fire by File!

Mickey Sullivan and his Lemonweir Minute Men were just left of center as the 6th Wisconsin reached the Chambersburg Pike fence, the soldiers resting their muskets on the top rail. "Fire by file! Fire by file!" came the order. The sudden and steady ripple of musketry from right to left along the regiment's seventy-five-yard front caught the rebels in the flank. "The Johnnies were so intent upon following up their advantage that they did not for some time discover what was going on [on] their right," recalled one Wisconsin soldier. On the left side of the Wisconsin line, Loyd Harris with the Brigade Guard watched as the Confederate line wheeled to face the sudden threat. "I could not help thinking, how, for once, we will have a square stand up and knock down fight. No trees, nor walls to protect either, when presto! Their whole line disappeared as if swallowed up by the earth." The Confederates had moved into the deep unfinished railroad cut. To Private Sullivan, it seemed "as if the ground had opened and swallowed them up; but we soon found that they were still on top if it—as they opened a tremendous fire upon us . . . ."[1]

With the fighting beginning in earnest Sullivan discovered he was in serious trouble—his musket would not fire. He quickly pulled another percussion cap from his pouch, but that failed as well. Along the fence, rebel bullets splintered rails and ripped furrows in the grass. "In the road our fellows straightened up their lines and waited for all hands to get over the fence," explained the private. Then they were over a second fence and in an open field facing the musketry from the railroad cut about 175 yards distant. It was "a galling fire," confirmed one 6th Wisconsin man. "Several of our poor boys [were] left dangling on the fence." Lieutenant Colonel Rufus Dawes described the incoming small arms fire as "murderous," and said "to climb that fence in the face of such a fire was a clear test of mettle and discipline."[2]

The Wisconsin regiment and two companies of the Brigade Guard slowly began moving out into the smoky field, loading and firing as fast as they could in an attempt to beat down the Confederate return fire. Still at the fence, Sullivan finally concluded his musket was double-loaded and that was why he could not get it to discharge. When he spotted Adjutant Edward Brooks, he called out, "Brooks, my gun won't go off." Brooks handed him a musket he had picked up and Sullivan moved up to his company only to find the second musket did not fire, either. And then he realized the problem: "I knew my caps were bad." The private ran up to Captain John Ticknor of his own Company K, who pointed to a downed soldier (Corporal Charles Crawford of Kildare). "We rolled him over and I took the cartridge box and buckled it on myself." As Sullivan turned around, he saw "Ticknor start for the rear in a spread out, staggering sort of way. After a few steps, he fell." Standing nearby, Sergeant Erastus Smith announced, "I think he is killed and I am going to see about him." He was right; Ticknor was dying.[3]

The captain's loss would be sharply felt throughout the regiment. A sawmill worker in Juneau County, Wisconsin, when Fort Sumter was fired upon, he was one of the first to sign the roll to be a volunteer. In camp, he was known as "Jerky," for reasons never discovered, and was a regimental favorite. The men carried Ticknor up and down his company street when his commission as lieutenant was approved, his men laughing and singing as they hoisted him on their shoulders. He was six feet tall, "straight as an arrow," and incredibly brave.[4] The young officer was also one of the regimental singers, and the Wisconsin men insisted he had a role in creating the great war song of the Civil War. The opportunity came following a review at Washington as they marched back to their camp. "[O]ur leading singer," said Dawes, "Sergeant John Ticknor, as he was wont to do on such occasions, led out with his strong clear and beautiful tenor voice, 'Hang Jeff Davis on a sour apple tree.' The whole regiment joined the grand chorus, 'Glory, glory hallelujah, as we go marching on.'" A lady visitor, Julia Ward Howe, rode in a carriage near the soldiers and said later she was inspired to the composition of the Battle Hymn of the Republic. If Ticknor and the

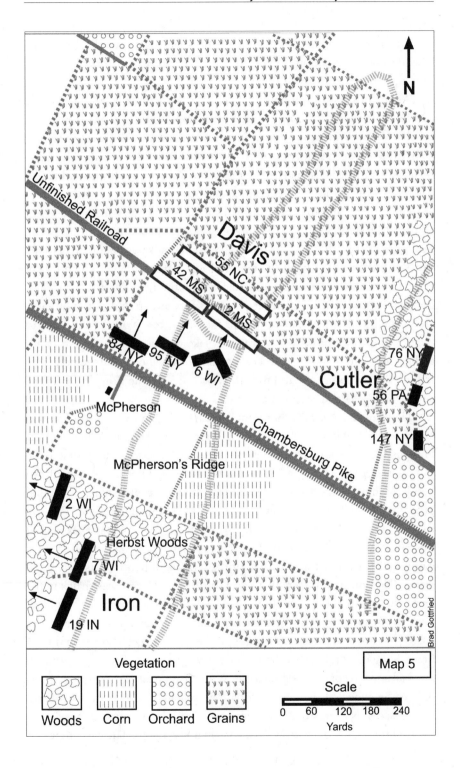

Wisconsin men were not singled out for the honor, said Dawes, "We at least helped to swell the chorus."[5] Now, the beloved Badger captain was bleeding out in the fields along the Chambersburg Pike.

As the 6th Wisconsin line surged across the fence toward the railroad cut, Dawes shouted "Forward! Forward charge! Align on the Colors! Align on the Colors!" Holding those colors was Sergeant Thomas Polleys of Trempealeau. The regiment carried just the national flag, for the blue state regimental had been used up and sent back to Wisconsin. Before midday, all eight men of the color party would be dead or down.[6]

Confederate fire from the railroad cut was "fearful" and "destructive," recorded Dawes, crashing "with an unbroken roar before us. Men [were] being shot by twenties and thirties and breaking ranks by falling or running. But the boys . . . crowded in right and left toward the colors and went forward." The advancing line was quickly into the field. On the left side of the line, Harris watched as the flag moved forward and knew the order to charge had been given. As he passed the 95th New York he ran over to them, shouting at an officer, "For God's sake why don't you move forward and join our left!" But the New Yorkers did not advance. A frustrated Harris ran back to his command and the 6th Wisconsin and the Brigade Guard, he later wrote, "charged, singly and alone."[7]

Halfway into the field, Sergeant Michael Mangan of Fond du Lac was struck in the ankle by a ball and was hopping to the rear. When Francis Deleglise of the color party moved to help him, he was also shot, first in the calf of his right leg and then a second time in the right knee. Dropping down beside Mangan, Deleglise tried to bandage the sergeant's ankle, but found his muscles rigid from his own injuries. When Captain Joseph Marston found the wounded pair, he ordered Private Harry Dunn to take Mangan to the rear. Nearby, Lieutenant Orrin Chapman, who had listened to a harmonica playing "Home, Sweet Home" the night before, was down and dying. The officer who blew that harmonica, Loyd Harris, was struck in the neck by buckshot but somehow managed to continue moving forward. Dick Marston, spared from a potential death sentence for sleeping on a guard post just a few days earlier, was struck and killed. The premonition of Frank King of Fond du Lac also came true when he was hit in the stomach by a ball and left sprawled on the field. With the men falling all around, it was only to be expected that the national flag would go down, and so it did. Within seconds it was back up again, waving in the warming Pennsylvania air. And then it fell once more. Once again it was raised. The cycle repeated itself several times. On one of those occasions, Captain Earl Rogers watched Dawes pick up the colors, only to be shouldered aside by one of the few members of the color party still standing and still willing to shoulder the honor.

In Company I, the Bad Ax and Dane County boys were getting knocked apart. Andy Miller of De Soto went down. Near him, Gottlieb Schreiber of Hillsboro fell wounded. A few yards more and Lewis Boughton of Tomah was killed, and William Sweet of Wonewoc dropped to the ground wounded. Jim McLean of Webster and Alfred Thompson of Harmony were shot and George Sutton of Viroqua killed. John Goodwin of Plymouth was wounded and just ahead of him, Corporal Charles Jones of Mauston, a member of the color party, fell. The edge of the railroad cut was a handful of yards ahead when Levi Stedman of Brookville fell mortally wounded and Edward Lind of De Soto was hit. In the flurry bullets and shouts, a bullet struck and staggered Private James Kelly of Company B. Somehow the soldier managed to keep his feet, but he dropped his musket and moved to grab Dawes' coat sleeve. As the two jostled forward in the press of soldiers, Kelly opened his "woolen shirt" to show Dawes a "red bullet mark" on his chest. "Colonel, won't you tell my folks I was a good soldier?" Dawes nodded his understanding. "Yes, Kelly, I will." Satisfied, the private turned to head for the rear.[8]

Private Amos Lefler
Co. E, 6th Wisconsin Volunteers

The young farmer enlisted in Bragg's Rifles in June 1861. He was wounded at South Mountain in 1862 and shot in the face at Gettysburg in the charge on the railroad cut. He transferred to the Veteran Reserve Corps in November 1863.

Larry Lefler

The Wisconsin line was now a "V-shaped crowd of men," remembered Dawes, "with the colors at the point, moving hurriedly and firmly forward, while the whole field behind is streaming with men plunging in agony to the rear or sinking in death to the ground." To his dismay, the young officer watched his wounded men "leaving the ranks in crowds."[9] The rebel bullets were taking a heavy toll. One ball smashed Sergeant George Fairfield's canteen and slashed his hip, but he plunged forward. Amos Lefler of Eden was shot in the face and went down, spitting out blood and teeth. Sergeant Henry Schildt, a native of Prussia and one of the older men in the regiment, was putting a percussion camp on his rifle when a charge of buck and ball struck him in the left side. Two of the buckshot entered Schildt's left side between the fourth and fifth ribs, about one inch apart.[10]

Fewer than thirty yards from the cut, Sergeant Fairfield realized that Davis' Confederates were holding their fire "and it became evident we should get a volley." The massive discharge was delivered at point-blank range. In all the smoke and noise, he believed "half our men had fallen." Not far away, Corporal Frank Wallar of De Soto ran forward in a "general rush and yells enough to almost awaken the dead." As Harris described it, the "fire was the worst ever experienced, yet not a man failed to move promptly forward and closed in to the right as the men fell before the murderous fire of the rebels in the railroad cut." The killing at a distance was over. The two lines crashed together near a Confederate flag fluttering on the edge of the yawning smoky depression.[11]

When Lieutenant William Remington spotted the Confederate flag, he recognized his chance to capture it. Moving quickly to his right behind his battle line, he ducked his head and ran through a break in the line. A bullet nicked the left side of his neck, but he quickly closed on the enemy banner. So he could reach out for the staff, he transferred his sword to his left hand, which was still holding his revolver. "I saw a soldier taking aim at me from the railroad cut," he said. "I threw my right shoulder forward and kept going for the flag. He hit me through the right shoulder and knocked me down." Remington staggered to his feet and stumbled backward through his line, where he "got d——d" by Major John Hauser for going after the flag. He started for the rear at his best run. "Flag-taking," he concluded, "was pretty well knocked out of me." According to the lieutenant, he made it within twenty feet of the Confederate flag before being hit, when two other soldiers passed him—Cornelius Okey of Cassville and Lewis Eggleston of Shiocton. Okey said he reached the flag ahead of Eggleston and "bending

Unfinished Railroad Cut
Gettysburg

This picture was taken after the battle and shows the installed railroad tracks. The cut was under construction in 1863 and was filled with large rocks and debris. This photograph was included by the Dawes family in a 1936 edition of Rufus Dawes' 1890 memoir.

over grasped the staff low down, but he was so close to me that before I could draw it from the ground, the staff having been driven well down in the dirt, Eggleston had also got a hold of it. I noticed a rebel corporal on his knees, right in front of men in the act of firing, his bayonet almost touched me; as quick as thought almost I made a quarter face to the left, thus pressing my right side to him and bringing Eggleston, who still retained his hold on the flag, as well as my self, at my back." The rebel fired and his buck and ball charge passed through the skirt of Okey's frock coat and lodged in his left forearm and wrist. Eggleston also fell, shot through both arms.[12]

Fighting amongst the tangle of soldiers was John O. Johnson of Stevens Point, who tried to save Eggleston, a member of his mess "whom I loved as a brother." But Johnson's musket ramrod was jammed halfway down the barrel. "Seeing other rebels raising their guns as if to shoot or bayonet Eggleston, I stepped in front of him and raised my musket to defend him as best I could. While thus in the act of stroking, I received a wound that disabled my right arm. Poor Eggleston also went down, and I think from the same bullet that wounded me."[13] As Eggleston fell, David "Rocky Mountain" Anderson of Minneapolis[14] swung his musket like a club, crushing the skull of the rebel who fired the fatal ball. Nearby, John Harland of Glendale was shot as he moved toward the Confederate flag, his body sliding into the railroad cut at the foot of the soldier who killed him. Levi Tongue of Hillsboro, aimed his musket point-blank at the rebel. "Don't shoot! Don't kill me!" the Johnny cried out. "All hell can't save you now," yelled back the embittered Levi Tongue, who squeezed his trigger, the ball knocking the rebel onto the body of his friend. In the tangle of "shooting, thrusting and parrying thrusts," Frank Wallar of De Soto, his brother Sam at his side, closed in on the Confederate flag.[15]

Struggling to hold aloft the 2nd Mississippi's flag staff was Corporal W. B. Murphy. He was carrying the flag that July morning because the regular

Color Sergeant, Christopher Columbus Davis, was sick. "My color guards were all killed and wounded in less

Captain Joseph Marston
6th Wisconsin Volunteers

Marston captured a sword in the the fight at the Railroad Cut at Gettysburg on July 1, 1863. He later attempted to reach the 2nd Mississippi Infantry officer who surrendered it so it could be returned.

Buck Marston

than five minutes, and also my colors was shot more than one dozen times, and the flag staff was hit and splinted two or three times," recalled Murphy. A group of Federals rushed toward him, but all were killed our wounded," but others "still kept rushing for my flag and there were over a dozen shot down like sheep in the mad rush for the colors." He saw Captain William Remington shot down along with a dozen or so others. "Then a large man [Corporal Frank Wallar of De Soto] made a rush for me and the flag. As I tore the flag from the staff he took hold of me and the color. The firing was still going on, and was kept up for several minutes after the flag was taken from me . . . ."[16]

As Wallar pushed though the soldiers and reached for the flag a Confederate pointed a musket at Wallar's side, but his brother, Sam Wallar, parried the barrel as the gun went off, then reversed his musket and clubbed down the Johnny. According to Frank, "soon after I got the flag there were men from all the companies there. I did take the flag out of the color bearer's hand . . . " He thought about making for the rear with the trophy, but "then I thought I would stay, and I threw it down and loaded and fired twice standing on it. While standing on it," he continued, "there was a Fourteenth Brooklyn man took hold of it and tried to get it, and I had threatened to shoot him before he would stop. By this time we had them cleaned out."[17]

The tide was now turning in favor of the Badgers. Only minutes earlier, Davis' Southern infantry had spotted the unfinished railroad cut and deemed it a blessing—a defensive entrenchment perfectly aligned to repel the charging Union soldiers. What they did not realize was that although shallow on both ends, much of the rest of the cut was too deep to utilize as a

Sergeant Albert E. Tarbox
Co. K, 6th Wisconsin

A native of Necedah, Tarbox enlisted in June 1861 and was soon promoted to sergeant. Wounded at Antietam, he was shot and killed in the Railroad Cut on July 1, 1863, as he tried to assist the wounded James Sullivan of his company.

Carroll College Civil War Institute

defensive position. Once the men by the hundreds crowded into the cut, they found themselves stuck below ground level, unable to shoot at their enemies or respond to orders. For so many, the position was now nothing more than a giant open grave.

While the fighting for the flag was concluding, the rest of the charging Wisconsin men crowded up along the edge of the cut, pushing and firing their musket barrels into the upraised faces of hundreds of Confederates trapped below. "Throw down your muskets! Down with your muskets!" the soldiers in tall black hats screamed over and over. "The men [were] black and grimy with powder and heat," remembered one of the Wisconsin officers. "They seemed all unconscious to the terrible situation; they were mad and fought with a desperation seldom witness."[18]

With most of the rest of his survivors, Dawes found himself on the edge of the cut with his men yelling for the Confederates to surrender. "I found myself face to face with hundreds of rebels, who I looked down upon in the railroad cut, which was, where I stood, four feet deep." On his right, a fast-thinking Adjutant Edward Brooks threw a dozen men across the east end of the cut, where they began firing into the trapped and now helpless Confederates who, deep in the depression, were unable to see more than a handful of their attackers.

"Where is the colonel of this Regiment?" Dawes shouted.

Major John Blair of the 2nd Mississippi looked up at the Union officer. "Here I am. Who are you?"

Dawes jumped into the cut, pushing and pulling aside still-armed rebels as he shoved his way toward the major. "I command this regiment. Surrender or I will fire." Blair handed over his sword without a word. The Confederates around the pair of officers began dropping their muskets. "The coolness, self-possession, and discipline which held back our men from pouring in a general volley," claimed Dawes, "saved a hundred lives of the enemy, and as my mind goes back to the fearful excitement of the moment, I marvel at it."

The young officer took Blair's sword and other side arms offered by various Southern officers until the bundle in his arms grew to an awkward size. Brooks walked up to assist him. "It would have been a handsome thing to say, 'Keep your sword, sir,'" Dawes reminisced years later, "but I was new to such occasions and when six other officers came up and handed me their swords, I took them also."

Loyd Harris later said he heard the exchange of swords in the bloody railroad cut did not go as smoothly as Dawes testified. According to Harris, someone told him that Blair demanded Dawes' surrender, but the Wisconsin officer defiantly answered, "I will see you in hell first!" Harris doubted the story, and said Dawes did not remember it. A Wisconsin private who was there said that when the Confederate major was told he faced the 6th Wisconsin, he replied, "Thank God. I thought it was a New York regiment."[19]

Captain Marston of Appleton also captured a sword. His prize came just as Private Lyman White of his company was about to bayonet a Confederate captain. As Marston recalled it, he "sprang and caught Lyman's gun and saved the captain's life." The Southern officer handed his sword to Marston and surrendered. A Wisconsin soldier said the Union men "would have made a great slaughter down the cut had they [the Confederates] not surrendered." Most of Davis' men were in the cut and "could neither fight nor retreat . . . .on account of the high banks." Some rebels ran for it out of the west end of the depression "as the cut was too deep for them to see the scarcity of our numbers or make attack. The 2d Miss. lay in the water, mud and blood at the east of the cut where the cut was coming out to a grade."[20]

Not far from where Dawes accepted Blair's surrender and Marston saved a Southern officer, Private Sullivan captured his own blade. Just as the shooting north of the Chambersburg Pike was sputtering to a fitful halt, Sullivan jumped into the railroad cut to help gather prisoners when an officer handed him a sword in surrender. "Some of the Johnnies threw down their guns and surrendered. Some would fire and then throw down their guns and cry 'I surrender,' and some broke for the rear," Sullivan wrote. As he was climbing up the other side of the embankment, "a big rebel broke for the rear and I called on him to halt, to which he paid no attention, and I flung the rebel sword at him with all my might . . . " Sullivan was in the act of launching the weapon when "a bullet hit me on the left shoulder and knocked me down as quick as if I had been hit with a sledge hammer." He said he first thought he had been hit with a musket butt, "for I felt numb and stunned, but I was not long in finding out what was the matter." If he had not tried to throw the sword, he said, he would have been shot square in the body." As Sullivan lay on the ground, Sergeant Albert Tarbox of Necedah moved up next to him. "They got you down Mickey, have they?" and then Tarbox fell forward dead, said Sullivan, shot by a rebel who had already surrendered. "They did a good deal of that kind of work that day." It was a terrible moment, he remembered: "I never saw so many men killed in such a short time, as it was not more than fifteen or twenty minutes from the time we saw the rebels, until we had them officers, colors and all."[21]

To the left of the 6th Wisconsin, the 95th New York and the 14th Brooklyn held their positions and fired into the Confederates seeping out of the western end of the railroad cut. Fighting erupted along the whole line temporarily, but just as quickly died out amidst cries of "Surrender!" and "Throw down your muskets!"

The fighting at the railroad cut resulted in the capture of seven officers and 225 enlisted men, including Major Blair, eighty-seven men from the 2nd Mississippi, and the regiment's battle flag.[22] Of the 300 men in the ranks that morning, the 6th Wisconsin loss included two officers killed, six wounded, 27 enlisted men killed, 105 wounded and 25 men missing.[23]

From a woods on Seminary Ridge, John Kellogg of the 6th Wisconsin, serving on the staff of his old colonel, Lysander Cutler, watched his regiment overcome the rebels. It was "three minutes" after the 6th Wisconsin reached the unfinished railroad cut, he said, before the 95th New York and 14th Brooklyn arrived to fire into the fleeting rebels. Not far away, an excited James Wadsworth and his staff also watched the stunning regimental charge. When the national flag lifted in victory, Wadsworth swung his horse around, waiving his hat. "My God, the 6th has conquered them!" he shouted.[24]

As the firing died away, Private Sullivan lay sprawled on the edge of the railroad cut with his left shoulder wound. "After a while I began to feel better, and like a true Irishman I spoke to myself to see if I was dead or only speechless, and finding it was only the latter, I picked up my gun and tried to shoulder it, but I found that my left arm was powerless," he wrote. "I went around to the other side of the cut where our fellows had a heavy line of prisoners and a very thin skirmish line of themselves, and took my place outside the rebs, intending to help guard them." By this time Sullivan was "sick and faint and the blood was running down inside my clothes and dropping from my pants leg and my shoe was full and running over." He had a canteen of fresh milk and one of the Confederates, seeing his discomfort as he tried to get it, "took it off me and held it while I took a big swig, which helped me a good bit."[25]

Chapter 16

What Became of That Sword I Gave You?

ong afterward, when Gettysburg was already regarded as the baptism by blood that brought the Union what Abraham Lincoln described as a "new birth of freedom," old soldiers remembered the fighting. Rufus Dawes of Marietta, Ohio, late colonel of the 6th Wisconsin, exchanged friendly letters with John Blair, late major of the 2nd Mississippi. Former Confederate Color bearer W. A. Murphy added letters from Mooresville, Falls County, Texas: "My Dear Genl.," he wrote, using Dawes' honorary rank. "I would like very much to have my old flag back again for a keep sake, there is nothing that I would appreciate more highly than to see it once more in my life as I am now 50 years in July 13, 1892, and by the time you receive this letter say July 1st 1892, twenty nine years ago since you or some one of your command took the flag out of my hands."

Blair was practicing law in Tupelo, Mississippi, and Dawes sent him a copy of his 1890 memoir *Service with the 6th Wisconsin Volunteers*. Inside was a note saying the fight at the cut at Gettysburg involved two fine regiments, and that he believed Blair's men certainly had given as good as they got. Blair responded with an equally gracious letter, asking Dawes and his family, if the occasion should present itself, to visit him in Mississippi. His letter included a final, perhaps unexpected question: "What became of the sword I gave you?" Dawes was forced to admit that the swords taken in the railroad cut that morning so long ago had been lost when the Confederates captured the town of Gettysburg just a few hours later.[1]

Turning back to evaluate the past and put demons to rest was happening all through the aging ranks of veterans of the old regiments. Now, decades after the war, explained editor Jerome Watrous of *The Milwaukee Sunday Telegraph*, late adjutant of the 6th Wisconsin, the men who once were young soldiers "look back to the stirring times from '61 to '65 and recall the experiences and incidents with the keenest of pleasure. . . . We may account in part for the readiness of comrades to talk about the war from the fact that all who participated in the great struggle are more proud of that service than anything they have done in the whole course of their lives. Is it not something to be proud of?"[2] But Watrous admitted (accentuated by a sharp recollection of his brother's cruel death at Port Hudson) that the July anniversary of the epic battle always brought back memories that did not make the heart glad or lift the spirit.

One of the troubling memories drove one-time Captain Joseph Marston of the 6th Wisconsin searching for the officer whose sword he had captured in the railroad cut. Marston wrote to the newspapers published in Mississippi telling how he blocked the shot that would have killed a Confederate officer. "I have the sword in my possession. Now, I call to mind the manly appearing officer, I have but one wish, and this is, if he is living, to return him his sword, as I drew my sword not in hatred." He asked only for the "inscription on the scabbard" and "any little incident that he may remember in connection with this charge." Within a few weeks, R. W. Leavell of Verona, Mississippi, late captain of Company I, 2nd Mississippi, replied with a friendly letter: "I am strongly inclined to believe from many indications that I am the person from whom the capture was made." The details were not always clear: "I determined to surrender, and as a signal of my determination, raised my hat from my head and moved back to the end of the cut from which I had started. Stepping out of the cut and advancing, as I remember only a few paces, I was met by an officer who demanded in a somewhat excited manner the surrender of my sword. I had not, up this moment, thought of grounding my arms, and was therefore exposed to the fire of your men. . . . On the demand being made, I at once handed my sword to the officer." No record exists whether Marston returned the sword.[3]

George M. Keyt of Rockford, Illinois, was forever haunted by the face and the dying words of his friend Frank King of Fond du Lac, who fell wounded at Gettysburg in the field by the Chambersburg Pike. King was "a rollicking young fellow," always "cheerful, full of stories and the delight of his comrades," remembered Keyt. He was shot through the body and was dying. He called out over and over to passing soldiers for help: "You are my friend. I beg you to end my misery, shoot me!" But those tough young men who could stand almost anything could not stand that, and they hurried away. Finally it was Keyt's turn, and he found himself staring down on King. "I have asked a dozen of the boys to help me, Keyt, but they declined. I am shot through the body and must die. I want to die now. Please shoot me." Keyt said he drew back for a second and brought up his musket. But he could not do it and broke and fled, running "as [I] never ran before." King's body was found three days later where Keyt (and so many others) had left him.[4]

But all of the attempts at emotional healing and putting the past right would come later. About noon on July 1 at Gettysburg, the fighting may have come to a sputtering halt along much of the length of McPherson's Ridge, but it was obvious to nearly everyone that the battle was far, far from decided.

Dawes was reorganizing his command along the railroad cut when Corporal Wallar bought him the square red battle flag of the 2nd Mississippi. On it were the names Manassas, Gaines Farm, Malvern Hill and Seven Pines. "It is a rule in battle not to allow sound men to leave the ranks," replied Dawes, who gave the flag to Sergeant William Evans, who was shot through the upper legs and making his way to the rear using two muskets for crutches. Dawes wrapped the flag and tied it around Evan's body under the coat, telling him to keep it safe. Adjutant Brooks also came up with a bundle of captured swords he handed to another wounded man. The swords were delivered to Surgeon A. W. Preston in town, but were lost when Confederates overran his temporary hospital later in the day.

Just as this was going on, some of the captured Confederates made a run for the end of the unfinished railroad bed. "They are getting away!" the Wisconsin men shouted, and the escape was cut off. Another lone Confederate jumped up and started to run up the ridge, but Enoch Jones of Portage and Isaiah F. Kelly of Prescott both fired and the rebel fell. They ran up the ridge and found the downed Johnny with a broken leg. Nearby was a soldier from the 56th Pennsylvania, shot through the body. But the ridge was clear of Confederates and the two soldiers returned to ranks. "I . . . had just taken my place . . . when two shots were fired from the old fence from which I had just returned," recalled Kelly. One of the heavy bullets struck Color Corporal Charles W. Mead of Newark on the head and killed him. The other went through the brim of Kelly's hat, "so close to my head that it almost burned a blister. Mead was the last one of the brave color guard who went into the fight."

Captain John Hyatt picked up the flag dropped by Mead and asked several soldiers to take the banner, but they all refused. Kelly turned to Dawes, standing behind him, and said he would carry the flag. "All right, Corporal," Dawes responded and Kelly, wounded in the knee in the charge up to the railroad cut, so sick with dysentery he was reduced to "a skeleton" and had barely kept up on the march to Gettysburg, was handed "the old flag" of the 6th Wisconsin. He would carry it through the rest of the fight.

Sullivan, his left arm useless, was also having a hard time staying on his feet. General Wadsworth, who ridden his way over to the scene of Dawes' victory, noticed the Irishman's distress. "My man, you are too badly hurt to be here," said the general. He ordered a cavalry sergeant to take Sullivan onto his horse and take him to a hospital being set up in Gettysburg. The sergeant was told not to leave the wounded private "until he saw [him] in the care of a doctor."[5]

As Sullivan left the field, Dawes released members of the Brigade Guard to return to their regiments now moving to the defensive position in the woods on McPherson's Ridge. An artillery battery was brought forward between the Chambersburg Pike and the railroad cut where it was supported by the 6th Wisconsin, 14th Brooklyn, and 95th New York. The three other regiments of Cutler's brigade extended the Union line north along the ridge. Cutler's men and the 2nd and 6th Wisconsin of Meredith's brigade had been roughly handled. The 6th Wisconsin lost one of every two men in the rush to the railroad cut. The other regiments suffered fewer casualties, but had still been badly shot up. The initial fighting was at an end: Archer's and Davis' Confederate brigades were routed, and other Union commands and officers were now moving onto the hard-won field.

* * *

Earlier that morning, Colonel Charles Wainwright of the Artillery Brigade had been finishing his monthly returns when an order came to move at once. He rode ahead where he met John Reynolds, who told him he did not expect any fighting and that the infantry was only moving up to support Union cavalry northwest of Gettysburg. Reynolds rode ahead to catch up to Wadsworth's division and Hall's 2nd Maine Battery, camped three miles in advance. By 10:30 a.m., Reynolds would be dead.

As Wainwright moved up the road, his horse "Billy" threw two shoes and the officer stopped at farm house and ordered up an artillery battery forge to replace them. He waited another ten or to fifteen minutes for a heavy rain shower to clear before moving up the roadway. When he came upon General Abner Doubleday about two miles south of Gettysburg, the two officers chatted. Doubleday took the opportunity to grumble over his lack of promotion. It was, Wainwright said, between 10:30 and 11:00 a.m. when the two began to hear the distant rumble of cannon fire. A staff officer pounded up with "orders to push on as fast as possible," as Reynolds was engaged over beyond a Lutheran Seminary Building.[6]

As he drew near the sound of the fighting, Captain Clayton Rogers of Wadsworth's staff pushed forward with eagerness, "greatly elated at the prospect of seeing a cavalry fight, having been two years in the service without seeing one." His hope of seeing horse soldiers in action ended in disappointment when he encountered only "dismounted cavalry falling back." Among the Federal wounded walking from the field was a familiar face. Colonel Lucius Fairchild of the 2nd Wisconsin was making his way from the woods with a shattered arm that would be amputated a few hours later.[7]

Lieutenant James Stewart of Battery B, 4th U.S. Artillery, finished a long night of making out returns for his unit. No sooner were they sent off than an orderly rode up with an order to send all wagons to the rear. Before Stewart mounted his horse to ride ahead with his bugler "to see what was going on," he told Lieutenant James Davison to have "boots and saddles" sounded in case there was a call for his guns. Climbing on his mount he rode ahead to find Thomas Devins' cavalry brigade. He watched the battle for some time before realizing the Union horsemen would not be able to hold much longer. "Having the battery field-glasses with me, I took a good survey of the field, and was surprised to see their [Confederate] strength as they were advancing." When Stewart was told Reynolds had been killed, he found Wadsworth at the front and offered to place three guns on Chambersburg Pike and three more on the other side of the railroad cut. The general told the artilleryman he would be "much obliged," and Stewart sent a rider at the gallop with orders to Davison to bring up Battery B.[8]

Stewart's famous Battery B was equipped with six Model 1857 muzzle-loaded 12-pound bronze smoothbores (often called Napoleons or "Light Twelves") to distinguish them from an earlier model. They were officially categorized as "gun-howitzers," and got their name in part by the weight of the ammunition: a 4.62-inch caliber, 12-pound solid shot. Newer rifled batteries were already in service, but Napoleon smoothbores (named after a light, mobile field gun of the type favor by Napoleon III in France) were considered the workhorses of the Army of the Potomac. In addition to solid shot, the guns fired bursting shells using a timed fuse. They also fired canister, a thin iron can containing lead or iron balls packed in sawdust. Canister was an anti-personnel charge, used against infantry at close ranges with a result not unlike the blast from a giant shotgun.

The operation of a battery was complicated. It involved not only well-trained artillerymen to fire the smoothbores, but horses to move it and mechanics to keep it in operation. On the march—a full six-gun battery occupied nearly one-half mile of roadway—each gun was attached to a two-wheeled cart called a limber that carried an ammunition chest over the axle. Each gun and limber was normally drawn by a team of six horses harnessed two abreast. The teams were controlled by three drivers who rode the left horses. Each gun was usually accompanied by a caisson carrying two ammunition chests with a spare wheel attached to the rear chest.

The battery train also included a battery wagon, mobile forge, and extra caissons. The battery wagon carried items for the maintenance of the gun. These ranged from grease and oil to paint, tools, extra wheel spokes, 200 pounds of spare harness, and a grindstone. The forge was basically a blacksmith shop on wheels and carried 300 pounds of horse shoes, nails, extra iron, and additional equipment. Under ideal conditions, a battery employed eighty-four draft horses with another two dozen horses used as spares and as riders. The regulation gun crew required nine men. Capable of firing two aimed shots a minute, they were especially lethal using canister against advancing infantry.

An earlier example of their lethality came about when the battery was nearly captured in the fighting near the Cornfield at Antietam on September 17, 1862. The six 12-pounders were firing from an open field, with one gun unlimbered on the Hagerstown Pike. Attacking Confederates surged to within point-blank range of the gun crews and horses. Some crews were down to one or two men and using double and even triple charges of canister, and even then it seemed nothing could hold back the Southerners. Brigadier John Gibbon in command of the Western infantry brigade but ever watchful over his old battery, was on foot among the gunners. He spun up the elevating screw on one gun so the canister blast would glance off the ground into the Confederates. The general jumped away and nodded to pull the lanyard, yelling, "Give them hell, boys!" The gun bucked and Gibbon watched as the blast blew "away most of the fence in front of it" and produced "great destruction in the enemy ranks." The Confederate charge crested and retreated in disarray. In front of the hot muzzles, dead and wound Confederates were "found piled on top of each other."[9]

Stewart's Battery B and its gunners were badly used up in the campaigning of 1862, and it was only the respite of winter camp, the additional of more infantry volunteers, and Stewart's stiff drills and training that brought the unit back to effective strength. It was little used in the Chancellorsville campaign, and by the end of June 1863 there was no battery in the army more ready or eager for service. Even though it was officially a Regular Army unit, ninety percent of the battery's gunners were volunteers from the five Iron Brigade regiments. It was "The Iron Brigade Battery" in both truth and nickname.[10]

The opening infantry fighting at Gettysburg on July 1, 1863, involved just four brigades—Archer and Davis on the Confederate side, and Cutler and Meredith's Iron Brigade on the other. In the lull that followed, both sides moved reinforcements to the field. With Reynolds down, Doubleday of the First Corps commanded the Union forces on and approaching the field. He arrived only minutes before Reynolds was shot and was left without instructions of what the fallen general planned to do. Doubleday believed the woods to be the key to the McPherson's Ridge line, and he kept the four Iron Brigade regiments in the trees despite protests from Meredith that the position was not strong enough. Doubleday placed two of the arriving Union brigades on the ridge, one on each side of the hard-hit Iron Brigade, and sent two more across the Chambersburg Pike to extend the line north along the ridge. Doubleday also ordered Cutler's damaged regiments to once again move forward to McPherson's Ridge. "It's just like cock-fighting to-day," Cutler told his men. "We fight a little and run a little. There are no supports."[11]

Doubleday was famous in the army for his role as second in command at Fort Sumter in 1861. He was a New Yorker and West Pointer, and was an abolitionist whose views were sometimes expressed with too much force. Doubleday was enough of a solder to realize that the Union position northwest of Gettysburg could not be held indefinitely, but that holding it would provide additional time for other regiments of the First Corps to reach the field. "Upon taking a retrospect of the field, it might seem, in view of the fact that we were finally forced to retreat, that this would have been a proper time to retire," Doubleday later wrote in his official report. He explained, however, given the decision of Reynolds to fight northwest of Gettysburg, "I naturally supposed that it was the intention to defend the place." A short time later, when General Oliver Howard of the Eleventh Corps reached the field and assumed command because of his senior commission, he ordered Doubleday to hold Seminary Ridge at all hazards if driven from McPherson's Ridge. Howard left a division of the Eleventh Corps under General Adolph von Steinwehr along with some artillery in reserve south of the town at a place called Cemetery Hill, and ordered his two other divisions through the town to meet the Confederate threat developing from the north.

* * *

Confederate Henry Heth's inaugural debut as a major general and division leader in Lee's Army of Northern Virginia had not gotten off to an auspicious start. His decision to recklessly push Archer and Davis toward Gettysburg on an early morning reconnaissance—the former leading Heth's smallest brigade and the latter an inexperienced commander—triggered a bloody setback. With half his division roughly handled, Heth brought up his batteries to rake the strengthening Federal position on the ridges in the distance, while simultaneously preparing his two remaining brigades under Brigadier General James Pettigrew and Colonel John Brockenbrough to press the attack.

Chapter 17

I Can Stand it No Longer

he fighting west and north of Gettysburg and the movement of soldiers and artillery through streets and backyards sent the town's civilians scurrying for safety. The excitement and danger also aroused patriotism in former Town Constable John Burns, a cobbler and 68-year-old veteran of the War of 1812.

Burns had seen armed rebels on the streets of Gettysburg when a Confederate column occupied the town on June 26 after scattering a makeshift regiment of home guards and militia. The rebels burned and razed a nearby iron foundry owned by Congressman Thaddeus Stevens, an outspoken abolitionist and hard-line proponent of putting down the rebellion by force. An advance party of rebel cavalry ("the filthiest looking pack of men we had ever seen," recalled a town girl) galloped through Gettysburg yelling and firing revolvers, scaring citizens off the streets. The troopers then took to looting barns, stores, and chicken coops as well as leading off pet horses.

Confederate Major General Jubal Early arrived from nearby Mummasburg a short time later and found about 100 of the captured local militia under guard in the town square. He lectured them about the consequences of rash action, told the old fellows that they should have used more sense, and the younger ones that they should have stayed with their mothers. Early paroled the lot of them.

The general, sitting on his horse, wrote a list for town officials of supplies he required of them, including 7,000 pounds of bacon, 1,200 pounds of sugar, and 1,000 pairs of shoes. If the materials were not available, he said, he would take $5,000 instead. Town Council President David Kendlehart sent back a note saying neither food nor cash was available, but town merchants would open their doors to furnish what ever they could of such provisions. The man he selected to take the message to the general was John Burns, who worked for Kendlehart. Early read the reply, handed both papers back to Burns, and said, "I will see my commissary about it." His soldiers soon turned up 2,000 military rations in a rail car. The food was intended for the Pennsylvania militia. Early rode off, but a Confederate band spent the night in Gettysburg playing rebel airs. The enemy left the next morning.[1]

Now the Confederates were back in force, and old Burns was restless and eager to take a hand in driving them away. What happened over the next few hours was a story told and retold so often no one was sure of the truth of it. Gathering his old musket, Burns went out on the streets to rouse his neighbors. Despite his curses and swearing—a pious towns woman claimed Burns berated a neighbor as a "damned coward, a chicken hearted squaw, a tallow faced sissy"—he had little success. Finally, declaring he could stand it no longer and that he "must have a hand in the fight," the old cobbler put musket to shoulder and started toward the sound of the fighting on the rolling ridges northwest of Gettysburg.[2]

In the center of the line was the woods on McPherson's Ridge and the four regiments of the Iron Brigade—the 2nd and 7th Wisconsin, 19th Indiana and 24th Michigan—posted along a low crest running east of Willoughby Run. To the south and slightly to the east were the 121st Pennsylvania, 8th New York, 142nd Pennsylvania and 151st Pennsylvania. To the north, the 150th Pennsylvania, 143rd Pennsylvania, and 149th Pennsylvania were in line, but they were in the open and thus susceptible to an attack from the north.

North of Gettysburg, meanwhile, two divisions from Confederate Lieutenant General Richard Ewell's Second Corps, one under Robert Rodes and the other under Jubal Early, were moving toward the town. Ewell had been marching to the rally point at Cashtown when he turned south on the Carlisle and Harrisburg roads to head toward Gettysburg. Oliver Howard had some Federal units from his Eleventh Corps units just going into line, but they were reaching the field piecemeal and the Confederates were already arriving in heavy numbers. In the early afternoon, Ewell's divisions under Rodes and Early arrived and attacked the extended Union line posted on largely on indefensible ground northwest and north of town. Rodes, one of the leading lights of the Virginia army, kicked off one of his worse days on the battlefield by launching a clumsy, piecemeal assault south off Oak Hill. Two of his brigades under Edward A. O'Neal and Alfred Iverson suffered heavy losses storming a strong position held by John C. Robinson's division, part of the First Corps. Temporarily, at least, the Southern advance in that sector stalled. Directly north of town, however, Early's men caught Federal Francis C. Barlow's division of the Eleventh Corps in a weak formation and overran what was the right flank of the position, wounding and capturing Barlow in the attack and driving thousands of Eleventh Corps men rearward.

South and west of this fighting in the woods on McPherson's Ridge, the Black Hats could see Heth's Confederates massing on Herr Ridge to their front. The Union position on the east bank of Willoughby Run was slightly up the slope. It was apparent the brigade could be overlapped on both the left and the right, and that the left of the line was almost invisible from the right because of intervening trees and brush. The right flank of Colonel Henry Morrow's 24th Michigan was awkwardly curved back to unite with the 7th Wisconsin while his left edged down a hillside to a hollow in an effort to reach the right side of the 19th Indiana. In Morrow's opinion, the Federal line should be moved back to the crest of the ridge. Three times he petitioned headquarters to correct his line, but three times the request was refused.

The buildup lasted until mid-afternoon when the Confederates gathered like the dark cloud of a coming storm, first atop Herr Ridge and then moving in heavy lines down into a wooded area halfway down the slope where they halted. The Black Hat veterans could see there were at least three and possibly five or six brigades arrayed against them—more than enough to easily sweep them back. Only three small Union brigades were available face them—the Iron Brigade in the center, General Thomas Rowley's brigade to the south, and General Roy Stone's brigade to the north. Farther north, where the regiments of the Eleventh Corps were sent, the sounds of artillery and heavy rips of musketry were clearly heard by all.

It was now nearly 3:00 p.m. Some 3,000 soldiers from Heth's two remaining brigades, together with some of Archer's survivors, stepped off to clear McPherson's Ridge and open the way to Gettysburg. John M.

Brockenbrough's Virginians were on the left, Pettigrew's North Carolinians in the center, and Archer's men on the right. Formed behind the advance line were the brigades of William D. Pender's large and fresh division. Edward Thomas' Georgia regiments were deployed north of the Chambersburg Pike, with the brigades of Alfred M. Scales, Abner Perrin, and James H. Lane aligned south of the roadway.

The line of advancing Confederate soldiers, muskets at the shoulder, moved down into the swale with a swaying step. The Black Hats held their fire, watching as the Confederates stepped over a weak rail fence into a field of oats. An order was yelled out by someone and the Johnnies came on with that chilling and wild yell heard on so many battlefields. Heading directly for the 24th Michigan and the right side of the 19th Indiana was the 26th North Carolina with 800 men in perfect lines of battle.

The 26th North Carolina was a well-known regiment led by a man who might have been the youngest colonel in the Confederate army, 22- year-old Henry King Burgwyn, Jr. Burgwyn had been an outstanding student at the Virginia Military Institute, where one of his professors, Thomas Jackson, described the young cadet in a recommendation as "a high-toned Southern gentleman." The first colonel of the 26th North Carolina was former Congressman Zebulon B. Vance, but he left after a year to become wartime governor of North Carolina leaving Burgwyn—despite Vance's grumbling over his youthfulness—to be named colonel. He was just 21.

The young colonel was already a man with a reputation. The son of a highly regarded planter, he entered the University of North Carolina at age 16 and graduated with honors and joined the corps of cadets at the VMI, where he graduated at the top of his class. Burgwyn was among the cadets that guarded abolitionist John Brown following his ill-fated raid on Harpers Ferry in 1859. Burgwyn proved a capable and brave officer despite being a sharp disciplinarian. The men who marched across the field into the battle of Gettysburg under his command were both proud of their young colonel and a bit fearful of him.

The 26th North Carolina held the left of Pettigrew's brigade line with the 11th North Carolina, 47th North Carolina, and 52nd North Carolina extending the front to the right (south). The four regiments were midway through the field when the Western men fired their first volley, a shower of bullets that mostly fell short of their mark. The Confederate line halted and fired a volley of its own. A second Union volley followed, this time high, and the Confederates came forward again at the quick-step. The third hard volley from the Iron Brigade staggered the advancing North Carolinians and opening holes in the advancing line. Suddenly, in a great swirl of shouts and gunfire and swarming bullets, the Confederates leaned forward and pushed toward the wood line. Within seconds the 24th Michigan and 26th North Carolina found themselves locked into a fierce firefight that would make the valor of both units famous and forever link them by blood.[3]

Just southeast of the town of Gettysburg near a place called Cemetery Hill, the ammunition wagons of the First Division of the First Army Corps were parked alongside the Emmitsburg road. Ordnance Sergeant Jerome Watrous, who was in charge of the train, rode ahead and found several infantry regiments, some artillery, and excited staff officers preparing a defensive position around a small cemetery. Away to the north, Watrous could hear the sound of musketry and artillery fire from Howard's ongoing defensive effort against Ewell's attack. The roadways leaving Gettysburg were crowded with civilians and their buggies and wagons, as well as large numbers of wounded and demoralized soldiers.

Word from the front was mixed. The Confederate army was coming down hard on the regiments and brigades of the First and Eleventh corps that had pushed through earlier in the day to the ridges west and north of Gettysburg. It was now common talk that Reynolds was down and probably dead, and that Watrous' own First Division was heavily involved in the fighting. The Confederate army had been found, and the expected battle that might decide the war was now fully underway.[4]

Watrous returned to his wagons to make sure they were ready when needed. The division's ordnance officer, who had orders to stay with the train, waved his hat and galloped off toward the sound of the fighting. Not long afterward, a rider arrived from the front, helloing for Watrous and carrying orders to bring ten wagons of ammunition forward as quickly as possible. The sergeant rode along the wagons picking out the best teams and drivers. One of the men selected was Bert O'Connor of the 7th Wisconsin, known by Watrous to be a steady man under fire. "Bert, you run your team to the front." Within a few minutes, Watrous had the wagons in a line, two men on each seat. His orders were straight forward: each driver was to whip the mules into a "keen run" and do not stop until the order came to do so.[5]

The road into Gettysburg was a good one, O'Connor remembered, and "you can bet we made those 10 mule teams spin along." The train careened at reckless speed. "It seemed as [though] those mules knew that glorious old Wadsworth's gallant men were getting short of ammunition, and that we must get it to them without a moment's delay." Watrous rode alongside the moving wagons shouting over and over for the drivers to go faster.[6] After all, much was riding on their timely arrival at the front.

Chapter 18

Yelling Like Demons

C olonel Henry Morrow could see his 24th Michigan was at the very point of attack in the enemy effort to clear McPherson Ridge. His soldiers were firing steadily from their line just east of Willoughby Run, the low ground around the creek already full of smoke. But the Michigan line was bowed forward, and his men were having trouble concentrating fire on the advancing enemy infantry. It was soon point-blank shooting at fifty to eighty yards. The Wolverines, sporting their new black hats and still concerned they had something to prove to their veteran comrades, had done little to throw up any protection. It was a time when Iron Brigade men still believed there was a certain honor in a "stand up and knock down" fight against a brave foe—a prideful notion that would be knocked out of them in the next hour.

The fighting raged at close range, the air full of bullets, and the boys going down at a fearful rate. One Black Hat said usually the charging party was forced to retire without reaching their objective or the troops attacked would break and fly. But the 26th North Carolina—"yelling like demons" and still in step— pressed forward without hesitation, and the 24th Michigan men stood firm in the face of the storm of bullets.[1]

The battle flags of the opposing regiments were clearly visible in the smoke and noise and the bright banners became the target of soldiers on both sides. The Michigan regiment carried only the magnificent and beautifully embroidered national color made by Tiffany & Co. of New York.

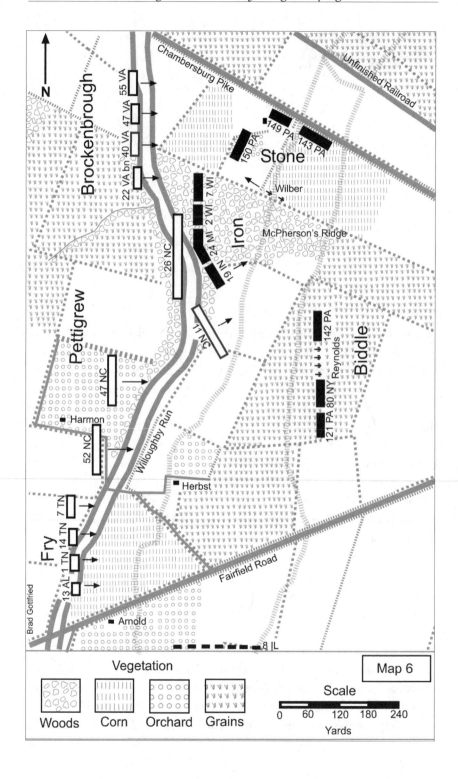

Brad Gottfried

Map 6

It was presented to the regiment in August 1862 on behalf of F. Buhl & Co. of Detroit. At the time, Color Sergeant Abel G. Peck was given a check from a Detroit citizen for $100, which Peck could keep if the banner was returned unsullied. He would not live to collect it. Peck was killed almost immediately that morning—the first of at least nine Michigan color-bearers to fall.[2]

Opposite the Michigan men, the red Confederate flag went down, only to be quickly raised high once again. The underbrush around Willoughby Run slowed the Confederate advance. A Federal battery was also firing into them, but the Rebels splashed across the shallow stream in fairly good order and halted briefly to reform. Michigan soldiers watched in wonder as a Rebel officer riding a mule behind the main line had his hat knocked off by a bullet, only to catch it in the air with one hand—all the while yelling out, "Give 'em hell, boys!" To the south, Confederates were flanking the 19th Indiana, with the Hoosiers bending back before the storm.

Other Federal regiments formed behind the 19th Indiana, but they were en echelon and could not prevent the heavy fire from tearing into the exposed Hoosier flank. The four Iron Brigade regiments had already been heavily engaged that morning, and ammunition was running low. As the 19th Indiana, with twenty men already dead and another 100 wounded, slowly recoiled, bullets swept the Union line from the front and left. To the north, the 2nd Wisconsin and the 7th Wisconsin were also heavily engaged, as were the Pennsylvania regiments in the open fields farther north. The woods were full of smoke, shouting, and shooting. Facing the relentless pressure of the advancing 26th North Carolina, the men of the 24th Michigan found themselves caught in a deadly crossfire from the flank and front. With their muskets fouled, steaming hot, and difficult to load, the Michigan men—already shot to pieces and face-to-face with a heavy line of Confederates, took a step backward; and then another. The Johnnies, just as determined to sweep them from the field as the Wolverines were to hold, took a step forward. And then another.

Somewhere in the noise and confusion as the North Carolinians moved up the wooded slope, Colonel Henry Burgwyn picked up the 26th's red battle flag from a downed color bearer. Just after he passed it to another soldier, a bullet hit the young officer in the side, passing through both lungs and knocking him down. John Randolph Lane, a 27-year-old farmer who rose from the ranks to become lieutenant colonel, took command of the Carolinians and continued pushing the regiment up the slope and into the woods. He was tall with a full black beard that made him seem older. Lane had been with the regiment from the beginning and was a favorite in ranks for his steady leadership. He had first met Burgwyn when the officer was only nineteen. Lane, who was then a corporal, went to headquarters to answer for a camp mix-up involving his new company of volunteers. "At first sight, I both feared and admired him," Lane said.[3]

The 19th Indiana, which also faced the onslaught of the large 26th North Carolina and the 11th North Carolina, carried two flags into battle that morning, a blue regimental presented by the ladies of Indianapolis in 1861 and a national color requisitioned from the Quartermaster Department when the complementary national flag from 1861 was retired. The national flag was carried first that morning by Sergeant Burlington Cunningham, but he was wounded in the opening flurry of bullets that also knocked down one of the color-guards. When Cunningham fell, Abe Buckles picked up the flag. Buckles was surprised at midday when Cunningham reappeared to take up the banner despite a wound in his side. As the 19th was bending under the heavy flank fire (Staff Officer Hollon Richardson said the Indiana regiment was disappearing "like dew before the morning sun."), Cunningham was wounded a second time in the leg and Buckles hit in the shoulder. Lieutenant Colonel William Dudley held the national flag while Sergeant Major Asa Blanchard looked for another color bearer, but Dudley was shot in the right shin before one could be found.

Blanchard grabbed the flag staff from the downed officer and gave it to another soldier. "Colonel, you shouldn't have done this. That was my duty. I shall never forgive myself for letting you touch that flag."

Blanchard ordered two soldiers to help carry Dudley to the rear; the Indiana flag fell yet again. At this point, eight Indiana color bearers had fallen and the regiment's loss in killed and wounded was about one of every two who marched into the fight. Unable to hold against the heavy fire from front and left, the 19th Indiana began moving backward.[4]

Before Blanchard could reach the fallen flag, Corporal David Phillips, who was carrying the Indiana regimental, scooped up the national banner and was waving it with one hand when he was wounded and fell on both Indiana flags.

"The flag is down!" someone shouted.

Captain William W. Macy ran over, yelling to a nearby private to "Go and get it!"

"Go to hell, I won't do it!" snapped back the soldier.

Macy, Lieutenant Crockett East, and Burr M. Clifford rolled the fallen Phillips off the flags. East, aware the bright silk was attracting bullets, furled the banner and was in the act of stuffing it into its case and trying to wrap the tassels when he was shot and killed. Macy and Clifford managed to get both flags in their cases only to be confronted by an angry Sergeant Major Blanchard, who demanded the flags. "No, there's been enough men shot down with it," answered Macy, but Blanchard appealed to Colonel Samuel J. Williams, who was passing by. The colonel told Macy to turn over the flags.

Blanchard pulled out the national colors and tied the case around his waist. "Rally boys!" he called out in a loud voice, waving the flag to attract their attention. Just then, a bullet severed an artery in his thigh and he fell in a gush of blood, dying almost immediately. Burr Clifford had seen enough. He picked up the national color and made a run for the town and safety.[5]

Brigade Commander Sol Meredith was also down, struck on the head by a piece of shell just as his large horse was killed by a bullet. Pinned under the kicking and dying animal, Meredith was pulled from the horse and taken to the rear. Sol was officially out of the battle and, although it was not yet known, out of the war. A staff rider was sent into the woods to find Colonel William Robinson of the 7th Wisconsin (one hopes it was estranged son-in-law Hollon Richardson who carried the news) to tell him that he was now in command of the Iron Brigade.

The line of the four Union regiments was about to fall to pieces. The 19th Indiana was already coming apart, and the 24th Michigan had already folded back its left companies against Pettigrew's flanking Confederates. The 7th and 2nd Wisconsin regiments were also suffering under a "galling fire," and the regiments in the open field to the right were just about played out. They fought on grimly, convinced the fate of the Army of the Potomac rested on their holding the McPherson Ridge position.

With them by this time on the ridge was citizen John Burns and his old musket. There are so many recollections of his presence there that it seems as if he was everywhere at the same time. Veterans claimed the old gent was given a new musket and cartridges that he stuffed in the pocket of his old-fashioned coat. Amos D. Rood of the 7th Wisconsin said he formally swore Burns into federal service just before the fighting by asking, "do you solemnly swear that you will obey all orders you may receive from any and all commanders placed over you until we knocked hell out of them?"

"Now that's just what I'll do," Burns replied—or at least, that's the way Rood remembered it.

Library of Congress

Citizen John Burns
Hero of Gettysburg

Old John Burns, a veteran of the War of 1812, shouldered his musket and went out to fight with the Pennsylvania and Wisconsin regiments on McPherson's Ridge. He was wounded and later won popular acclaim as the "Citizen Hero of Gettysburg."

The Burns stories were obviously romanced over the years. One soldier said he was first on the skirmish line of the 150th Pennsylvania in the open field near the McPherson farm buildings. Another claimed the old patriot was close to the 7th Wisconsin. Lieutenant Colonel John Callis recalled long after the battle that he saw Burns shoot a Confederate officer off a white horse, and that "the old man loaded and fired away" until he retreated with the skirmish line. As he moved back, said a Wisconsin man, Burns "was as calm and collected as any veteran on the ground." Hollon Richardson claimed he saw Burns fighting from behind a tree at the edge of the woods. Another Badger said the men around him watched Burns in action and remarked, "Ain't he a triumph." "See how cool he is." "Look at my old man." They also observed that Burns "did not slight a friendly tree, no more than we did."

The old man was also wounded on July 1. Accounts vary as to exactly where and how many times he was hit. Some claim seven injuries, or five, or three. But we know for sure that the ball that knocked him to the ground hit the old man in his leg, dropping him in some pain as the fighting moved off to the east. Worried about his status as a combatant in civilian clothes, he threw away his musket and used his knife to bury the four military musket cartridges still in his pockets. Burns rolled over the ground several times to mask the hole, and then waited for Confederate soldiers to discover him.[6]

The McPherson Ridge line was collapsing. The cartridge boxes of the Black Hats were empty and firing was slowed by fouled muskets and sheer exhaustion. Fresh Confederate units appeared and the line was severely flanked. Roughly one in every four Michigan men were still on their feet, Morrow claimed. He tried to swing a portion of his left to face the flanking fire. Before it could be executed, however, Confederate pressure forced him to fall back and take a new position a short distance in the rear. One of the Michigan officers killed trying to restore the flank was Lieutenant Gilbert Dickey, a member of Michigan State's first graduating class. At the new rally point, the Michigan men began a "desperate resistance" to slow the advancing Confederates with their cartridge boxes just about empty.

Chapter 19

I Grew About a Foot and a Half

Ordnance Sergeant Jerome Watrous and his train of ammunition wagons cleared Gettysburg on the run as the crippled Iron Brigade clung to the McPherson's Ridge line. Northwest of town, a line of blue infantry appeared and an officer waved for the wagons to halt, but they were not Wadsworth's men and Watrous shook off a call from a major to "Stop that wagon train. It will be captured!" His orders, the sergeant yelled back at the officer, were to deliver the ammunition to his division and, "by the Eternal," he was going to do it.

By this time, Watrous' wagons were in the open field beyond the Seminary building and in range of at least a dozen Confederate artillery pieces firing from the west and north. Somehow his wagons reached the area on the east edge of the woods on McPherson Ridge. Moving along the tree line, the second man on each wagon tumbled off one wooden box of ammunition after another. Running behind the wagons was Watrous, who used the blunt end of an axe to splinter open the boxes so the bundles of cartridges could be distributed to the fighting soldiers. Driving the lead team, Bert O'Connor said three wagon loads, almost 75,000 rounds, were distributed. "All this time the rebels were shelling us to kill. Nearly every wagon cover was hit with a shell, solid shot or minnie ball while we were there."[1]

Milwaukee County Historical Society

Jerome Watrous
6th Wisconsin Volunteers

He was still an ordnance sergeant when he took ten wagons of ammunition to Wadsworth's men fighting for their lives on McPherson Ridge at Gettysburg. His bravery won the admiration of Major General Winfield Scott Hancock. Watrous finished the war as adjutant of the Iron Brigade.

Watrous now faced the challenge of getting his train of wagons out of danger. He ordered the wagons back to town and told his men to issue the remaining rounds to any soldiers in need. The ten wagons contained the only musket ammunition at the front for the embattled First and Eleventh corps.

As the wagons turned around and headed onto the Chambersburg Pike, however, more Confederates appeared on the ridge and the roadway was swept by "a perfect storm of shot, shell and Bullets." O'Connor watched a solid shot strike the saddle mule of the team next to him, severing both the animal's hind legs. The driver of the wagon was a man everyone called "Indiana," O'Connor said, and "I shall never forget the look [he gave] . . . when the poor mule fell down on those stumps of legs." Someone cut the unfortunate beast from the harness and killed him with a shot from a belt revolver. Another artillery shot carved a flesh wound on the other wheel mule and a third round smashed the rear wheels of the wagon. A handful of Federal infantry ran forward to help unload the wagon, which was then dragged into town "with three mules hauling the front wheels and box. Two other wagons were also hit, but none of the ammunition was lost.[2]

Clayton Rogers of Wadsworth's staff watched as young Watrous held the wagons under fire to unload the damaged vehicle before bringing the train to the Chambersburg Pike near the unfinished railroad cut. "The sergeant had a very warm gallop across the railroad embankment into Gettysburg," remembered Rogers. "It seems impossible that a single man should have escaped through such a narrow passage...."[3]

Watrous found the streets of Gettysburg crowded with wounded and fleeing soldiers. O'Connor's wagon was at the rear of the train with Watrous riding at his side. "When we turned to the right . . . the rebels were shelling the town right lively." The Eleventh Corps had recently collapsed and broken, and hundreds of its members were clogging the streets and alleys in an effort to seek safety. The train was caught amid the "zip, zip and zipping of a shower of bullets" from a line of Confederate infantry just fifteen rods away. Federal officers responded with revolvers and O'Connor stood up on his wagon bed to add to the pistol fire. A nearby New York regiment fired a quick volley that broke the Confederate advance in confusion. "The street was packed with troops, mounted officers, artillery and cavalry, and such confusion I never saw," O'Connor recalled. "But there was method enough in the confused crowd to push forward at a good pace" for the rally point south of Gettysburg.

When he reached East Cemetery Hill, Watrous examined his wagons. Each had been hit from "one to a dozen times with solid shot, shell or bullets." The first general officer he found was General Howard "sitting upon his horse with as much coolness as though he was watching a Fourth of July parade." Just beyond, where the wagons cleared the ridge and moved to safety was Major General Winfield Scott Hancock, commander of the Second Corps. Hancock had just arrived with orders to take command of the field. Hancock, remembered Watrous, was "young and fresh and bright and constantly active." The young sergeant rode up with a salute and a request for orders. The general looked him over and soaked in the damaged wagons.

"Good God. What have you got here?" Hancock asked. "What have you got a wagon here for? You haven't been into action?"

Watrous nodded. "Yes sir, just came back with the rear guard."

Hancock gave him another hard look. "Well, did you lose all your ammunition?"

"No sir, distributed nearly all of it."

"Lose any of your wagons?"

"Well, I got back with some of them."

Hancock smiled. "Good. But it is the first Mule Train Charge I ever knew anything about. You did well, Sergeant. Just move your wagons down there and report to me in half an hour."

The "Mule Train Charge" cost the Union five mules, three wounded men, and a parcel of splintered wagons. O'Connor claimed he had never been in a hotter place, and indeed he had not. But Watrous and his wagons managed to provide ammunition to the soldiers of four divisions that played a key role in the delaying fight. This, in turn, allowed the Union to gain time and solidify the high ground south of Gettysburg. And it was that high ground that would prove the key to victory in the two more days of fighting waiting to unfold.[4]

Watrous, who would survive the war, always gave credit for the Gettysburg victory to Hancock. Twenty years later in a speech to veterans in Milwaukee during a memorial service on the death of the general, Watrous told of his chance meeting on the battlefield. It was the only time in his four years in uniform that he met Hancock. "It did me lots of good—I don't suppose it did the general any. I think I grew about a foot and a half [on seeing Hancock], and it was after a hard day's work too."[5]

Chapter 20

In a Tight Place

Lieutenant Colonel John Callis, now in command of the 7th Wisconsin with his colonel (William Robinson) leading the brigade, was fighting soldiers from his home state. A native of North Carolina, Callis and his family moved to Wisconsin when he was ten. Despite his father's warning that he was going to war against his own "flesh and blood," he decided to put on his sword to do "battle for the Nation's safety." Now, he discovered, what was left of his regiment was "in a tight place." Moving by right of companies to the rear toward the Lutheran Seminary building, the 7th Wisconsin halted and fired, and then moved to the rear again while loading. "We executed the same movement with terrible effect," he said.[1]

The Confederates paused at the crest of McPherson's Ridge to let the fresh brigades of Scales, Perrin, and Lane move forward just as the Iron Brigade regiments reached the rally point. The 19th Indiana ("now reduced to a mere squad," remembered one survivor) formed on the left of the 24th Michigan. A few 2nd Wisconsin men also joined the formation. As they watched, the fresh Confederate line lurched forward and the Black Hats realized the final push was coming.[2] The Western men knew they were not holding a good position, but the survivors prepared to fight on. "Every man on the fighting line supposed there was unity in this action and that Gen. Meade, with his whole army would soon be with us." As the new Confederate advance moved down into the swale, Federals still below the ridge realized the Union artillery behind them was ready to fire but could not get sufficient elevation to fire over them with safety.[3]

Lieutenant James Stewart's Battery B of the 4th U.S. Artillery was formed by half battery on both sides of the railroad cut closest to Gettysburg and abreast of what would become known as the Thompson House. The right half of the battery under Stewart was fighting the north side of the cut, slightly forward and facing west. The left half of the battery, under Lieutenant James Davidson, was in open order along the space between the turnpike and the railroad facing southwest. In a small grove to the north were the 11th Pennsylvania and the 6th Wisconsin.[4]

Facing the advancing Confederates in front of the Seminary building were remnants of the Iron Brigade and some Pennsylvania regiments (about 2,300 men), the 5th Maine Artillery and a battery of the 1st Pennsylvania Light Artillery. Battery B opened with case shot on the Confederates on the ridge and switched to murderous shotgun blasts of double-canister as they moved into the swale. The advancing lines slowed under the hail of metal, but a rebel line swung around to take the battery in the flank.

The heavy brass Napoleons fired with a fury equaled only by the fighting near the Cornfield at Antietam the previous September when the guns were nearly lost. "Feed it to 'em! God damn 'em, feed it to 'em!" Davidson yelled through the smokey confusion. Each of the guns fired savage blasts of double-canister that staggered the advancing Confederates. The battery was one of the best in the army and the volunteers and regulars stood to their duty. "Up and down the line men were reeling and falling," one battery man wrote later of Gettysburg. He continued:

> Splinters were flying from wheels and axles where bullets hit in the rear, horses were rearing and plunging, mad with wounds or terror, shells were bursting, shot shrieking over, howling about our ears or throwing up great clouds of dust where they hit; the musketry crashing on three sides of us; bullets hissing everywhere, cannon roaring, all crash on crash and peal on peal, smoke, dust, splinters, blood, wreck and carnage indescribable; but the brass guns of old B still bellowed and not a man or boy flinched or faltered.[5]

The Confederate line leaned forward as if marching against a stiff wind, braving the deadly storm of canister, "creeping toward" the battery "fairly fringed with flame." The soldiers of the 6th Wisconsin and 11th

Pennsylvania crawled over the bank of the railroad cut in rear of the caissons and added their musketry to the canister. Lieutenant Davidson was twice wounded (one ankle was shattered) and was so weak one of the men had to hold him up. The rebels fired volley after volley into the guns, hitting men and horses alike. Unable to remain in command, Davidson ordered Sergeant John Mitchell to take over the half-battery, "moving calmly from gun to gun, now and then changing men about as one after another was hit and fell, stooping over a wounded man to help him up, or aiding another to stagger to the rear . . ." The water in one bucket used for sponging, remembered one artilleryman, looked "like ink." Another gunner was smeared with burnt powder and "looked like a demon from below." North of the railroad cut, the three guns of the other half-battery under Stewart "flashed the chain-lightning . . . in one solid streak."[6]

Rufus Dawes of the 6th Wisconsin stood amid the guns watching the fighting. When the Confederates slowed under the weight of the canister and musketry, one of his infantrymen jumped forward, waving a fist and calling over and over again, "Come on, Johnny! Come on!" It was going to be very close, Dawes concluded.

Clayton Rogers arrived from General Wadsworth and was directed to Captain Rollin Converse. The two men shouted at each other above the noise for a time before Rogers ordered the regiment to retreat. Converse ordered the men to their feet and executed an about face. It was no sooner done than Dawes rushed through the ranks and jerked the National flag from the hands of color bearer I. F. Kelly and halted the regiment. Converse explained the orders and the Wisconsin men turned and poured in a volley to the Confederates who were so close, Kelly recalled, "that we could hear them yelling at us to halt and surrender."

The orders from Wadsworth were to retreat beyond the town and "hold your men together." Dawes said he was astonished at the orders, for the cheers of defiance along the line by the Seminary "had scarcely died away." But a single long glance to the right and rear was sufficient to convince him that the directive was indeed the right one. "There the troops of the eleventh corps appeared in full retreat," he later wrote, "and long lines of Confederates, with fluttering banners and shining steel were sweeping forward in pursuit of them without let or hindrance. It was a close race which could reach Gettysburg first, ourselves, or the rebel troops."

The officer wrote later that his regiment marched away with flag high and a steady step, but one of his big hats remembered a more direct order:

run for it! "We obeyed this literally, and how we did run!" he wrote. "As we came out of the smoke of the battle what a sight burst upon our gaze! On every side our troops were madly rushing to the rear. We were flanked on the right and on the left. We were overwhelmed by numbers. My heart sank within me. I lost all hope."[7]

Staff Officer Rogers found his brother Earl in command of his company. The younger Rogers was known in the regiment as "Bona" for what he claimed was a resemblance to Napoleon Bonaparte. The two shook hands and Clayton, looking at the approaching lines, said not entirely in jest, "Bona, those rebs look to me not less than sixteen feet high, and the flag-staffs at least twenty." With that, Clayton jumped up into the saddle and rode toward the town.[8]

With his infantry supports retreating, Stewart gave the order for for Battery B to limber up. The left half-battery withdrew along the Chambersburg Pike with the enemy scrambling within fifty yards, shooting down more men and horses. Stewart had to move his three guns across the shallow end of the railroad cut. When his three pieces were clear, he rode back to check on the left half-battery and found it gone and the place full of rebels. They called on him to surrender and fired, but Stewart jumped his horse over a fence and suffered two bullet holes in his blouse for his effort. Along the way he was struck in the thigh by a shell fragment that left him so nauseated he was forced to halt briefly and dismount. In pain, he wet his face and drank water from a furrow in a nearby field before continuing on to find his battery. The 6th Wisconsin opened its ranks to allow the guns to roll to the rear and relative safety. Stewart said the Wisconsin regiment and his battery were the last to leave the field.[9]

To the south, just before the line gave way, the fighting at the barricade along Seminary Ridge increased in its fury. During some of the heaviest shooting in the retreat across the swale, Hollon Richardson was seen on his horse waving the flag of a Pennsylvania regiment in an effort to rally it. He called on the men to "do their duty." It was all in vain. "But the captain, left alone and almost in the rebel hands," wrote an admiring correspondent for the *Cincinnati Gazette*, "held on to the flaunting colors of another regiment, that made him a conspicuous target, and brought them safely off."[10]

The barricade in front of the Seminary provided some welcome protection, explained Private William Ray of the 7th Wisconsin: "It being only 2 ½ feet high so we got behind it and just mowed the rebs, all in front of

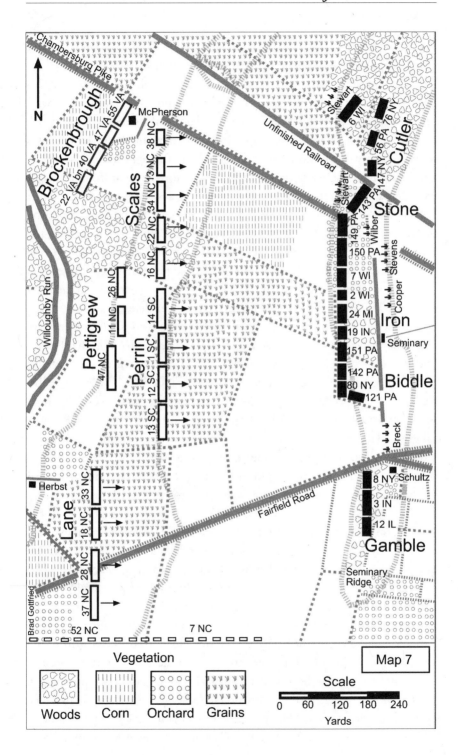

Vegetation

Woods   Corn   Orchard   Grains

Map 7

Scale

0   60   120   180   240

Yards

our Regt was just mowed down. But their line being the longer they kept swing[ing] around the end and getting crossfire on us."[11]

The fighting raged on for several minutes. John Callis of the 7th Wisconsin, afoot since his horse was shot from under him and already twice hit by buckshot, went down again, this time shot in the chest. The heavy ball entered his right side, broke a rib, and lodged in his lung. In the 24th Michigan, only one of every five men taken into the fight was still standing, and many of those were wounded. Colonel Morrow again found himself with the regimental flag. "Rally, rally!" he yelled as he was struck by a bullet that cut across his scalp. With blood streaming down his face and obscuring his vision, Morrow turned command over to Captain A. M. Edwards, the senior officer still on his feet, and made for the rear. Edwards went looking to find the flag and discovered a dead soldier had raised it up and locked it in the crook of his arm before dying. The officer took the banner and carried it to safety. The identity of the dead soldier was never determined.[12]

By now it was obvious to everyone that the position at the Seminary barricade could not be held much longer. "We had to abandon that Place," said Private Ray. "Battery B was just in the [right] rear of us when we lay behind the Rails and every gun poured in the grape which swept the rebs. But there being no Battery on the left to help the Boys so they couldn't hold up under double their number." As he turned to run for the town Ray was hit "by a Ball on the top of the head, came near knocking me down. But I straightened up, went on, another Ball hit the sole of my shoe cutting it nearly in two, it only making my foot sting a little." He limped toward Gettysburg, one of the fortunate few still able to do so.[13]

The 7th Wisconsin fought less exposed than the other regiments of the brigade, but was still raked with fire as it marched toward the town with the rebels 200 yards behind them in a long line of battle. Men "were falling at every step," recalled an eyewitness. "Many of our men that had fought gallantly all day, were taken prisoner by not keeping on the road." As the small column reached the town, Sergeant Daniel McDermott, carrying the regiment's national colors, was hit by a piece of shell that severely wounded him and splintered the flag staff. Alexander Hughes cut the flag from the damaged pole with a folding knife and handed the banner to McDermott, who clutched it to his chest, soaking it with his blood, as he was placed on a caisson moving ahead of the regiment. He feebly waved the flag in defiance even as he moved away. "He has carried this color through every battle in which the regiment has been engaged," Robinson recorded in his official report. In a few hours, on nearby Culp's Hill, soldiers of the 7th Wisconsin would cut and trim a sapling to replace the shattered staff of their beloved national colors.[14]

Despite defiance in the face of defeat, the famous Iron Brigade of the West, which had marched to the fighting with such a confident step at mid-morning, was completely wrecked.

Chapter 21

We Left Behind the Rebel Flag, That Dearly Bought the Prize

In the streets of Gettysburg, the retreating soldiers found panicked citizens and wandering soldiers, some wounded and others not. Artillery shells exploded in, around, and above homes and buildings while the buzz of spent bullets zipped closer. Injured soldiers were everywhere in the town square and around the railroad depot; more were being carried in from the fighting. Army surgeons set up makeshift hospitals before midday to deal with the causalities. More Federal troops and artillery, weary and dusty from hard marching, moved through the streets most of the early afternoon. The distant fighting flared again, and the trickle of wounded men became a river of miserable soldiers in blue marked by blood soaked bandages.

Amid the clamor, townsmen hid family horses and cows. Entire families, grim-faced men with nervous eyes, hysterical women, and frightened children, were in the streets carrying bundles or riding in wagons and carriages loaded with possessions as they fled. To the north and west were clouds of dust and the seemingly endless blasts of massed musketry. A 13-year-old boy watched his sisters and mother "making bandages and drawing lint for the wounded." Passing his front door on stretchers, he said, were "borne the bloody, mangled forms of tall Westerners, bearing on their black felt hats the red circular patch denoting their membership in the first division of the First Corps, many of them of the 'Iron Brigade'."[1]

Among the first of the wounded to arrive was Private James Patrick Sullivan of the 6th Wisconsin, riding a cavalry horse ordered up for him by General Wadsworth. There was no immediate sign of panic and citizens "had wine and refreshments of all kinds on tables and trays," he recalled, "and in their hands, urging them on every wounded man, and assisted them in every way." The private was dropped off at the courthouse where he found Dr. John C. Hall and Dr. O. F. Bartlett of his regiment along with a large number of civilians "busy cutting up and patching up the biggest part of the sixth regiment." Sullivan was put together "with sticking plaster and bandages" and given coffee. He felt faint but thankful as he lay on the floor and rested.

Feeling better after a time, Sullivan looked around to see how many of his Company K had got punched. "I found nearly every man in the company was in the same fix I was, and some a great deal worse," he wrote. Someone informed him there were more wounded from his company in the nearby railroad depot, "Though there were enough here out of the little squad of a company that went into the fight that morning." He found his uncle, Hugh Talty, among the injured. Talty—or "Tall T," as he was known by his comrades—was not feeling his wound just then, for some sympathetic citizen had filled his canteen with whiskey.[2]

Other 6th Wisconsin men were also reaching the city. Corporal Cornelius Okey, hit by buckshot while trying to grab the flag of the 2nd Mississippi at the railroad cut, made his way into Gettysburg. "On my way to town, near the seminary and passing a house, I noticed the door standing open, and, thinking I might get my arm bandaged up, I went in," he recalled. "Found the house deserted, a baby's cradle was standing there and looked as though the mother had hastily taken the child out of it and left all the little bed clothing in the cradle." Okey took a small pillow to support his arm and moved toward town.

Sergeant Michael Mangan was taken to the Washington Hotel, where his leg was amputated. Corporal Francis Deleglise was moving along to town with a group of Confederate prisoners who helped him until two Union cavalry troopers carried him to the cellar of a brick house. Inside were a dozen wounded soldiers, Confederate and Union alike, lying side-by-side on the stone floor. The wounded, he remembered, were "no longer divided by factional opinion, but united in a common suffering."[3]

In the afternoon, with the sound of heavy firing north and west of the town, Doctor Hall looked out a north window and watched as elements of the Eleventh Corps retreat in abject confusion. "Away went guns and knapsacks, and they fled for dear life, forming a funnel-shaped tail, extending to the town," he wrote. "The rebels coolly and deliberately shot them down like sheep. I did not see an officer attempt to rally or check them in their headlong retreat."[4]

The news caused consternation among the wounded and. "Solid shot and shell began to crash through the courthouse and burst in the yard," wrote Sullivan. The doctor ordered all who could move to leave and a hospital flag was stuck outside. The artillery fire slackened and a Southern officer entered the building a few minutes later to demand that all Federals surrender. "The doctor told him there were none there, only medical men and the severely wounded, and the band men who were nurses," said Sullivan. "After some palaver and a drink or two of hospital brandy, the rebel told our doctors to have the nurses tie a white string around their arm and the wounded to keep inside and they would not be disturbed. I was mad as the devil that all our hard fighting that morning had went for nothing and here was over two hundred of our brigade all smashed to pieces . . . ."[5]

In the press of retreating and defeated soldiers was Private Elisha Reed of the 2nd Wisconsin, who had been shot through the upper right thigh at the last stand. "I did not need a post-mortem examination to tell me that I was winged at last," he wrote. "At about the same instant another ball came crashing through the other leg, so very near to the artery that I felt sure that it must be cut." The rebels were very close. "To stop there and tie up my leg would be to fall into their hands in about one minute," he continued. "To run might insure my bleeding to death." Reed threw down his musket and broke for the rear, discovering in a rather unique way that he was not mortally wounded. "[N]o words can convey any idea of how rapidly I ran, even though, loaded down by my cartridge-box and knap-sack . . . I kept my eye right on my leg to see if arterial blood made its appearance," he said. "After running about half a mile and seeing no such blood, I was satisfied that artery was not cut."

Reed reached the Lutheran Seminary and found "the grounds outside and the whole of the lower story were already crowded with the dead and dying, while those who were able had gone up the stairs." He made his way to the third floor where an officer from the 24th Michigan got him to the speaker's stand of the chapel and went to get medical help.[6]

Three Wisconsin officers—Loyd Harris, William Remington, and John Beeley—were also nearby getting patched up for wounds. Young Harris was sitting in a chair as a surgeon was about to probe for a buckshot in the fleshy part of his neck. Assisting him was a "good old lady [who] declared her nerves" would not allow her to witness such a sight. Harris took his harmonica from his pocket. "Madam, the surgeon will be so gentle that while he is operating I will pay on this little musical affair," he said. "So, while he in no delicate manner probed around with his torturing instrument, [I] recklessly played 'Tramp, Tramp the Boys are Marching,' until he finished, when the old lady . . . explained, 'No wonder you men are called the "Iron Brigade".'"

No sooner was Harris bandaged than an orderly on the scene announced to Dr. Andrew J. Ward of the 2nd Wisconsin that wounded Lieutenant Colonel Lucius Fairchild was waiting. "Doctor, Col. Fairchild of the Second, sinds his compliments, and wants ye in a devil of a hurry to cut off his left arum." Harris and the three officers decided to cast about to find a place to stay and ask Fairchild's orderly whether there were "pleasant quarters" to be had. The aide left, but was soon back. "I have found a splendid place, wid such kind and beautiful ladies."

The three officers were taken to the home of "Mr. Hollinger, a true Union man." Harris romanced a bit on what happened next: "His wife was an invalid, but his daughters, two very pretty and sensible young ladies, assumed charge of the house-hold affairs, and we were soon made to feel that for the first time in two years of the hardest kind of campaigning, we were to enjoy a peaceful rest; under a roof, with comforts that too forcibly reminded us of home, sweet home."

The men were surprised to discover Sergeant William Evans in the same house with the captured flag of the 2nd Mississippi. The sight of "that crimson rag" brought a surge of emotion. "We had fought the bloodiest fight of the war to win it . . . and thirty brave comrades lay unburied on the field and one hundred and fifty more were maimed and crippled, all sacrificed to trail that haughty flag under ours; yet we had the esprit du corps to hold it before our new found young lady friends, and in a modest manner told the story of the charge [of the 6th Wisconsin on the unfinished railroad cut]." It was a moment the men treasured and remembered. "No Desdemona ever listed with more heartfelt sympathy than those two young ladies," Harris waxed poetically, "and the story finished, we felt that in their eyes every man of the old Sixth was a hero."

As Harris was inside looking at the "crimson rag," heavy cannonading swept the town. One "shell went tearing through a grape-arbor just in front of the house." Harris went to a window and said he never would forget the sight of the Union retreat. "My emotions were sickening, as I vainly gazed for the First Army corps, that Spartan band who had routed all before them in the morning fight. They were no where in sight—Brave men, I know they would sell their lives dearly: almost bewildered by the maddening scenes that were happening in rapid success, but a rifle shot distant." He decided his wounded friends Beeley and Remington "must not be captured."

Back in the kitchen, Harris told the two officers to make a run for it. "We have lost, and the rebels are in the next street." Beeley and Remington were quickly out the door. Evans, too badly wounded to be moved, was left in his bed. The mother fainted and the two young ladies were crying as they fluttered around her. Harris was about to bolt himself when he saw the despair on the father's face.

"Have you a cellar?" he asked. When one of the daughters nodded, Harris continued, "Then we must carry your mother there."

Helping the father with the wheelchair, the two struggled down a narrow staircase to carry the woman in her wheelchair to the cellar. With the family settled, Harris turned to leave, but stopped to say a few final words. "Good-bye, many thanks for your kindness," he began, "I shall always—" One of the young ladies cut him short. "Oh, hurry away or you will be lost!"

When Harris found rebels in the front street, he ran for a board fence and went over "as a dozen bullets rattled on it." Finding himself in another backyard, he crossed through a vacant house and into a street crowded with fleeing soldiers. In the surging crowd was an army ambulance. As luck would have it, Beeley and Remington were inside. The pair pulled Harris into the wagon. A Federal artillery battery was unlimbered on the street, and as soon as the crowd cleared the muzzles the guns fired. The blasts convinced some of the rebels to pull back as the ambulance moved along to safety.

"Oh, misery and shame, comrades forgive us," Harris said wrote. "We left behind the rebel flag, that dearly bought prize."[7]

Chapter 22

Are You Satisfied With the Twenty-Fourth?

The retreat from Seminary Ridge to the rally point on Cemetery Hill passed through the clogged streets of Gettysburg, the entire route fraught with danger and uncertainty. Lieutenant Amos Rood of the 7th Wisconsin said his regiment stayed until the Federal artillery was gone, then pushed toward the town. Raked by with artillery fire, a hot piece of razor-sharp shell sliced off Rood's left shoulder blade. "But as I was moving rapidly it did not knock me down nor go thro me," he remembered. "It had struck the ground and was rising or I would have been torn and killed. I did not give up tho, and limped and hobbled along . . . ."

To the dismay of many Union men, the Rebels were also in Gettysburg. Lieutenant General Richard Ewell's men had entered from the north, firing along the left cross streets, with Lieutenant General A. P. Hill's men moving and firing along the right cross streets. "I lost one-half of my men getting through town and to Cemetery Hill. Moving, fighting, best as I could!" exclaimed Rood. No men were in sight, he continued, but "lots of women and some children." They had tubs of water in the gateways and kept pumping fresh water for the passing soldiers. "Our men were suffering with thirst. Hot as hell too!"

Behind the 7th Wisconsin, the 6th Wisconsin was also trying to work its way through the streets of Gettysburg. "We know nothing about a Cemetery Hill," Rufus Dawes said. "We could see only that the on-coming lines of the enemy were encircling us in a horseshoe." On the porch of one of the houses they passed was Lucius Fairchild of the 2nd Wisconsin, who was somehow standing with the support of Doctor Ward. His left arm was freshly amputated, but he called out in a faint voice raising his good arm as he spoke, "Stick to 'em boys! Stay with 'em! You'll fetch 'em finally!" His appearance was both heartening and sorrowful at the same time.

The buildings of a small college sheltered the retreating 6th Wisconsin and Battery B of the 4th U.S. Artillery for a time. When he reached a street stretching from the school to Cemetery Hill, Dawes crossed it. He found Confederates in large numbers and turned south—unaware he was moving directly toward the designated rally point. One of the side streets was swept with musket fire, and Dawes ran his men one by one through a "hog-hole" in a wooden fence. The young officer stood at the hole. When a man stopped or hesitated, he pulled him clear to allow the next man through. Two men were shot in the street crossing, and it was obvious his soldiers were just about played out. "The sweat streamed from the faces of the men. There was not a drop of water in the canteens, and there had been none for hours." Farther on, the streets were "jammed with crowds of retreating soldiers, and with ambulances, artillery and wagons. The cellars were crowded with men, sound in body, but craven in spirit, who had gone there to surrender," Dawes recalled in his postwar memoir. "I saw no men wearing badges of the first army corps in this disgraceful company."

As the Black Hats passed, some of the men in the cellars thought they were advancing Confederates. "Don't fire, Johnny, we'll surrender," they called. The regiment was again halted by crowded streets. The rebels opened on them from houses and cross lots. At that desperate moment, an old man appeared with two buckets of water. "The inestimable value of this cup of cold water to those true, unyielding soldiers," Dawes wrote two decades later, "I would that our old friend would know." In response to the water, the Black Hats raised a cheer that attracted more Confederate shooting. The Wisconsin men returned fire and the exchange of bullets quickly cleared the street. "The way open, I marched again toward the Cemetery Hill. The enemy did not pursue. " Just ahead, they saw a line of blue and a National flag. It was the 73rd Ohio of the Eleventh Corps. The 6th Wisconsin had reached Cemetery Hill.[1]

General Abner Doubleday had waited until his artillery was gone before he and his staff rode through town. "As we passed through the streets, pale and frightened women came out and offered us coffee and found and implored us not to abandon them." His own First Corps "was broken and defeated, but not dismayed. There were but few left, but they . . . walked leisurely from the Seminary to the town, and did not run."

Private Robert Beecham of the 2nd Wisconsin scoffed at the officer's proud words. "It would be interesting to one old soldier to know where Gen. Doubleday waited until the artillery had gone," he wrote. "I did not wait a second, but dashed down the Chambersburg Pike, and while running my best, the artillery passed me. " There were also no frightened women on the streets with coffee and cookies, he continued. Any sensible women would be in their homes as the streets were no longer places for women. Beecham was cornered and captured by Confederates a short time later.[2]

Lieutenant James Stewart of Battery B found one of his caissons abandoned in the street with a broken rear axle. Working on the chest was a private, carefully destroying the charges as the regulations called for so they could not be used by the enemy. Stewart asked if he had been given an order. "No, but the Rebs are following us up pretty hard," he replied, "and if the caisson fell into their hands they would use the ammunition upon us." Stewart waited until the soldier was finished, mounted the men behind him on his horse, and rode ahead.[3]

Like so many others that day, Colonel Charles Wainwright also found the streets of the town crowded with soldiers: "There was little order amongst them, save that the Eleventh [Corps] took one side of the street and we the other; brigades and divisions were pretty well mixed up," he wrote in his journal. "Still the men were not panic-stricken; most of them were talking and joking."[4]

Behind them, wounded Lieutenant Colonel John Callis of the 7th Wisconsin was being carried from the field by his men when Confederates captured them alongside the Chambersburg Pike. The rebels took the soldiers prisoners and left the badly wounded Callis in agony on the ground.[5]

Colonel Henry Morrow of the 24th Michigan reached the city where "a true Union girl" dressed his bleeding scalp wound. The woman, Mary McAllister, found Morrow and other wounded soldiers in her home when she returned from assisting the wounded in Christ Lutheran Church across the street. "I saw the blood on his face and I asked, 'Can I do anything for you?' He said, 'Yes, if you would just wash this handkerchief out."

Also in the house was Lieutenant Dennis Dailey of the 2nd Wisconsin, still wearing the sword he took from Confederate Brigadier James Archer. The officer was furious at finding himself trapped. "I am not going to be taken prisoner, Colonel," he told Morrow and talked about hiding upstairs. Morrow replied sharply, "You will not. You must not endanger this family."

Dailey was "so mad he gritted his teeth" and then said to Miss McAllister, "Take this sword and keep it at all hazards. This is General Archer's sword. He surrendered it to me. I will be come back for it." She took the sword to the kitchen and threw it in a wood box and covered it with a newspaper.

Morrow handed Miss McAllister his diary, which she placed in her dress. "That's the place, they will not get it there." Other wounded soldiers in the house began giving her papers with their names and addresses. "Then, there came a pounding on the door," she recalled. "Colonel Morrow said, 'You must open the door. They know we are in here and they will break it.' By this time the rebels came in and they said, 'Oh, here is a bird!' They took Colonel Morrow's sword and led him away. Dailey, who Mrs. McAllister remembered as "so stubborn" and "so very solemn," was also taken prisoner.

The two officers and the others were added to a group of captives and marched four miles to a Confederate field hospital, where Morrow found fifty-four of his wounded men. "Colonel," one asked, "are you finally satisfied with the Twenty-fourth Michigan?"[6]

Another First Corps officer who was not having a very good day was Brigaider General Thomas Rowley, acting commander of the Third Division. Suffering from boils on his inner thigh, the largest "about the size of hen's egg," Rowley was not probably not physically able to perform on horseback. But the veteran of the War with Mexico was well aware that serving in the great battle would have political advantage back home in Pittsburgh. His mistake, however, was taking a drink or two to ease his suffering. By afternoon, he was red-faced and reeling in the saddle. When he fell from his horse at one point, his aides argued it was the result of the animal refusing to cross a ditch, and not because of the general's drinking. During the fighting late that afternoon, the fleshy general was seen on horseback rallying his men. "Here is for the Key Stone!" he shouted again and again as he rode behind his fighting troops.

In the retreat, however, Rowley seemed confused and out of control, brandishing his sword and cursing retreating officers and privates alike as cowards. Wainwright encountered Rowley on a street in town. "He was very talkative, claiming that he was in command of the corps. I tried to reason with him . . . but soon finding that he was drunk, I rode on to the top of

Cemetery Hill, the existence of which I now learned for the first time. Whether Rowley would have handled his division any better had been sober, I have my doubts."[7]

Doubleday reached the same conclusion. By the time he reached Cemetery Hill, Rowley was so intoxicated he could not do his duty. "His face was very red and he enunciated slowly," remembered Doubleday. What troubled him most, the general continued, was Rowley's mistaken insistence that he was now in command of the First Corps. "If I had succeeded General [John] Reynolds, General Rowley could not have succeeded me," Doubleday said.[8]

When the men of Battery B and the 6th Wisconsin reached Cemetery Hill, they found officers frantically trying to get defensive lines established. "I found everything in disorder," remembered Dawes. "Panic was impending over the exhausted soldiers. It was a confused rabble of disorganized regiments of infantry and crippled batteries." All around the rally point, Confederates were closing in, firing and yelling, and to add to "the confusion and peril" along came General Rowley who, Dawes related "had become positively insane." The general "was raving and storming, and giving wild and crazy orders." But, said the young officer, amid the confusion, "cool, courageous and efficient men, at that supreme crisis in the history of our country, brought order out of chaos."

One of these "cool, courageous and efficient men" was Lieutenant Clayton Rogers. Taking it all in, he rode up and without hesitation placed Rowley under arrest. Rogers turned to Dawes and the 6th Wisconsin to provide a detail to enforce the order. "This was perhaps the only instance in the war where a First Lieutenant forcibly arrested a Brigadier-General on the field of battle. I saw all that transpired and during the half hour of confusion, Rogers, who was well mounted, by his cool, clear-headed and quick-witted actions, did more than any other one man to get the troops in line of battle," related Dawes.[9]

Rogers wrote later that the general was "giving General Wadsworth's troops contradictory orders, calling them cowards, and whose conduct was so unbecoming a division commander and unfortunately stimulated by poor commissary [whiskey]. Not having seen General Wadsworth since the retreat commenced, the writer did not hesitate to arrest the crazy officer, on his own responsibility."[10] An embarrassed and likely enraged Rowley was escorted to the rear under guard.

In any evaluation, Rowley would have to be regarded as an officer of limited ability trying to do what he called "the honest discharge of a supposed duty" even though befuddled by strong drink. While giving credit to Rogers for his cool-headed action, it is difficult to to find fault with Rowley with much enthusiasm. It had been a long hard day for any soldier, and Rowley, suffering from boils, a veteran of two wars, and perhaps too old for active service, had been in the thick of it—drunk or sober.

Chapter 23

Our Best and Bravest

The survivors of the Iron Brigade reached the confusion that was the rally point at Cemetery Hill exhausted, "overcome by heat . . . almost dead with thirst." Many simply threw themselves on the ground to rest. Captain A. M. Edwards, carrying the flag of the 24th Michigan, arrived with about two dozen of his men. He planted the flag beside a battery to bring other Michigan men to him, and then sat down exhausted on a tombstone. Other Black Hats began gathering around the flag. A sergeant in the 6th Wisconsin counted only five men around his regimental colors. Two hours later the roll was called and about sixty-five answered. Color bearer I. F. Kelly's leg wound was dressed by an officer. The wound, he remembered, "bled profusely and filled my shoe with blood."[1]

With major Confederate forces gathering to the north and west around the broad sloping hill, the final outcome of the day was still in question. When General Hancock spotted rebel columns moving northeast, he ordered Abner Doubleday to extend the line in that direction by sending a division eastward to support a battery he had ordered to Culp's Hill, a largely wooded eminence that dominated Cemetery Hill. Doubleday replied that his men were just about played out, but Hancock insisted and the survivors of the Iron Brigade where once again on the move. A short time later, the rest of the 6th Wisconsin and Battery B arrived on Cemetery Hill. After a brief rest, Lieutenant Clayton Rogers arrived with orders to join the rest of the brigade. Stewart's Battery B unlimbered near the gate house by the town cemetery. It would remain there for the next three long days.[2]

The battery was in rough shape. Of the 145 or so men who went into the battle with the six guns, two had been killed, two more mortally wounded, and thirteen confirmed as seriously wounded. Two guns of the six pieces were disabled (but brought along), one caisson had been blown up, and three others abandoned with axles or wheels destroyed. Twelve battery horses had been killed outright and several more so injured they had to be shot with revolvers. Most of the losses occurred in the fifteen to thirty minutes of fighting during the late afternoon. Only four of the heavy Napoleons were serviceable, and these were placed on each side of the Baltimore Pike, the main approach from Gettysburg.[3]

The arriving 6th Wisconsin men were greeted with friendly calls and hellos as they reached the brigade. From a regimental wagon, a dozen spades and shovels were pulled out and the soldiers began constructing earthworks. Many in the army still believed that breastworks made a soldier cautious and sapped his will to fight, but such foolish notions had been forever knocked out of the Black Hats on McPherson's Ridge. "The men worked with great energy," remembered Rufus Dawes. "A man would dig with all his strength till out of breath, when another would seize the spade and push on the work." The spades were also passed to men from the other regiments. Before long, a strong defensive line was in place.

The Iron Brigade regiments, facing almost north, occupied the far left of Wadsworth's battered division in the new Union line strung along Culp's Hill. The 24th Michigan held the far left, not far from Cemetery Hill, with the 7th Wisconsin, 6th Wisconsin, 2nd Wisconsin, and 19th Indiana extending the line to the right. A 7th Wisconsin officer was generally pleased with the "rocky faced hill." The new position, he remembered, was "not hard to hold against attack. We piled stone along our front. Dandy for defence, and got water . . . from springs at the foot of the hill." Rations were issued, but coffee fires were banned. Men gobbled down sugar and hardtack instead, using "water [as] our helper with the cold grub."

With the work finished, the men settled in and reflected on what had been accomplished. Dawes tried to put it into words: "Our dead lay unburied and beyond our sight or reach. Our wounded were in the hands of the enemy. Our bravest and best were numbered with them . . ."[4]

One of those Dawes was referring to was John Callis, the former North Carolinian and now wounded veteran of the 7th Wisconsin. On Seminary

Wisconsin Historical Society, 3904

Lieutenant Colonel John Callis
7th Wisconsin Volunteers

A native of North Carolina, Lieutenant Callis was severely wounded in the last stand in front of the Lutheran Seminary Building. Left on the field, a Confederate officer from his home state came to his assistance when some soldiers stole his boots and wallet.

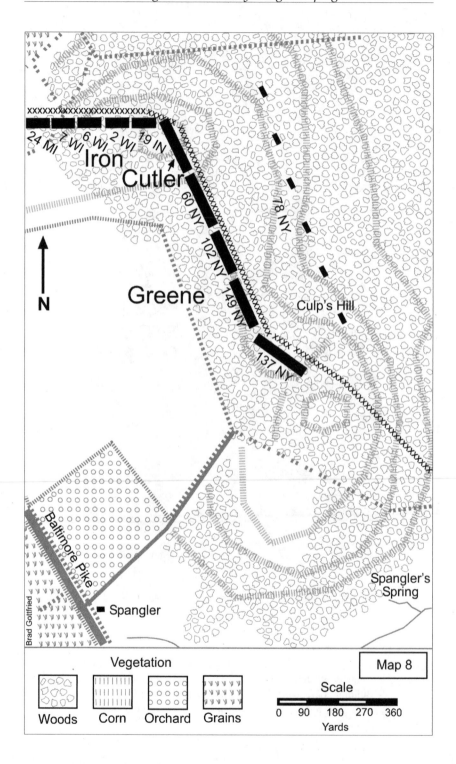

Iron

Cutler

24 MI 7 WI 6 WI 2 WI 19 IN

60 NY

102 NY

149 NY

137 NY

78 NY

Greene

Culp's Hill

N

Baltimore Pike

Spangler

Spangler's Spring

Brad Gottfried

Vegetation

Woods   Corn   Orchard   Grains

Map 8

Scale

0   90   180   270   360

Yards

Ridge when the fighting stopped, Callis found himself surrounded by rebels. The enemy roughly pulled off his jacket containing "$220 in greenbacks and gold" and other papers. The Confederates moved off and sat down by the railroad grading to go through the pocketbook when a Confederate officer approached. It was Lieutenant Henry C. Shepherd of the 43rd North Carolina. Callis took the opportunity to inform the officer that his family was from Fayetteville, North Carolina, which turned out to be Shepherd's hometown. Colonel Thomas S. Kenan of the 43rd North Carolina, Junius Daniel's Brigade (Rodes' Division, Ewell's Second Corps), was listening nearby. He leaned over to take a long look at the downed Wisconsin officer. "You are now my prisoner," he told Callis not unkindly, "and I'll treat you well. I may be yours later on." Kenan had to lean close to hear Callis' faint reply. He was convinced the Wisconsin officer was dying.

Callis explained he was wearing only one boot because some Confederate privates pulled off the other. Kenan spotted the boot nearby and placed it near the wounded officer, asking if they had taken anything else. My coat and money, Callis said, pointing again to the privates. The colonel ordered everything returned. Callis had two more requests: Would he please send the money to Callis' wife in Wisconsin. When Kenan agreed, Callis insisted the rebel officer take the fancy silver spurs on his boots. Kenan accepted with some reluctance, and then stood up to return to his regiment. He ordered two privates to carry Callis to the Lutheran Seminary, where he stood a better chance of receiving treatment. A slave accompanying the Confederate officers was sent along with the two soldiers. As the slave poured water on the wound, Callis told one of the privates, an Irishman, that he was glad he gave the spurs to Kenan. "Yis, sor, he's a mighty foine man, so he is, sor." The other private, a German, added: "Yah, he bin so better as good." The exchange made Callis smile.

Long afterward in 1893, Kenan was visiting Gettysburg to help mark Confederate lines and remembered the incident. He wrote Callis in Wisconsin to say he still had the spurs and prized them, and that he hoped they could meet again, "not on a hostile, but a friendly historic field [of Gettysburg]." Kenan explained in his letter to Callis that he fell wounded on Culp's Hill on July 3 and was captured. He spent the rest of the war as a prisoner. Callis wrote back a friendly letter a few days later, adding this postscript: "I shall be more than glad to meet you at Gettysburg as indicated in your favor, my health permitting." The two veterans never met again.[5]

Lieutenant John W. Bruce of the same 7th regiment was not far away, shot in the left breast and unable to walk. He was overrun by advancing Confederates who passed him with "discipline of the strictest kind, every man in his place, each officer in his, and the line dressed as if on review," recalled Bruce. When the fighting swept past him, he tried without success to receive assistance from captured Union soldiers. He gave $10 each to two different men, only to have them run away with his money. To his surprise, Bruce explained, General Robert Lee and members of his staff stopped to question him. A Confederate surgeon gave him some whiskey and promised to send assistance. There were thousands of wounded and dying on the field that day, however, and Bruce was but one of them. He would spend the next twenty-six hours lying in the open before being moved to a hospital.

During the night, crazed for water, the Wisconsin lieutenant called out to figures passing in the darkness. One rebel heard his pleas and approached him.

"Water, water," Bruce begged.

When the Confederate explained that he had none and did not want to try to find any because he might wander into Union lines, the Badger asked him to end his life. "I told him to kill me, then, to run his bayonet thorough me, as I could not live in such misery," Bruce wrote years later.

The rebel hesitated. "Tell you what it is, Yank. I have a canteen of milk which I gave my last quarter of your money for, and I will divide with you." The Confederate poured the milk into Bruce's canteen, spread a rubber and wool blanket under him.

The man's actions were so tender, said Bruce, "I could not keep back the tears . . . . I had a good cry. The pressure of his hands, as he tucked the clothes around me, carried me back to my home, my mother, and my little trundle bed. I must have fallen asleep then as I can remember nothing from that time till morning, when my friend, the surgeon came to administer the stimulant."[6]

Colonel Henry Morrow of the 24th Michigan was not far away in a Confederate field hospital. Before he had been marched away from Gettysburg with other prisoners, he claimed he was approached by Confederate Lieutenant General Richard S. Ewell. According to Morrow, Ewell claimed he was surprised the Michigan regiment fired on his advance as the Confederates had purposely held their fire to allow them to surrender. Ewell added it was foolish to fire and be badly shot up than to surrender. "General Ewell," replied Morrow—or so he liked to remember the exchange—"the Twenty-fourth Michigan came here to fight, not surrender."[7] Someone dressed Morrow's head wound and he settled down in an open field to sleep.

While Callis, Bruce, Morrow, and so many other Western men suffered out on the field, three wounded officers of the 6th Wisconsin—Loyd Harris, William Remington and John Beeley—were resting in a little church behind the Union line. Harris and Remington decided to find better quarters. They stopped at a farmhouse, but were refused admittance. After a time, the officers reached a blacksmith shop, where they stopped for the night. "I never felt so lonely in all my life," Harris remembered years later. "I thought . . . of the men who had been slain, the battle yet undecided. It was so dark and lonely in that old blacksmith shop; we were weak and hungry, but the fatigue of the day was so great we fell asleep like two 'babes in the woods'."

In Gettysburg, Private William Ray of the 7th Wisconsin rested after his head wound was treated. "Night comes on and we lay on our straw, some dying, some heaving their limbs amputated, others waiting," he wrote in his journal of those long and mournful hours. "I threw away my knapsack when hit and lost my haversack so I lost both Bedding & food. But can get along for that."[8]

Also in the court house hospital was Private George Frederick Neff of the 24th Michigan, who had been shot in the leg in the late afternoon. All the court house rooms were crowed with wounded except for the locked judge's chambers off the main courtroom. Neff made his way outside the building, broke a window, and crawled in and bedded down with two others. When the Confederates did occupy the town, they never checked the locked room and the three enjoyed a peaceful night.[9]

Nearby, Private Sullivan of the 6th Wisconsin, his shoulder wound finally bandaged, rested the sleep of the unwell. Along toward night, Sullivan said he began "to skirmish around for some better place to sleep than the floor of the court house where having no blankets or knapsack for a pillow, I was not very comfortable." He and Corporal William Hancock discussed the matter, with Hancock observing "our fellows had a good place in the railroad depot. They found the place crowded with wounded soldiers, but made the best of it. I slept with a dead officer who had been mortally wounded in the cavalry fight; and some citizen had brought out a feather bed and some bed clothes and had fixed him on it; not being able to roll him off I lay down with him and some time in the night I went to sleep."[10]

Chapter 24

The Finger of God Paralyzed his Brain

Robert Beecham of the 2nd Wisconsin, captured at Gettysburg and sent to a Confederate prison, was exchanged several months later. He was promoted as an officer in a U.S. Colored regiment only to be captured again in the fighting at the Crater in Virginia in 1864. After another eight months as a prisoner, he escaped and made his way to Union lines. In 1900, Beecham returned to Gettysburg and spent two weeks walking the battlefield, carefully stepping off the distances from McPherson's Ridge eastward to Seminary Ridge.

Beecham first wrote at length about Gettysburg in a memoir entitled "Adventures of an Iron Brigade Man," which appeared between August 14 and December 18, 1902, in the *National Tribune*, a weekly newspaper aimed squarely at veterans that was published in Washington. He also began working on a history of the battle, published in 1911 as *Gettysburg: The Pivotal Battle of the Civil War*. The book was generally praised, although one ex-Confederate claimed it was prejudicial against General Lee.[1]

Beecham believed the Confederates could have won the battle of Gettysburg if they had pushed ahead and seized Cemetery Hill late on the afternoon of the first day's battle. He called the failure to do so Lee's "great mistake" of the campaign. Up to 5:00 p.m. on July 1, he wrote, Lee "had everything going his way" except for the surprising resistance by the First Corps and Eleventh corps of the Army of the Potomac. Union forces had been soundly driven from their first positions west and north of town, and they "fully expected to be attacked in their second," Beecham explained. But the attack never came.

The Confederate Army of Northern Virginia was weary after the long day of marching and fighting, he continued, but the Union First Corps had lost 5,500 men and the partially engaged Eleventh Corps another 2,600. Facing most of Lee's assembled army, the Federals only had slightly more than 21,000 men on the field, including cavalry. "Why he did not follow up the advantage gained with his wonted vigor is beyond the comprehension of everyone familiar with conditions," Beecham wrote after his 1900 visit. Lee was a "man of genius, a great man. Great men are apt to make great mistakes. . . . It would seem that the finger of God had paralyzed his brain in the very moment of victory."[2]

In fact, Lee recognized the strength of the Union position and believed "it was only necessary to press those people in order to secure possession of the heights." But his orders to General Richard Ewell were that Cemetery Hill and Culp's Hill should be taken "if practicable." Ewell, new to command of a corps and facing the coming darkness, hesitated. Despite being pressed by several of his subordinates to attack—or so they later claimed—he decided not to make the assault. It was the first time Ewell served under the direct orders of Lee. He previously answered only to the fallen "Stonewall" Jackson, who rarely if ever issued discretionary orders.

Beecham's flowery language about "the finger of God" notwithstanding, the lack of attack as evening drew near on July 1, 1863, offered a welcomed respite to the decimated Black Hats. The officers of the regiments called the rolls on Culp's Hill; the final numbers staggered even the hardest veterans. The brigade had taken 1,883 into the fighting that morning. Now, only 691 remained around the battle flags. The 6th Wisconsin, which escaped the heavy fighting on McPherson's Ridge, still sustained losses of forty-eight percent. The 7th Wisconsin suffered similarly casualties, leaving forty-two percent of its men on the field. The 19th Indiana and 2nd Wisconsin, however, had been decimated, losing seventy-two percent and seventy-seven percent, respectively. The newest and largest regiment of the brigade, the 24th Michigan, suffered a staggering eighty percent loss—the largest number of casualties any Union regiment suffered during the first day of the battle. Three of the five regimental commanders were among the captured and wounded: Lucius Fairchild of the 2nd Wisconsin, John Callis of the 7th Wisconsin, and Henry Morrow of the 24th Michigan. Also down was Sol Meredith, the Iron Brigade commander. Two of the fallen 2nd Wisconsin men were Sergeant Joseph Williams and George Legate. Their morning premonitions to Cornelius Wheeler of not getting through the day alive had proven true.[3]

After his crippling arm wound, Lucius Fairchild was carried to the home of Reverend Charles F. Schaeffer, the principal of the Lutheran Theological Seminary. He kept telling his stretcher bearers he was going to get his arm bandaged and then return to his regiment. Returning to the field proved impossible and a surgeon from the 2nd Wisconsin was summoned. He carefully cut off Fairchild's vest, removed the bandage and examined the wound. The shattered limb could not be saved and the arm was amputated above the elbow. When Fairchild awakened, he looked at his bandaged stump and exclaimed, "Thank God! I still have one left."

A short time later, a Confederate officer came to the door to search the house. Fairchild's sword was found hidden in the coal bin. Seeing Fairchild's condition, the officer scribbled out a parole and left. Sitting in the parlor, Fairchild watched out the window while Reverend Schaeffer buried his amputated arm in a tin box in a small garden outside his window.[4]

Despite some movement in front of Cemetery Hill and Culp's Hill, the victorious Confederates did not attack in force that evening and the sun slowly set on the bloody first day of fighting at Gettysburg. Around the four guns of Battery B near the cemetery gate, the artillerymen began taking stock of the day's events. The gunners generally agreed that most of the deaths and wounds came as the battery retreated into the town. One of the rumors passing among the men was a whisper that Lieutenant James Stewart used his pistol to escape capture. The gruff Regular Army officer never verified it.

Another oft-told story involved a Confederate officer who rode up, placed his hand on the tube of a Napoleon, and demanded its surrender just as the battery was hitching up to make for the town. When the driver ignored the demand and rode off, the Confederate shot the driver in the back. The survivors agreed the wheel driver was shot, and though mortally wounded, stuck to his saddle until the gun got into town. But no rebel officer put his hand on the gun, they said. "It was always our proudest boast that she was a virgin battery!" the battery historian wrote, and that "though in battle many times, and in the wide-open jaws of death more than once, not one of her bright guns had ever been defiled by the touch of a Rebel hand!"[5]

In the fading light of dusk, the old battery veterans observed with some relief that the new position was "much stronger than the old." Union reinforcements were also coming up. It was generally agreed that the Eleventh Corps "had behaved well enough to redeem themselves from their disgrace at Chancellorsville," and the "Old First had covered itself with glory and every man in ranks knew it." Any examination showed they were not whipped, they continued, for they had held the ground outside Gettysburg for a long while against superior numbers. The men believed they "had punished the enemy terribly" and made "an orderly and respectable retreat to a much stronger and better position." A few grumbled that the Twelfth Corps, which was not far from Gettysburg, should have hurried to the assistance of the embattled First and Eleventh corps. Around the four guns of Battery B and in the lines of the five Iron Brigade regiments, the men in ranks "knew that we had done as desperate work as ever befell an army corps, and we were almost as proud of the record as we would have been of a victory."[6]

Looking back from the distance of three decades, Rufus Dawes saw the truth of the day and night of July 1, 1863—at least for the Iron Brigade of the West: "We had lost the ground on which we had fought, we had lost our commander and our comrades, but our fight had held the Cemetery Hill and forced the decision for history that the crowning battle of the war should be at Gettysburg."[7]

Chapter 25

This Battle Will go by the Name of Gettysburg

In the darkness on Culp's Hill, along the makeshift breastworks of stacked rocks, fence rails, and overturned earth, the Black Hats ate what hardtack remained in their haversacks and tried to sleep. About 1:00 a.m., a soldier in the nearby 7th Indiana "cried out so loudly in his sleep" it roused the slumbering men around him. Lieutenant Colonel Rufus Dawes, still half asleep, ordered his 6th Wisconsin to "Fall in!" and some shooting erupted in the darkness when the soldiers opened fire on shadows and trees in front of them. It took a few minutes to calm the nerves and quiet things down. At 3:00 a.m., soldiers on the Culp's Hill line were awakened to take their firing positions in case of a pre-dawn rebel attack.

Private Levi Tongue of the 6th Wisconsin took a few moments to scribble a brief letter to his wife Anna. "Yesterday we were in another engagement, and a severe one it was too. We lost 17 out of our company . . . [T]his battle will go by the name of Gettysburg, for it is right by it. We are in the rear of the city behind some piles of rails we have thrown up. This is all I have time to write. I can count myself lucky. I will write again and let you know more of this when it is over, if I live." Tongue was 20-years-old.[1]

In Gettysburg, the wounded Private James Sullivan watched rebels plundering stores and houses, "carrying away pails of sugar, molasses, and groceries of all kinds, clothing and bales of goods, silks, calico and cloth." Except for a surly officer or two, Sullivan found the Confederates generally friendly to the Union wounded, sharing "whiskey, tobacco and baker's bread freely." There was one incident when an officer directed a rebel soldier to take Sullivan's "good pair of balmoral shoes." Sullivan bristled, and warned "there would be an Irish row first, and the fellow said they could not fit him, that they were too small." The Irishman also managed to catch a good look at Confederate Major General Jubal Early riding his horse down one of the town's congested streets. Sullivan described the general as a "short, pussy, grey-haired, bull-headed reb, with no great amount of intelligence in his look."[2]

Nearby, Private Francis Deleglise of the 6th Wisconsin remained in a cellar with other wounded when a Confederate officer entered. The officer looked over the situation with a grim face. Seeing two seriously wounded men under a quilt, he asked about their regiments. "The 25th Georgia" answered the first man. "I belong to the Federal army," replied the second. The officer, Deleglise continued, "drew from his pocket his canteen filed with milk punch and first gave a drink to the Union soldier and afterward to the man who belonged to his own side."[3]

Private George Frederick Neff of the 24th Michigan spent a relatively comfortable night behind a locked door in the judge's room of the court house. Restless and bored, he decided to take a walk around and soon found himself in a conversation with Confederate soldiers, including "one who gave me a drink of whiskey." When rebel officers appeared and began taking the names of wounded Yankees out in the street, he went back into the judge's room, where he spent most of the day.

Private William Ray of the 7th Wisconsin was another Western man who walked the streets of Gettysburg on July 2. He was surprised by the number of able-bodied Confederates "laying around town." That situation changed when heavy firing erupted far to the south and provost squads began driving them toward the front. "Lots of wounded secesh" were coming back from the front, Ray recorded in his journal. "They don't say much, seem mum. That tells me that they were not victorious."[4]

Henry Morrow of the 24th Michigan slept that first night in a field, had his head dressing changed, and was told by a friendly rebel surgeon with a wink that he was not fit to be moved. Sometime in the early morning of the second day, he made his way to a Union hospital in Gettysburg where he cut off his shoulder straps and tied a green cloth around his waist to signify he was a doctor. Morrow found a Michigan surgeon and began helping him. In a nearby barn packed with 200 wounded, he found Private Patrick Clarey of

Colonel Henry Morrow
24th Michigan Infantry

The colonel suffered a minor scalp wound in the final stand outside the Lutheran Seminary. He was in Gettysburg being treated when he was captured. Morrow helped with the Michigan wounded in the town and saved his diary.

his own regiment. Surgeons looked at his wounded leg and told Clarey he not had long to live unless the limb was removed, but the private would have none of it. "Colonel, if you'll not have my leg taken off, I'll be with the regiment in a week." Despite the dire prediction of the doctors, however,

Clarey would keep his leg, survive, and meet again with the colonel in Detroit in a happier time.

There was one close moment when a rebel lieutenant approached Morrow with a smile. "You don't seem to recognize me. Your regiment captured me at Fitzhugh [Crossing]."

"Glad of it," said the colonel. "Didn't we treat you well?

"Bully," said the officer, and Morrow replied, "Then treat me the same."

"We will. Where are your shoulder straps?"

"I have lost them for the time being."

"All right, I'll not say a word." The rebel officer smiled and walked off.[5]

Well outside of town a group of wounded Federal officers was trying to find shelter. When Lieutenant Loyd Harris of the 6th Wisconsin found a "fine brick mansion" he approached the elderly owner. "Sir, I am here with nine wounded officers and hope you can give us a room where we can spread our blankets and rest for the night." The old man refused. "Then can we occupy the barn?" asked Harris. The reply was "No sir, my barn is filled with horses." When Harris explained that the horses could be moved, the owner resisted, claiming he was worried the soldiers would steal them. With that, young Harris lost his temper, pulled his belt revolver ("and it was a good one, presented to me by Mr. John Lawyer, Chas. Rau and John Conger, at old Prairie du Chien"), and aimed it squarely at the old man's head. "You have refused to do a kind act," Harris said. "Now if you have a wife you can retire to your room with her, and that room shall be held sacred; the rest of this house is for hospital service, for this night, at least." Before he could march the owner back to the house, an orderly called from the roadway that a special train was ready to convey wounded officers to Baltimore. The officers were soon on their way to safety.[6]

Behind the Union lines, news was read at the morning roll call that Major General Abner Doubleday had been replaced as commander of the First Corps by John Newton of the Sixth Corps. The announcement was met with "instant disapprobation by the men." While Doubleday was not the sort of officer "to excite much enthusiasm," remembered one soldier, the men believed the general's handling the First Corps displayed "skill and courage which the dullest private could not help commending." The ranks were "disgusted when they learned that a stranger had been put over them."[7]

On Culp's Hill, the Black Hats waited on the battle line, but nothing developed except for a shelling now and then. From the high ground, they could see troops "were hurrying to different points of the field to take the positions assigned them. . . . Batteries were being placed in advantageous positions as fast the already jaded horses could be lashed into drawing them. Ammunition wagons came to the front on a keen gallop. Cartridge boxes were replenished. All was, noise, hurry and confusion." According to one soldier, each man "felt that a desperate struggle was to come and that the result no one could foretell. All felt they must nerve themselves for the ordeal."[8]

Later that afternoon about 4:00 p.m., heavy fighting erupted on the far left of the Union line. Most of James Longstreet's First Corps was now up, and his men were attacking Meade's left. The effort was an attempt to either roll up the Union line or cause significant reinforcements to be sent south, leaving weaknesses elsewhere to be exploited later in the day by other Confederate commands. As the Southern attack rippled its way en echelon northward along Seminary Ridge, Richard Ewell's Second Corps prepared to make what was referred to as a "demonstration" against Culp's Hill and Cemetery Hill against the far right side of the Union line. The demonstration was to be turned into a full assault if the situation developed favorably. As the fighting escalated, Meade shuttled heavy reinforcements (nearly 20,000 soldiers) to stabilize his position along his crumbling left, stripping other parts of his line to do so. The subsequent fighting at places that became known as the Devil's Den, Little Round Top, the Wheatfield, the Peach Orchard, and lower Cemetery Ridge included some of the most savage combat of the war.

"We could plainly see that our troops were giving ground," said one Wisconsin officer watching from the relative safety of the right side of the line. "Our suspense and anxiety were intense. We gathered in knots all over the hill watching the battle. . . . As the sun was low down a fine sight was seen. It was two long blue lines of battle, with twenty or thirty regimental banners, charging forward into the smoke and din of battle. To all appearances they saved the field."

The fighting, however, was not yet over. In the fading light, about 7:00 p.m., the rebel yell went up in front of Culp's Hill and the far right of the Union line was attacked by Confederate Major General Edward "Allegheny" Johnson's Division. Another attack hit East Cemetery Hill, which had been stripped of troops to stem breaches elsewhere in the line. Confederates from Jubal Early's Division managed to drive off the defenders and, for a short time, capture the critically important high

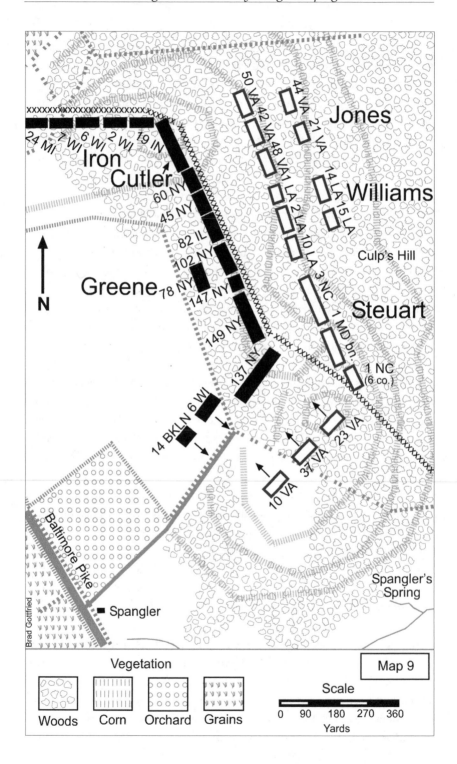

Map 9

ground—the hinge in the long fishhook-shaped Union line. When Robert Rodes fumbled his grand opportunity for what was to have been a coordinated attack from the opposite side, however, Union reinforcements drove the Southerners off and re-secured the heights. Johnson's men farther to the right also came within a hair's breadth of success. Most of the Culp's Hill defenders from the Union Twelfth Corps, had been sent to the far left to help repulse Longstreet's attacks, and only a single brigade of New Yorkers under Brigadier General George S. Greene remained in position. Greene's insistence on constructing defensive works proved the difference, although a portion of the abandoned Federal entrenchments on the lower part of Culp's Hill fell to the attackers.

As the lines on the far left were trading volleys, an officer rode up looking for Rufus Dawes with orders in hand for him to report to General Greene. The 6th Wisconsin and the 14th Brooklyn were sent to the right to assist in repelling part of the attack by Johnson's Division against Culp's Hill. Wisconsin Color bearer I. F. Kelly remembered struggling through the brush, darkness, and trees with his 11-foot flag staff.

The first mounted officer Dawes encountered was Greene, who took a card from his pocket and wrote on it in the darkness his name and command before handing it to the young officer. He ordered Dawes to move his regiment into the supposedly abandoned breastworks. Dawes ordered, "Forward—run! March!" As the 6th Wisconsin reached the line, rebels hiding amongst the dark rocks rose and fired a volley. Greene was unaware that Confederates were occupying that part of his breastworks, and the rebels were just as surprised by the arrival of the Wisconsin men. After the volley, the exhausted and confused Confederates tumbled back down the slope. "This remarkable encounter did not last a minute," confessed Dawes. "We lost two men, killed—both burned with the powder of the guns fired at them." One of the wounded was color bearer Kelly, struck by a spatter of lead off a rock that sliced open his neck. The wound bled freely. Soldiers around him found a rag, wet it from canteens, and wrapped it around his neck. The 6th Wisconsin remained in the line until about midnight, when it was relieved by returning troops from the Twelfth Corps. The Wisconsin and New York regiment returned to their original positions without further incident.[9]

In town that night, two surgeons set up a mess in a saloon where the wounded soldiers were served coffee, tea, and hardtack. Some of it they shared with wounded Confederates. James Sullivan and William Hancock of the 6th Wisconsin went looking for a place to sleep and went back to the bed Sullivan used the night before. The dead cavalry officer was still there. The two Black hats rolled him off and took possession. "I did not enjoy our conquest very much," admitted Sullivan. "What added to our uneasiness was the fact the Rebs might clean out the Army of the Potomac and take Washington, then 'Old Abe' and the country was gone for certain."[10]

Chapter 26

A Shot From a Smoothbore Gun

The third morning of the battle at Gettysburg came with a flurry of artillery fire and fighting on Culp's Hill even before the sun had made its appearance. Robert E. Lee hoped to build on his limited successes of the previous two days by once again assuming the offensive. His plan was to open with a large artillery bombardment to soften the right-center of the Federal line, followed immediately by an attack with a strong infantry column under the command of James Longstreet to drive the defenders off Cemetery Ridge and split Meade's army in two. Richard Ewell's men under General Edward Johnson, meanwhile, reinforced by four additional brigades, would press their advantage against the far right of the Union line on Culp's Hill.

In a brilliant preemptive strike, the Federals launched a sharp pre-dawn attack of their own in an attempt to push the Confederates from the captured trenches on the right side of Culp's Hill. Twenty Union artillery pieces were placed to pound and enfilade the Confederate position. The artillery bombardment convinced Johnson he could not stay where he was, so he opened his own attack prematurely. The Southerners attacked, were repulsed, and reformed and attacked again. For more than three hours the fighting surged and ebbed up the heavy corpse-strewn slopes of Culp's Hill. One Confederate survivor claimed he stood in an ankle-deep stream of blood as he fired up the slope. Later that morning, a Federal countercharge forced the Confederates to withdraw, ending the fighting for Culp's Hill.

The field fell quiet except for an occasional flurry of artillery or exchange of musketry along the picket lines. As the minutes passed, there was great anticipation in the Union ranks, for it seemed nothing as yet had been resolved. What was uncertain was whether the Confederates would attack again, withdraw, or move to slip around one of the army's flanks.

The clock edged its way toward noon with no heavy action interrupting the relative solitude. The thin regiments of the Iron Brigade manned their breastwork line along the top of Culp's Hill and waited. It was the first time in almost two years of fighting the Western men threw up branches, stones and earth for protection and it was an indication of how the desperate fighting and heavy losses of July 1, 1863, had unsettled them. Of those first hours of Friday, July 3, one soldier remembered the "zip of the sharpshooter's bullet, the 'where is you' of cannon shot and the ringing whistle of the ragged fragments of bursting shell."[1]

Wounded James Sullivan of the 6th Wisconsin found the streets oddly quiet under a clear sky that July 3. George Frederick Neff of the 24th Michigan again left his hideout in the locked judge's room to discover a brigade of Confederate infantry standing in the street, muskets stacked. They were behind buildings and out of view of the Federal line, and Neff and some of the other prisoners tried to think of a way to alert the Union forces of their presence. One Union prisoner found a cache of firecrackers and set them off. The startled Confederates jumped up "and seized their rifles and made ready to defend themselves," but the joke was soon discovered. The rebels "had a good laugh over their discomfiture," Neff said, "believing one of their own had set off the fireworks."[2]

The four guns of Stewart's Battery B were still facing northwest near the gate of the cemetery. Confederate artillery shelled the position from long range, but no serious damage was done and there was no movement of rebel infantry along their front. The battery had engaged the enemy during the dusk hours of July 2 when Confederate seized East Cemetery Hill, but the assault ended in failure and little movement of the lines of both sides. The fighting that flared up for a time that morning along the far side of Culp's Hill triggered some concern within the battery's ranks. The men wondered aloud that perhaps the rebel army had them surrounded and was much bigger than first thought. "And this ugly impression was not abated when we saw, looking to the front and left, glimpses of columns of infantry moving about on Seminary Ridge, and a palpable concentration of their artillery near the Seminary and to the southward of it," said the battery's historian. "It is safe to say that at no time since the beginning of the struggle had things looked more 'skittish' to the average man in ranks than they did the forenoon of the third day." Finally, the firing died out and a short time later the battery men could see rebel infantry falling back through the fields north of Culp's Hill, "evidently retreating from that position and making for the main line of the enemy on Seminary Ridge."[3]

One incident nearly everyone seemed to recall related to sharpshooters. The pesky and deadly snipers had been actively shooting in their direction from houses and fences in the town. In the immediate front of Battery B, the "most annoying of this sharpshooting came from a small brick house just off the Baltimore Pike. The gabled end of the two-story house with two windows in each story faced the guns only about 600 yards distant. When Private Lyman W. Blackley fell wounded from a sharpshooter's round, Sergeant John Mitchell decided to take matters into his own hands. He ordered the gun in the road loaded with case shot, cut to explode at 600 yards. The brass gun tube was a new one, having been issued the previous month to replace one with a worn bore. It had only been fired at Gettysburg and with a new bore "was as accurate as a smooth-bore can be."

Mitchell sighted the gun and had Corporal Jimmy Maher, one of the Regulars attached to the battery, check his aim. "When they got her right, they pulled lanyard, and the case shot went right through the brick wall behind the two windows in the second story, exploding beautifully inside the house. The Rebel

Sergeant John Mitchell
Battery B, 4th U.S. Artillery

This Regular Army artillery sergeant used a 12-pound piece in a successful duel against Confederate sharpshooters firing from a house in Gettysburg.

Scott D. Hann Collection

sharpshooters evidently did not consider it a desirable residence after that." It was later discovered the case round (one artilleryman said it was "one of the best shots I ever saw from a smooth-bore gun") killed one Confederate sharpshooter and wounded another.[4]

Elsewhere in Gettysburg, Union prisoners and wounded were freely walking about, keenly aware something was about to happen. In a final desperate decision, Robert E. Lee decided to move forward with his massed infantry attack against the Union center. The assault would include George Pickett's Virginia division of Longstreet's Corps and six brigades from two other divisions pulled from A. P. Hill's Third Corps. Other troops may have also been tasked to follow up the attack. Available Confederate artillery was positioned to concentrate its fire against the center of the line to drive away enemy guns and defenders. The long-arm's goal was to render the position indefensible, so the infantry ordered to follow the bombardment could reach and carry the ridge. About 150 to 170 Confederate guns would be involved in the grand effort.

In town, a lookout in the observatory of the train depot called out that Confederate infantry and artillery were being massed on the right side of town. "We knew they meant to make trouble pretty soon," said Sullivan. After the midday meal, the observer said the Johnnies were moving. "Just then 'bang, bang' went a couple of guns, and then such a roar of artillery as I have never heard before or since; the ground shook and the depot building fairly trembled. Our fellows answered just as loud, and it seemed as if the last day had come."[5]

On Culp's Hill, General James Wadsworth and his staff were sitting around "a cracker-box table" when the first artillery shells from "a furious cannonade" swept the position. A dozen shells burst around the officers, covering their dinner with dirt, recalled John Kress of Wadsworth's staff. The general and the other officers moved a few feet away to a safer location, which gave them what Kress called "a fine view of the whole field of battle."

Despite a lack of adequate artillery, the Confederate gunners increased their rate of fire and about eighty Union guns answered them. After an indeterminate time (some witnesses claim as few as fifteen minutes, and others as long as two hours) the firing eased. Kress and the others watched "lines over a mile long of gray coats forming on the opposite ridge, saw them move across the valley and the low ground under the terrible fire of our artillery, posted as thickly along our lines as the ground permitted, blowing great gaps in the ranks." The Confederates came on in a seemly irresistible wave marked by their bright battle flags. Lee was attempting to break the very center of the Union line with a concentrated infantry assault. If successful, the attack might break and drive away the Army of the Potomac.[6]

After it was all over, the Black Hats discovered their opponents of the hard-fought first day's battle took part in the grand infantry assault. Joe Davis' Brigade—much reduced after its battering on July 1—once again found itself battling the circumstances of ill-luck. Someone positioned Colonel Brockenbrough's weak Virginia brigade on the far left of the attacking line. When the Virginians broke shortly after the attack began, Davis' left flank lay exposed to a galling fire as his men, including the 2nd Mississippi survivors of the railroad cut debacle, tramped their way toward Cemetery Ridge. Pettigrew's Brigade, including the 26th North Carolina, was also in the fight, as were the shattered regiments of captured James Archer's Brigade. In the Union line facing these attackers were two former Iron Brigade men now serving with the Second Union Corps—Brigadier General John Gibbon and his aide Frank Haskell. Gibbon would fall wounded, but Haskell would live to write about the fighting in a long letter he would send within two weeks to his brother at Portage, Wisconsin.

Long after the war, Haskell would become Wisconsin's most widely known Civil War soldier—not for his service with Gibbon's Black Hat Brigade, but as "Haskell of Gettysburg," the officer who rallied the Union line in the final Confederate attack at Gettysburg on July 3, 1863. His lengthy letter was published long after Haskell's death at Cold Harbor in 1863, but his description was so important no historian writing of Gettysburg could ignore it.

In Gettysburg, Private Sullivan found one of the band members to help him and, hanging onto the railing on the stairs, climbed to the cupola of the depot. "I saw what appeared like the whole Rebel Army in a chunk start for our lines with their infernal squealing yell. It seemed as if everything stood still inside of me for a second or two, then I began to pray." Kress, watching from Culp's Hill, called it an irresistible sight: "On they came, banners waving in the battle smoke, cannon roaring, men shouting, horses neighing, small arms crashing in volleys! Still they came on . . . nothing stops them. They almost reach our main line of battle with a fairly well-filled line of their own, as it seemed from our location."

Sullivan's prayer (though he admitted he "was, and am not yet noted for the frequency and fervency of my prayers") was that the Confederates would "catch h—l." It seemed after a few long, anxious minutes he said, as "if the fire from our lines doubled and doubled again, and I could see long streaks of light through the Rebel columns, but they went forward. I was afraid they would capture our guns." Another Wisconsin soldier watching the heavy Confederate losses said he "felt bad for the poor cusses who went down, but it had to be."

On Culp's Hill, Wadsworth could "keep quiet no longer" and sent Kress off at the gallop to Meade to "ask him if he did not want our division." The young officer rode through the scattered bullets and shells and found the army commander "close in rear of our main line where the enemy had but a moment before pierced it, and a large body of the brave fellows who had charged so recklessly, were just surrendering by individuals and detachments." Meade received Wadsworth offer with a smile and shook his head. "Tell the general I am much obliged for this tender of service, but we are all right and do not need his troops here."

From the railroad depot cupola Sullivan watched as the Confederate infantry melted away when the Union infantry opened on them. "[W]e could hear the Northern cheer. We knew that the rebs were scooped, and the old Army of the Potomac was victorious," wrote Sullivan. The dozen or so wounded soldiers around Sullivan "were wild with joy, some cried, others shook hands, and all joined in with the best cheer we could get up. I forgot all about my wound and was very forcibly reminded of it when I went to shout as I had to sit down to keep from falling." A Confederate officer came to see what the clamor was about. "[W]hen told that Lee was cleaned, he growled out if we d——d Yankees were able to cheer we were able to go to Richmond," recalled Sullivan, who admitted "our fellows felt good anyway, and the reb went out and we saw no more of him."[7]

George Neff was in the streets during the attack on July 3. As Confederate staff officers rode through, onlookers called out, asking about the progress of the battle. One officer told the listening soldiers everything depended on driving the Federals off the hill. Later, after most of the firing ceased, another officer rode through "looking terribly dispirited," Neff remembered. The Confederates gathered around him and in a sad voice he said, "All hell could not drive the Yanks off the hill. We will have to fall back."[8]

At the Lutheran Seminary, a dozen wounded and captured Federal soldiers—including Elisha Reed of the 2nd Wisconsin—watched the battle's progress from the cupola. The failure of the attack brought shouts and cheers, and the viewers went below to the chapel to tell the others. The news triggered more yells and rejoicing. A rebel lieutenant came in "slowly, sadly, and silently," remembered Reed. He walked around the room looking at no one. Finally, the officer—"like the pent-up thunder in the earth beneath"—poured out "a raging torrent of long suppressed wrath. Imagine if you can an enraged Southern fire-eater pouring out volcanic clouds of vigorous and vehement volumes of profanity." The lieutenant said that Lee was "a fool" for "undertaking to dislodge Meade from the position over there. 'He can't do it—and he knows he can't do it; then why in hell does he try to do it'." The Confederate swore some more then uttered, "there was not a private soldier in the whole Confederate army but would know better than to undertake to dislodge Meade from such a position." Finally, the officer turned and left the chapel.[9]

Still wearing a green scarf around his waist marking him as a surgeon, Colonel Henry Morrow watched the failed charge from a church steeple. In the street a short time later, he came upon Confederate General John B. Gordon and his staff. Morrow saluted and said, "General, I am informed that the wounded of our first day's battle lie uncared for where they fell, and I ask your assistance in having them attended to." Gordon, mistaking Morrow for a doctor, turned to his staff. "Is this so, and if so, why is it?" A surgeon told him the wounded of both armies had been cared for, but they had been unable to visit that extreme part of the field. Gordon promised to help and that evening a train of twelve Confederate ambulances arrived to go to the site of the first day's fighting. In the darkness, with lanterns held high, hospital stewards and nurses moved among the "blackened and swollen corpses" seeking any wounded still alive after two days and a night. "The moans and cries for assistance and water were heart rendering," said one person in describing the scene. "Some were delirious and talked of home and friends and wondered that they neglected them so long, while others, in their wild delirium cheered on their comrades as they fought over in imagination the terrible battle."

One of the wounded men was Corporal Andrew Wagner of the 24th Michigan. Wagner had been shot through the breast while carrying the colors. As he lay helpless, his shoes and money were stolen by a small party of Confederates who thought he was dying. At least they took the time to make a pillow for his head. Wagner was the only survivor of the two entire color guard detachments that served with the 24th Michigan on July 1.

It was not until after midnight the wounded survivors were finally taken to hospitals. By then, however, after two days on the battlefield, one soldier recalled, "the maggots began to crawl and fatten in their festering wounds."[10]

Several wounded men brought in were from his 7th Wisconsin, explained William Ray, but there were no survivors from his company. "They look bad, having nothing to eat or drink since wounded and some were wounded early on the first," he wrote on his journal. "We all know that the rebs havnt broke our lines and the general impression [is] that they will retreat."[11]

Chapter 27

The Old Army had Come to Itself Again

James Sullivan spent an uneasy night in Gettysburg despite the fact the Confederate army was turned back the previous day and had begun evacuating the field. "My wound had now got so far along that the numbness had left and was very painful," he wrote, "and I was unable to sleep during the night." The quiet he so longed for was disturbed by the steady rumble of rolling wagons and artillery. At daylight on July 4, Sullivan and William Hancock walked out into the street intending to try and reach the 6th Wisconsin—wherever their regiment happened to be. "It was raining a drizzling sort of rain and I had no coat on and Hancock went back for one of the bed quilts for me," Sullivan recalled, "but before he returned a skirmish line came down the street, followed by a support and the battle flag of the 11th Corps, and then I knew that my fellows had Gettysburg." The two Black Hats told an officer about the movement of Confederate artillery and, after sending a courier back to headquarters, the Eleventh Corps men followed the retreating Confederates.[1]

The streets of Gettysburg were almost empty except for some wounded Union men when injured Private William Ray of the 7th Wisconsin took a look around. "All the Rebs gone someplace, ambulances, wagons & all." Without warning, a Confederate cavalryman thundered down the street with his horse in a dead run, yelling to the Union men to "keep in your heads, your skirmishers are coming!" No sooner did he yell out the warning than a gun went off and a bullet whizzed down the street past him. Union cavalry galloped after the gray trooper, followed by trotting Eleventh Corps infantry who "searched every Barn & horse taking a great many prisoners right in the town. I guess nearly as many as they took of our Boys when they could." Soon the streets were full of walking wounded, wrote Ray, who "scratch & hobbled along" in an effort to return to their regiments.[2]

Private George Frederick Neff of the 24th Michigan watched several U.S. Sharpshooters round up prisoners. Citizens began to appear on the streets waving handkerchiefs and flags. The hungry private crossed a street to a small home where many of the Michigan men lay wounded. He was drawing water from a well to wash when the lady of the house invited him in to eat. Neff was surprised to discover both a table full of men, and that it was the third breakfast the woman had served that morning. One of the men at the table was Lieutenant Hollon Richardson of the 7th Wisconsin. Neff said the young officer tried to pay the woman when he was finished, but she would not take his money. "Cleaning out the Rebels was all I ask or want," she told him.

The front room of the house was full of wounded men. An old lady was breaking bread and feeding it to a soldier shot through both arms. The woman and friends were making bread and coffee and carrying it across the street to the wounded in the courthouse. "It was a sight to behold," Neff remembered. "Women were carrying sheets, pillows, quilts, bandages and everything else which would make a soldier comfortable, while men staggered under crates and baskets full of eatables." He returned to the courthouse to gather his things before joining wounded men instructed to move to an army hospital on the outskirts of town. Neff found the hospital a dreadful place and there was nothing there to eat. "I would rather take my chances marching than starve to death," he told some of the wounded Michigan men. He set off on his own to find the regiment.[3]

The pre-dawn rain woke Rufus Dawes from what called the "troubled and dreamy sleep of the battlefield." Half awake behind the makeshift breastworks manned by his regiment on Culp's Hill, he wondered whether the fighting would be resumed and realized with somewhat of a start that it was July 4—Independence Day, 1863. His 25th birthday. As the day brightened, Dawes pulled a letter from his pocket he had started the night before and added a few lines: "I am entirely safe through the first three of these terrible days of bloody struggle. The fighting was the most desperate I ever saw. O, Mary, it is sad to look now at our shattered band of devoted men. . . . Tell mother I am safe."

By midmorning it was apparent that there would be no more fighting. The realization puzzled the Iron Brigade men. From their perspective, it seemed as if nothing besides the senseless deaths of thousands of good men had been resolved during the three days of intense combat. Except for the first few hours of fighting, the armies had maintained their relative positions on the battlefield. True, General Lee had been unable to drive away the Army of the Potomac and win a major victory on Pennsylvania soil, but the wounded Union army had also proved unable to respond with a decisive blow.

With the Virginia army pulling away, the Western men who survived the ordeal of Gettysburg turned their immediate thoughts and efforts to finding out what had happened to their missing comrades. The horrors they discovered on the battlefield challenged the mettle of the men who moved across it on that fourth day of July. Colonel Henry Morrow located his 24th Michigan and told stories of his grim night trying to find the regiment's dead and wounded northwest of Gettysburg. The Confederates treated the wounded well, but stripped and robbed "the bodies of the dead who still lie there so bloated as to be unrecognizable." Jerome Watrous of the 6th Wisconsin found the farm fields "covered with unburied dead, hospitals, homes, sheds and barns were crowded with bleeding, dying men." Watrous came across a veritable flood of men moving out of the town toward the Union position, an exodus he described as "wounded squadron with broomsticks for crutches, and any means of assistance they could lay their hands on." Put another way, ambulatory injured men were trying to find their regiments. Several of them wore the black hat of the Iron Brigade.

William Ray discovered only nineteen men left in his company of the 7th Wisconsin. "They all seemed as glad to see me as if I were their Brother and I assure you I was just as glad to see them." James Sullivan found his 6th Wisconsin "about the size of a decent company." Company K was down to "seven or eight men" with a sergeant in command. It had marched to Gettysburg on the morning of July 1 with thirty-four soldiers in its ranks. The 6th Wisconsin carried 340 soldiers into the battle; more than 160 were down, dead or missing. Six of twelve company officers were shot with two killed outright. With some dismay, it suddenly dawned on Sullivan that the five regiments of the Iron Brigade "would not make one." The 19th Indiana was in sad shape, he observed, with most of its officers killed or wounded.[4]

One of the arriving wounded was Sergeant William Evans, who presented Dawes with the captured flag of the 2nd Mississippi. He had kept the banner hidden in his bed in town during the Confederate occupation of the city. Another wounded soldier brought the young officer a bouquet of flowers and a note with the compliments of "Miss Sallie Paxton." She had watched the regiment's charge on the railroad cut the morning of July 1. Sergeant Michael Mangan of the 6th Wisconsin told anyone who would listen how the sight of Union soldiers clearing the town lifted his spirits: "It would be impossible to describe my feelings when our boys rushed in . . . took our guards prisoners and released us, as I had given up all hopes of such an event." A Michigan soldier wrote home: "The day for us was fearful and our thoughts turn to those at home whose dear ones lie on yond field; some in their last gory sleep, others suffering from wounds and no aid near them."[5]

After a time, when all that needed to be said was spoken, the wounded men made their goodbyes and began walking to the First Corps hospital two miles distant. The next morning most of them made their way to Littletown, so they could be transported to Harrisburg and Philadelphia for treatment. Sullivan and about twenty-five others spent the night in a barn. "The old Pennsylvania farmer furnished us with quilts, supper and breakfast," he wrote with satisfaction. The next morning the farmer hitched a wagon and carried them to Littletown, where Sullivan and others were sent to an army hospital in Germantown, Pennsylvania. Sullivan was lucky to have survived his wound, and remembered that "[i]t was a long time before I was able to go back to the regiment."[6]

Back on the Culp's Hill, Dawes added another few sentences to his ongoing letter. "What a solemn birthday," he began. It was 6:00 p.m. on July 4. "My little band, now only two hundred men, have all been out burying the bloody corpses of friend and foe. No fighting to-day. Both armies need rest from the exhaustion of the desperate struggle. My boys until just now have had nothing to eat since yesterday morning. No regiment in the army did better service than ours." A Michigan soldier agreed, adding that "Our wounded were full of enthusiasm, though unable to move with limbs crushed and swollen, and without food."[7]

Independence Day at Gettysburg in 1863 was "chiefly a day of gloom" thought one Badger. "Nearly every survivor had lost from one to a dozen of his company comrades. It was a day like a funeral, a quiet day, save the labor called for in burying the dead and caring for the wounded." William Ray represented the feelings of most of the Black Hats when he noted in his simple prose, "This has been rather a dull fourth to me as well as a hard one."

Dawes carried the captured flag of the 2nd Mississippi to headquarters with hopes of getting permission to send it to Wisconsin as a trophy. The request was denied, and as he returned with it draped over his arm he passed over the ground where the grand Confederate attack of July 3 had been made. A badly wounded Confederate pulled himself up on an elbow and called to him in a faint voice, "You have got our flag!" Dawes stopped to discover the injured man was a sergeant of the 2nd Mississippi, part of Joe Davis' Brigade. The wounded Southerner offered the Wisconsin officer "many particulars" in regard to the history of his regiment. "I do not know whether this sergeant survived his wound," Dawes wrote later. "I did all in my power to secure for him aid and attention."[8]

About sunset, remembered Watrous many years later, General Meade "ordered all of the bands to move up close to the men who had fought and won one of the greatest victories that any army had ever won and play the patriotic airs." He continued:

> At first the music had but little effect upon the victorious army, but when the bands came to "America" and the "Star-spangled Banner" hearts were touched . . . and by and by a cheer started. It was taken up and went along the five mile line of battle and was repeated several times, and the old army had come to itself again and the next day was ready to start in pursuit of Gen. Lee and his brave army in gray.[9]

Chapter 28

They Have Played Their Hand Long Enough

The small regiments of the Iron Brigade left Culp's Hill the morning of July 5, 1863, for Cemetery Ridge near what a Michigan man called "the scene of the rebels' desperate and final charge." The area was scarred and shell-ripped with evidence of the struggle—"the ground trampled down; buildings riddled with shot or in black ruins, trees cut and fences splintered with grape." Here and there, in a growing stench under the hot sun, details of soldiers pulled Confederate corpses into piles for mass burials. Civilians were also moving on the fields in small groups on foot or in wagons and buggies. Many were simply onlookers—curious to see the battlefield and perhaps collect souvenirs. Others sported red eyes as they grieved for friends and family members missing in the maelstrom of battle. Some carried shovels to open fresh Union graves to see if a loved one lay inside. "There is an unusual stillness everywhere," wrote one Badger in his diary.[1]

After waiting for a time and not getting orders, the Western soldiers put up what small tents they had and rested through a "rainy night." The campfire talk centered on whether the Confederate army was making a run for Virginia and safety. There was also some discussion about Meade's handling of the army. He was steady and capable, they agreed, having been thrust into command of a scattered army less than a week before Gettysburg. Meade had somehow avoided disaster.

At noon the next day, July 6, Lieutenant Amos Rood of the 7th Wisconsin found a horse and rode back to Gettysburg to "to see after our wounded and who fell in the first day's fight." He found most of the surviving wounded being cared for around the McPherson barn buildings, but on the field "our dead lay as they fell." Union skirmishers pushing after the retreating Confederate army encountered scattered opposition and captured knots of stragglers.

The Army of the Potomac, however, was as disorganized in victory as the Virginia army was in defeat. Meade's men were exhausted, their commander structure had been decimated, and stocks of rations, ammunition, and shoes were in short supply. Complicating matters was the weather: steady rains had turned all roads to mud. The long and short of it was that the army was not immediately in a condition to mount a vigorous pursuit. Still, Meade had fresh brigades on hand to mount whatever effort he chose to attempt. John Sedgwick's Sixth Corps soldiers, for example, had hardly pulled a trigger. Meade, however, was a generally cautious officer, and not about to lose what he fought so hard and long to gain. He wired Washington that he was having "great difficulty in getting reliable information," but believed "the enemy is retreating, very much crippled and hampered by his trains." The delay in pursuit ended early on July 6, as a Michigan man announced in a letter home: "The army is in motion towards the retreating invaders."[2]

The main portion of the Army of the Potomac took to the roads "very early" on July 6 with the telegraph line from Washington (unmindful of often "knee-deep mud" slowing the soldiers) frantic with messages to press the retreating Confederates. It was raining again, and one of the soldiers in the 24th Michigan recalled that "the very heavens seemed to weep at the dreadful carnage just past." The regiments halted near Emmitsburg, Maryland. There was little coffee, even less quality food, and many of the men did not have blankets. "May God save me and my men from any more such trials," grumbled a Wisconsin officer. The column containing the Black Hats halted when it reached Bellville by nightfall on July 7 after a grueling twenty-four mile march. The Westerners tried to sleep in a hard rain that lasted through the dark hours. Lieutenant Rood "sat up against a nice big tree. Pulled hat rim down around. Poncho over my feet, and, by George, I never slept sounder. . . . Everybody else too, I reckon."

When the column lurched through Middletown, Maryland, and finally halted, the Iron Brigade found itself bivouacked on the western slope of

South Mountain. Without orders, the soldiers piled up rails and a Michigan man explained, with the hindsight of having been in a hard place or two, that "a rail fence properly disposed, and covered with a few shovelfuls of earth, doubles the defence of the troops as well as gives strength to their confidence." The regiments did not move all that day, which prompted a Wisconsin soldier to write in his diary that "never was a day of rest more welcome." Word reached the Union column that the Confederate stronghold at Vicksburg, Mississippi, had finally fallen to General U. S. Grant's besieging army. "Hooray! Hooray!" a Wisconsin officer wrote in his journal. "[W]e celebrated as best we could."[3]

Meade and his generals, however, were not as immediately successful. The general telegraphed Washington that his army was "assembling slowly" and rain "made all the roads [and] pikes almost impassable. Artillery and wagons are stalled. It will take time to collect them together."

"We have marched night and day and we have beaten the rebel army," Dawes wrote in his letter home. "At last the Army of the Potomac has done what, well-handled, it might have done long ago." Dawes added to his missive whenever the opportunity presented itself. From Boonsborough, Maryland, he wrote: "Our men have toiled and suffered as never before. Almost half of our men have marched barefooted for a week. . . . We have had severe rains since the battle. I have not slept in a dry blanket or had on dry clothing since crossing the Potomac [River] before the battle. If we can end this war right here, I will cheerfully abide the terrible risk of another battle." Later that day: "We are again near the rebel army and unless they escape over the river, we may expect a battle. . . . General Meade has shown himself equal to the emergency." Dawes' letter was not all good news. "The oldest of the Iron Brigade regiments, the 2nd Wisconsin," he penned home, "cannot muster fifty muskets." What was left has been with the advance since the battle, "and will probably open the next fight as it did the last."

Back in Gettysburg, meanwhile, Colonel Henry Morrow of the 24th Michigan rode to the home where he left his diary. Mary McAllister was inside when she was told a man on horseback wanted to see her.

"Miss Mary, don't you know me?" asked the rider when she failed to reveal any hit of recognition.

She looked at him a second time. "No! You do look a little like Colonel Morrow, but the Rebels took him."

The rider laughed. "Why, God bless you. I am Colonel Morrow, safe and sound, and I called for my diary. I am going on to join the army"[4] Miss

McAlister returned the book and said she still had General James Archer's sword. She gave it to the colonel with his promise he would return it to the officer who had captured it.

Two days later another man showed up carrying a gun and wearing an old hat. She recognized him immediately. "Why look here, you were taken prisoner." It was Dennis Dailey of the 2nd Wisconsin.

"I have come for my sword," he told her.

When she told him she had given it to Colonel Morrow, the Wisconsin man looked so disappointed she offered to feed him. Dailey explained that he had managed to escape when his guard fell asleep. A few days later he wrote her to tell her that he had found Colonel Morrow and he had returned the sword, as promised.[5]

On July 12, nearly one week after leaving Gettysburg, the Union army caught up with the retreating Confederates along the banks of the swollen Potomac River at Williamsport, Maryland. The days of the retreat had been filled with fighting waged largely by the opposing cavalry commands as Lee's crippled army and his long wagon train of wounded sought to reach the river and the safety offered by its distant shore. Recent rains had flooded the wide waterway, and for a time the Army of the Potomac had Lee's men trapped against the wrong side of the river. Confederate engineers had worked tirelessly for days throwing up powerful earthworks to discourage an attack against the trapped Virginia army. Southern troops aggressively manhandled Union skirmishers trying to ascertain the strength and depth of the enemy line. With the hours slipping past, Union commanders moved here and there, probing for weaknesses in the extensive defensive line. Meade, however, was justifiably worried that an ill-planned assault against the massive lines studded with artillery would end in failure and further cripple his army. Finally, an attack was ordered for July 14. Daylight that morning, however, brought with it word that one of the great Union opportunities to end the war had passed: Lee's army had crossed the Potomac River during the night on a makeshift pontoon bridge. It was only later that the survivors of the 24th Michigan learned one of the last Confederate units to escape was the 26th North Carolina, which had fought "such a terrible duel" with the Wolverines at Gettysburg on July 1.[6]

A troubling incident was scribbled into the diary of a Wisconsin man during this phase of the campaign: "Rebels are retreating; we followed them almost to Williamsport, but arrived too late. In a barn we found a Negro branded with hot irons because he refused to flee with the retreating rebels."

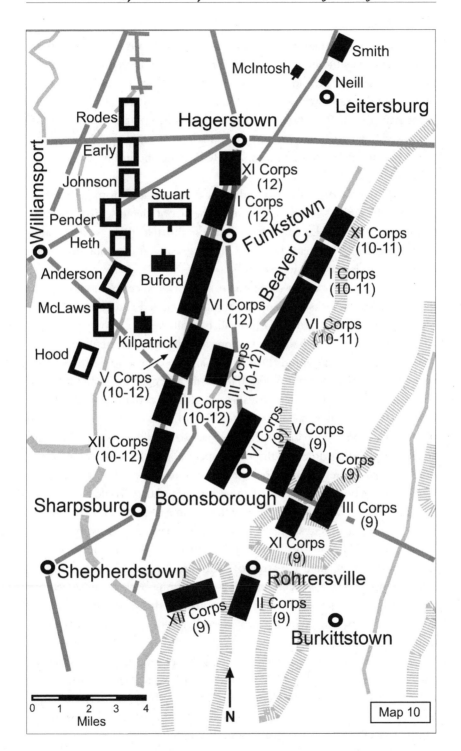

Smith

McIntosh

Neill

Leitersburg

Rodes

Early

Johnson

Hagerstown

XI Corps
(12)

I Corps
(12)

Stuart

Pender

Funkstown

Beaver C.

XI Corps
(10-11)

Heth

I Corps
(10-11)

Anderson

Buford

McLaws

VI Corps
(12)

VI Corps
(10-11)

Hood

Kilpatrick

V Corps
(10-12)

III Corps
(10-12)

II Corps
(10-12)

XII Corps
(10-12)

VI Corps
(9)

V Corps
(9)

I Corps
(9)

III Corps
(9)

Sharpsburg

Boonsborough

XI Corps
(9)

Shepherdstown

Rohrersville

XII Corps
(9)

II Corps
(9)

Burkittstown

Williamsport

0 1 2 3 4
Miles

N

Map 10

The weather had turned very hot and a squad of 7th Wisconsin men found another runaway hiding in a straw stack. When they forced him out at the point of a bayonet, he told them his master was a Confederate officer killed on the first day along with his son. "He was scared and about sick," recalled Lieutenant Rood. "Had no grub for 2 days, except a pint of honey and that physicked him and weakened him. Fed and doctored him up. Mustered him as my servant at 10 $$ per month. . . . He became about the best servant I ever had about me."

A short time after the Confederates crossed the Potomac to safety, Meade telegraphed Washington that the Confederates had escaped. President Abraham Lincoln, upon reading the telegraph, said in bitter disappointment, "We had them within our grasp. We had only to stretch forth our hands and they were ours."[7]

In truth, of course, it was not that easy. Northern celebrations over the twin victories of Vicksburg and Gettysburg included sour muttering that Meade and the Army of the Potomac had allowed Lee to escape. Iron Brigade men who watched events from a front row seat at Williamsport were not of the same mind. Dawes was among a group of officers who examined the Confederate works. He found them very strong and well-constructed: "I think General Meade would have certainly failed to carry them by direct assault," he later wrote. "Both flanks of the works were on the Potomac river. We had no other alternative than direct assault. I take no stock in the stuff printed in the newspapers about demoralization of the rebel army after Gettysburg. They were worn out and tired as we were, but their cartridge boxes had plenty of ammunition, and they would have quietly lain their rifle pits and shot us down with the same coolness and desperation they showed at Gettysburg." A Michigan man agreed with Dawes' assessment: "Many in the North still seem to think that Meade's army should have annihilated it [Army of Northern Virginia]," he began. The army "won a great victory in defeating and turning back the invaders, but the opposing armies were too nearly equal, both before and after the Gettysburg battle, for each to destroy the other. Our victory had cost us too dearly to be rash."[8]

Dawes wrote what many already knew: his regiment, the Iron Brigade, and the whole Army of the Potomac needed rest. "The incessant and toilsome marching from Fredericksburg to Gettysburg, the terrible battle, and the hurried pursuit of the enemy to their point has been the most trying campaign of this army," he wrote home. "Our men have become ragged and shoeless, thousands have marched for days barefoot over the flinty turnpikes. The army has shown a willingness and alacrity under its toils, sufferings and privations, that entitle it to the gratitude of the Nation and I think for once we will receive it."[9]

One of the Federal prisoners moving with the retreating rebel army was the 2nd Wisconsin's Robert Beecham. As he moved along a road, Confederate General Robert E. Lee was pointed out to him. "His long, grizzled beard was neatly arranged; his clothing was clean and faultless; his horse had been groomed and saddled with care; there was nothing about his personal appearance to indicate haste, uneasiness or even weariness; he bestrode his steed apparently cool and confident, not as one who had suffered defeat, but rather as a conqueror," remembered Beecham, who continued:

> Then I looked from him to his shattered battalions, and read the evidence of his terrible conflict and his humiliating defeat, and it was plain to see that Lee himself must have full recognized the fact that the glorious dream of his ambition could never be realized. . . . Lee was the only man of the defeated army, so far as I saw it on the retreat from Gettysburg, who did not reveal the marks of defeat, but it is fair to presume that beneath this outward show of pride and unyielding courage there was an ambitious heart that was very sore.[10]

And so the Gettysburg campaign waged on Northern soil (the armies would move back through Virginia to take up positions nearly equal to those given up in early June) effectively ended at the Williamsport river crossing. The sometimes troubled, usually hard-luck, and always politically-racked Army of the Potomac had finally triumphed over its nemesis, the Army of Northern Virginia. It was a great victory forged in noise and death of unexpected magnitude. It was a great victory despite, or perhaps because of, the unlikely situation of a new general thrust into command just days before the battle. And it was the great victory that Iron Brigade survivors believed was a turning point on the long and hard road of civil war started more than two years before. "I think the backbone of the rebellion is broken, or soon will be," a Wisconsin private wrote home. "They have played their hand long enough."[11]

Gettysburg, they would eventually come to realize, was the last great battle for the bright volunteers who flocked to the Union banners in 1861.

Stand-up battle lines and bold charges would still take place—and 1864 would prove to be the bloodiest year of the war—but their days were passing. War was taking on a grim, harder face; the change would be fully noted in the letters, diaries, and journals of the Western men. After Gettysburg, the throwing up of makeshift earthworks took place at almost every halt. Without orders, the Wisconsin, Indiana, and Michigan men gathered logs and brush and piled up soil using bayonets, shovels, canteen halves, and tin plates. It was as if they instinctively knew that by conserving themselves, their small regiments and famous brigade might continue to exist.

And that was the very question they were afraid to consider: What would become of the Old Iron Brigade of the West? The four original regiments each carried 1,000 volunteers to Washington in 1861, with the 24th Michigan adding 1,000 more in late 1862. Now, less than 700 of the original 5,000 men were still in the ranks. The brigade was about used up. "It is awful to soldier in this kind of way, only five or six men in a company," a 2nd Wisconsin man wrote home. He continued:

> [W]ere we N.Y. troops, we would be taken home, or at least relieved from the front. But we have no friends at home to speak for us, and our Generals know very well that the Wis. Boys will fight and not run, they just shove them ahead like a lot of cattle going to slaughter. Well, it will take but one more shove for the Second, and the "jig is up." Then, some man who saw us fight will be promoted to Brigadier General as a reward for our gallantry.[12]

The "shove" came July 16, 1863. In complete disregard for tradition and morale, the 167th Pennsylvania was added to what was once the all-Western brigade. The Pennsylvania unit had 800 men—more than all the survivors of the five original regiments combined. The Keystone men had not seen any serious fighting. What most angered the veterans from Wisconsin, Indiana, and Michigan was the simple fact that the new arrivals were nine-month men—draftees. The Pennsylvanians were also sulky and mutinous because they believed their nine months had expired and they were entitled to go home. The first "little difficulty" with the new regiment (as a 7th Wisconsin man called it in his diary) came two weeks later on July 30 when the Pennsylvanians refused to go on guard duty. They only changed their mind after two or three of the mutineers were arrested. Two days later, the drafted men refused to march.

The acting commander of the brigade was Lysander Cutler, the former colonel of the 6th Wisconsin. The grim and serious New Englander had little patience for such behavior. Cutler, recalled one witness,

> ordered the rest of the Brigade to fall in and to load their guns. They formed in line of battle on two sides of the Reg. And they had 5 minutes given them to fall in and take their arms. The 2nd and 6th [Wisconsin] were marched up in a line of battle and the order was given to them to halt and right dress. Then the Gen. gave the order to make ready and then to aim , and quick as that was done the whole of the 167th fell in double quick time and they got out of that camp quicker than any Regt I ever so go out of camp.

A company of the 6th Wisconsin followed the reluctant soldiers with orders to shoot any man who fell out of ranks. A final report of the event came in an August 5th diary entry: "The 167th drafted Regiment started for home. The brass band belonging to the Iron Brigade serenaded them part way to the R.R."[13]

The departure of the Pennsylvania regiment and the return to all-Western status lasted only a few more days when four companies of the 1st Battalion New York Sharpshooters were added to the brigade. The New Yorkers were at least three-year men and would stay with the brigade for most of 1864. As veterans, they were generally welcomed, but the old brigade was not the same as the one which had done such great service at Gettysburg. No longer would the brigade be the deciding force in battle. The men in ranks were beginning to realize that perhaps the Iron Brigade's greatest days of service were behind it.

There was, however, one more shining moment.

A group of citizens, proud of the brigade's record at Gettysburg and elsewhere ("one of the most glorious organizations in the entire army," a *New York Times* correspondent called it), raised $1,000 and commissioned Tiffany & Co. of New York to produce a banner of the richest construction "as a testimonial of the appreciation in which the Brigade is held for its bravery, gallantry and valor." The banner carried the names of the five regiments and their various battle honors. It was mounted on a special staff with a massive silver spear head. The new flag was to be presented on

Wisconsin Historical Society 25598

Iron Brigade Presentation Flag

Funds for this special Tiffany & Co. presentation banner were raised by citizens in Wisconsin, Indiana, and Michigan. The flag was is presently housed in the Wisconsin Veterans Museum in Madison.

September 17, 1863, the one-year anniversary of Antietam, with a great flourish. Several dignitaries planned to attend, including Alexander Randall, Wisconsin's first war governor. A "beautifully decorated bower" was prepared by regimental work details for the "grand affair," but before the event could take place, orders put the brigade on the march.[14]

Nevertheless, on the appointed day W. Yates Selleck of Milwaukee, Wisconsin's military agent at Washington, caught up with the brigade at Culpepper, Virginia. The regiments were drawn up in a square. The presentation had "no splendid bower nor distinguished guests," recalled one officer, but "victuals" were on hand, as were "the liquors." Selleck gave a brief speech and presented the flag to Colonel William Robinson, who was just then commanding the brigade. It was somehow fitting that the oldest regiment, the 2nd Wisconsin, served as the escort for the new colors. One of the highlights was the reading of a letter by Selleck from the army's former commander, General George B. McClellan. "My heart and prayers are ever with them, and that, although their new colors can witness no more brilliant acts of patriotism and devotion than those which the old torn flags have shared in," Little Mac wrote, "I know that on every future field, they and the whole Army of the Potomac, will maintain their part, and the honor of their country and their colors."[15] Afterward, the officers made for the full tables. A Wisconsin officer noted for his temperance views wrote his sweetheart that the event quickly turned into "an affair that conferred little honor on the brigade, as gentlemen. I feel glad to say there were a few exceptions." He also reported the brigade officers and visiting generals "and staff officers within any convenient distance of us were almost unanimously drunk last night. We will see an account of the presentation in the *New York Times*, as I saw the 'graphic and reliable' correspondent of that paper guzzling champagne and wine with the rest of them." It was a spree of such epic proportions that it disturbed the sleep of the enlisted men although one private claimed the "rank and file got what they could swipe, which was not a small amount."

Unfortunately, the new glorious flag had no place with the brigade. Unable to keep it because regulations forbid all but official banners, the officers of the five regiments resolved to send the flag to Washington with Wisconsin Agent Selleck.[16]

Chapter 29

I Guess He is All Right on the Fight Question

The Union victories of July at Gettysburg in Pennsylvania and Vicksburg on the Mississippi River rocked the Confederacy with two hard blows, but Southern armies were still in the field and the war was still a long way from over. In the East, George Gordon Meade worried that what had been accomplished at Gettysburg might be just as quickly undone, and was cautious about his next operation. Confederate Robert E. Lee and his veteran army remained a viable and threatening force, though its days of major offensive operations above the Potomac River were at an end. In Tennessee, Union forces suffered a potentially crippling setback at Chickamauga in the middle of September 1863, but regrouped to push Confederate troops away from the hills surrounding Chattanooga in late November, setting the stage for a campaign the following summer to capture the important logistical city of Atlanta, Georgia.

The mid-summer fighting of 1863 left the Iron Brigade much reduced, and resulted in a wholesale shuffling of the organization's command structure. General John Newton of the Sixth Corps, the stranger who replaced Abner Doubleday in Pennsylvania (after Doubleday had moved up to replace the fallen John Reynolds) remained in command of the First Corps. First Division commander James Wadsworth, exhausted by the active campaigning, went on extended leave on July 17. He would return several months later only to be killed in the desperate fighting in the

Wilderness in early May 1864 when a bullet drilled him through the brain. The Iron Brigade's commander Sol Meredith, injured at Gettysburg, went home on medical leave to Indiana. He returned in November, but it was apparent after two weeks that field service was now too much for him. He transferred to light duty posts at Cairo, Illinois, and then Paducah, Kentucky. Colonels Lysander Cutler of the 6th Wisconsin and William Robinson of the 7th Wisconsin shared brigade command in Meredith's absence.

In the regiments, several promotions were approved. John Mansfield took command of the 2nd Wisconsin, replacing Lucius Fairchild, who went home to a political career helped by the empty sleeve of his coat—a never-ending reminder to voters of his selfless service at Gettysburg. Lieutenant Colonel Rufus Dawes remained in command of the 6th Wisconsin in place of the injured Colonel Edward Bragg. Colonel Samuel Williams led the 19th Indiana, as did Colonel Henry Morrow with the 24th Michigan.[1]

As 1863 came to an end, the weather added to the misery of a bleak winter camp. The winter proved to be the coldest in recent memory, and the last week of the year proved the most stormy. A strong wind carrying a wet snow swept in from the northwest and covered the Rappahannock River camps to the depth of a man's boot tops. The storm finally blew itself out. Christmas Day dawned cold and still. It was an uncertain holiday. "Fences had to suffer," recorded one veteran, and the weather—"much like our western winters"—reminded the young soldiers huddled around big fires of places and loved ones far away.[2]

It was their third Christmas in the grim civil war of unexpected magnitude, and to the common soldiers it seemed that, despite the thousands of deaths and bloody fighting, little had been resolved. The rebel army lay across the river and there was quiet discussion of a possible Confederate invasion of Kentucky or Ohio—or even another offensive against the Army of the Potomac on Northern soil. But some Black Hats argued during the coffee fire debates that the war had turned at Gettysburg, and the hope of the Confederacy now rested on the success of a peace candidate over Abraham Lincoln in the upcoming presidential.

It was not the weather or winter duty that filled soldier talk, but the vexing "veteran question" and the warm prospect they might be going home, at least for a short time. It was a matter discussed in quiet, serious tones and with boastful shouts and wild laughter. After three years of the harshest service, after long weeks and months of hardship, death, illness, and suffering, the thought of home was almost beyond comprehension. It had been some thirty months since the Wisconsin and Indiana regiments left their states amid shouts and cheers and the music of town bands. Home to most of the men in the ranks was now reduced to a few pictures, a packet of folded letters, and dim memories of the places and loved ones they left behind. Now, at least for those willing to reenlist, there was the promise of warm homecomings, soft beds, and kitchens with good smells and full tables. There was more to going home than the expected welcome on the family doorstep. They had marched off full of innocent patriotic zeal, caught up in the great crusade for the Union; now they would return as heroes in one of the most famous organizations of the Union armies—veterans in the Iron Brigade of the West.

The question now waiting to be answered was whether the boys who enlisted in 1861 were willing to stay to see the war through to its conclusion. Many of the volunteer regiments were reaching the end of their three-year enlistments just at a time when victory seemed a possibility. Would the men and boys who had been the first to volunteer and who had borne the brunt of the fighting just pack and go home? In the Army of the Potomac alone, the enlistment of more than seventy-five regiments would expire before the end of August 1864. Worried Army officials published an order just one week before Gettysburg on June 25, 1863. The word passed through the army gave authority for veteran re-enlistments of "all able bodied men between the ages of eighteen and forty-five years, who have heretofore enlisted and have served not less than nine months." If three-fourths of the men on the roster of a volunteer unit would reenlist, the order continued, each soldier would receive a $402 bounty paid in installments (this at a time when privates collected $13 a month) and a thirty-day furlough—the "veteran volunteers" to be sent home "as a regiment" to enjoy it.

The order caused a great stir. Some Black Hats argued the war probably could be brought to a successful conclusion within the year and reenlistment would allow them to "share the glory of a continuous service to the end of the war." If the month-long furlough was a most "tempting bait," however, other matters were considered just as important: "Down in the hearts of the men there was the manhood of patriotism," one veteran recalled, "the feeling that the country needed them, and that they would not be contented at home while armies were contending."

The quandary vexing the Western men was outlined in the diary of Charles Walker of the 7th Wisconsin:

October 5, 1863:
There is quite an excitement in camp about going into the Veterans'
Corps. The 19th Ind. took a vote on it tonight and they were all for it
to a man.

October 6, 1863:
Went over to the Co. and put my name down for to go into the
Veterans' Corps. The boys are all going to a man. . . . A lot of
conscripts came in for the 2nd Brigade.

December 18, 1863:
Very wet and sloppy underfoot. No inspection, but at noon we fell in
without arms...to find out how many were willing to go into the
Veteran Crops and go home on a 30 day furlough . . .

Dec. 31, 1863:
Was mustered in to serve 3 years longer.

January 1, 1864:
Signed the payroll and got my pay amounting to $194.50.[3]

In the end, the veteran question ended forever the brigade associations
started in the Washington camps of 1861. The 7th Wisconsin, with 249 on
its rolls, re-enlisted 211 as veterans. The 6th Wisconsin, with 290 men,
signed 227. The 2nd Wisconsin, however, was used up and mustered only
forty veteran enlistments with the remaining 170 on the rolls destined to be
sent home in June 1864. The 19th Indiana reenlisted 213 men, but was
somehow ruled short of the goal. The 24th Michigan's three-year enlistment
ran until 1865. One Wisconsin veteran wrote home with some pride in the
veteran status of his regiment: "The men, who have stood by the old flag
through fair and foul weather, and through many bloody battles, almost to a
man dedicated their lives and services anew to their country."[4]

The month on veteran furlough in Wisconsin during the early weeks of
1864 was remembered with fondness for the rest of their lives. The road
home started on a hard note, though. The soldiers were piled into unheated
freight cars and suffered from the cold weather on the first sixty-mile leg.
One man was frozen so severely he was left behind in an Alexandria,
Virginia, hospital. At Washington, the veterans "replenished their wardrobe

Mary Beman Gates
Marietta, Ohio

She met Rufus Dawes when he visited his hometown of Marietta, Ohio, during the war and became his correspondent. Dawes always said his letters addressed "MBG" always stood for "My Best Girl." They were married in 1864.

Service With

The Sixth Wisconsin Volunteers

with fine suits of clothes and new hat trimmings." Colonel Edward Bragg of the 6th Wisconsin made his way to the War Department for the flag of the 2nd Mississippi captured at Gettysburg. A few days later the regiment carried it down Milwaukee's main street in a foot of snow to nail the banner to a wall at the Chamber of Commerce hall so citizens could come to look at it. The local newspaper reported that the "men all look rugged and hearty." Another weekly in central Wisconsin announced the veterans had monopolized all "horses, cutters, sleighs and young lady's to be found in the vicinity." There were also several social notices: Lieutenant William S. Campbell was wed to Millie Pixley in Portage City, and William Palmer of the Sauk County Riflemen "took a wife in the person of Miss Clara Kern of Sumpter."[5]

Rufus Dawes left the 6th Wisconsin at Pittsburgh to go home to Marietta, Ohio, where he married Mary Beman Gates at a 5:30 a.m. service Monday morning, January 18, 1864. There were few guests besides family. The young officer and his new wife immediately took the train to Milwaukee to join the regiment. At one point, the journey was delayed by a strike of locomotive engineers and the couple rented a sleigh for a twelve-mile ride across country to another rail connection to continue the journey in a freight train. "Of course under such circumstances," Dawes recalled, "the trip was in every respect delightful." The new Mrs. Dawes never saw her husband's regiment. The closest she came was a glimpse inside a hall, where she spotted "stacks of muskets with belts and cartridge boxes hanging upon them, as left by the column when broken for the men to visit their homes." Dawes' mare, wounded at Gettysburg, had been shipped with the regiment and as he rode along an icy Milwaukee street the animal fell at a corner, dislocating the officer's ankle. The injury left Dawes unable to return to active duty for several weeks. Given the circumstances, wrote the injured officer, "This accident was regarded as a great piece of good fortune."[6]

The month ended too quickly and the 6th and 7th Wisconsin men were back in their old camps by early February 1864. There were new developments: U.S. Grant, famous for his service in the Western Theater in general, and at Vicksburg in particular, was elevated to commander of all the Union armies. (One private called the appointment a gift from President Lincoln—"A cigar, with a silent, successful man behind it." Grant's demands that opponents succumb to terms of "unconditional surrender" also made him a popular choice.) Although General Meade remained in command of the always politically intrigued Army of the Potomac, Grant's decided to maintain his headquarters *with* the army rather than in the nation's capital. He often pitched his ten near the Iron Brigade camps.

The cold weather lingered well into 1864. Dawn came overcast and damp in the Iron Brigade camp on March 29. A six-inch snowfall two days earlier was still sitting in piles of slush on the muddy ground. The Black Hats and other veterans of the old First Corps were marched to a railroad track near Culpepper, Virginia, where the small regiments were formed in a drizzle of cold rain. The First Corps, used up by hard service, was no more. It was dismantled over the winter months and removed from the Army rolls, its survivors merged into Gouverneur Warren's Fifth Corps. It was a bitter disappointment to the soldiers who were with the famous old unit organized by General McClellan in the Washington camps of 1861. The Black Hats were now officially the First Brigade of the Fourth Division of the Fifth Corps. The only bright spot was that the order allowed First Corps men to retain and wear the red wool disc badges marking their original organization.

The regiments were formed in the rain that March day for a scheduled review by General Grant. They had been mustered twice before only to have the general fail to appear. As Dawes and his regiment waited shivering in the rain, he was reminded of another review in November 1861. On that occasion, a party that included President Lincoln, McClellan, and other dignitaries rode along the line at a dashing gait, cheer upon cheer filling the air as they passed the regiments while the soldiers flung their caps high into the air. In those innocent days of new soldiering, the young officer recalled that it was regarded that perfect silence and ranks—not wild cheering and throwing of caps—was evidence of the true and well-disciplined soldier. As the General McClellan and Lincoln passed, the new brigade of Westerners stood silent and made only the proper salutes. McClellan did not acknowledge them.

Now there was a new commander and another review. Grant was two hours late when he and his escort finally appeared. The small party passed slowly along the line and Grant was given cheers. He made no recognition of their compliments. The general rode in "a slouchy unobservant way," one soldier observed, "with his coat unbuttoned and setting anything but an example of military bearing to the troops." Another thought "Old Grant" not "so hard-looking a man as his photographs make him out to be, but stumpy, unmilitary, slouchy and Western-looking; very ordinary in fact." A third soldier wrote home that the new commander (perhaps comparing him with the dashing Little Mac) "is a pretty tough-looking man for Lieutenant General but I guess he is all right on the fight question." Dawes' impression was more favorable: "He looks like a plain common sense man, one not to be puffed up by his position nor abashed by obstacles."[7]

Still, the 25-year-old Dawes, who had learned his soldiering in the Army of the Potomac, was provoked by Grant's indifferent manner. There was, he admitted, some lingering resentment that the government had turned to a general—even though a Western man—not from the Army of the Potomac for the final push to end the war. Some soldiers welcomed the appointment because they hoped and believed Grant would force the issue, while others were fearful because Grant had never had confronted Robert E. Lee and the Army of Northern Virginia on a battlefield. It was during that swirl of emotions Dawes that turned to face his regiment: "As General Grant does not seem to think our cheering worth notice, I will not call for cheers. Maintain your position as soldiers."

When Grant reached the 6th Wisconsin he was met with military salutes performed with exact precision, the hard veterans as motionless as statues. The lieutenant general was pulled up by the silence. Taking it all in an instant, Grant removed his hat and made a slight bow as regimental colors dipped in salute. Dawes said his Westerners understood the gesture immediately. "It was to say, 'I did not come here for a personal ovation.' It was a genuine Grantism and our men were highly pleased at it." Afterward, the Wisconsin soldiers told all that "Grant wants soldiers, not yaupers."[8]

Chapter 30

No Man Can Fight Surrounded by Cowards

The Army of the Potomac of 1864 was forever changing. Reorganizations, expired enlistments, and battle losses brought in a flood of conscripts to fill the ranks of the old regiments. There were a few real volunteers, but most arrivals were drafted men or those who accepted bounties to join the army. The tough veterans were troubled by the new men—or "cattle," as one soldier derisively referred to them. The bounty men were the most suspect and roundly despised. The drafted men were given a grim acceptance by the veterans as fellows who just had bad luck to be conscripted, but were there doing their duty and making the best of it. Among the new arrivals from Wisconsin were members of the Indian tribes, who had been previously barred from military service. No one knew quite what to make of them. Rufus Dawes of the 6th Wisconsin wrote home that thousands of soldiers from other regiments gathered in wonder on the eve of the battle of the Wilderness in May 1864 to watch a "war dance" by newly arrived Ojibwa serving in the 7th Wisconsin.

Initially, Indians were considered "members of an alien nation" and not allowed to enlist in the Union army. Nor were they subject to the draft. One of the first turned away was Robert Grignon of Wisconsin, who offered "200 Menomonee warriors, well armed with rifles, who are sure hits at 40 rods." Another rejected was George Copway, a Methodist minister whose territory included Minnesota, Wisconsin, Illinois, and Iowa. He proposed to raise a regiment of Indians from the Great Lakes area, "not to be employed for using the tomahawk or scalping knife upon the people of the South but as scouts and runners for the army. They will be young men inured to hardship, fleet as deers, shrewd, and cautious." A group of 200 Michigan Indians from the Mackinac area offered their services "to fight for the Stars and Stripes." Each offer was turned away. At Saginaw, Michigan, six Chippewa under Thomas Ke-chi-ti-go tried to enlist, but they too were rejected. "As a race, they have not yet reached that degree of civilization which should entitle them to all the rights, and place on them all the responsibilities of citizenship," trumpeted the Detroit *Advertiser and Tribune* in an 1863 editorial that objected to the idea of using Indians in any way in the Union armies. "Very few of them can read and by far the greater portion neither speak nor understand our language. At the best they are but semi-civilized. . . . They are a poor, ignorant and dependent race."

That sentiment was not echoed by the Board of Supervisors in Oceana County in Northern Michigan. It notified state officials ninety-four white men, "citizens of the county of Oceana," enlisted together with "thirty-four indians whom we regard as citizens of said county."

Some French-Indian "mixed bloods" or "Métis," seeking adventure and to avoid hard times at home, enlisted early in the war by claiming to be "French Canadians." The dire need for more soldiers eventually ended the restriction on putting Indians in uniform, and unscrupulous agents looking for substitutes to replace drafted white men soon worked the Wisconsin reservations with a promise of $100 to any young male tribal member willing to sign the muster roll. This effort came at a time when the agents were getting up to $300 for substitutes and disease and starvation were a common part of reservation life.

In the Wisconsin regiments, the tribal recruits were accepted with some coolness. In fact, all the units were inflated by the arrival of drafted and bounty men, but the new soldiers were a different breed than the "enthusiastic and eager volunteers" of 1861. No longer were the companies made up of hometown boys—brothers, cousins, schoolmates—of those first months of the war. The influx brought about a radical change in the makeup of the regiments; most of the soldiers were from the same state but hailed from different communities—strangers in many ways, serving in each company. There were also changes among the brigade's officers. Many of the men wearing shoulder straps in 1864 were the same non-commissioned officers of 1861. The veterans, distrusting the new men, clung to themselves in small messes even as they attempted to get the companies and regiments ready for the campaign of 1864.

In early May 1864 the Army of the Potomac lurched its way across the Rapidan River at three points to plunge into what Dawes called that "strange and terrible struggle" in the Wilderness. Commanded by General Meade but accompanied by General Grant (an uncomfortable situation for both men), the army slid into the same general vicinity where Joe Hooker had come to grief almost exactly one year earlier. The heavy terrain included scrub growth, brush, briars, and trees fed by small creeks, the whole crisscrossed with but few roads worthy of the name. Unlike Hooker, however, Grant had no desire to fight within the thickets, and wanted to march through into the open as quickly as possible. For General Lee, however, fighting in the Wilderness offered advantages for his outnumbered and outgunned army.

Driving ahead with Richard Ewell's Second Corps on his left and A. P. Hill's Third Corps on his right on roads running roughly parallel to one another, Lee came into contact with the Union soldiers on May 5. The meeting triggered one of the most desperate, confusing, and terrible battles of the war.

When the Warren's Fifth Corps encountered Ewell's Confederates along the Orange Turnpike, an attack to force them aside was ordered. One of the units deployed for the effort was Lysander Cutler's Iron Brigade, which advanced into heavy woods south of the turnpike to take up a position just north of Mill Branch. The brigade was arrayed in two lines with the 24th Michigan on the left, followed by the 19th Indiana, 2nd Wisconsin, and 7th Wisconsin extending the line to the right. Dawes' 6th Wisconsin took up a position in the second line, with the 7th Indiana alligned on its right. As soon as the men moved out they lost their way in the dense underbrush. After moving only a short distance it was struck on the flank by a heavy line of Confederates and tumbled backward in some disorder. "I ordered a change of front on the color company to bring the regiment to face them," remembered Dawes of the initial fighting on May 5. He continued:

> We here lost 40 to 50 men in a very few moments. The brush now served us well. The rebels came on yelling and firing. Our little band, as always under fire, clung around its colors. We rallied and formed twice or three times and gave the enemy a hot reception as they came on. When the rebels ceased pursing us, we found ourselves alone as a

regiment and lost in the woods, and we lay flat on the ground, not knowing certainly which way to go to join our troops. . . . We were in the woods between the hostile lines and we felt our way cautiously back to the open ground around the Lacy House, where our corps was being formed after this repulse.[1]

The fighting raged all that day and ended in a stalemate. Despite massive assaults, broken lines, and hand-to-hand fighting on May 7, neither side had anything substantial to show for its terrible losses. By the time night fell on May 6, the Wilderness fallen included two prominent officers associated with the Iron Brigade. Old James Wadsworth, who had done well at Gettysburg under difficult conditions, accidently rode into rebel lines and was shot in the back of the head by an Alabama soldier. He lingered for two terrible days before dying in a Confederate hospital. Colonel Samuel Williams of the 19th Indiana was also killed. He left behind a wife and six children.

When the fighting ended in the Wilderness, Grant did something no other Union commander had done. Instead of withdrawing to return to his camps, he turned his army south, forcing Lee to either intercept him and fight again, or risk losing the Confederate capital at Richmond. When the horrendous Spotsylvania Court House fighting begin around Laurel Hill on May 8, the Iron Brigade was, as usual, in the thick of it. Cutler, who had taken over division command for the mortally wounded Wadsworth, aligned his men west of the Old Court House Road and moved south, the Westerners thrust into the center position. When a flank attacked seemed imminent, the 2nd Wisconsin formed at a right angle to the 7th Wisconsin. It was too late, remembered Dawes. A tactical assault of Alabama troops swept through a ravine. "Outflanked both ways and pressed by the enemy on both sides," wrote the Badger officer, "the line broke in disorder." The disastrous experience at Gettysburg, coupled with the rough handling in the Wildneress, had taken its toll on the Iron Brigade.

Some relief arrived when the Western men were held in reserve before being moved forward a few days later through a driving rainstorm within shooting distance of a place history has popularized as "the Bloody Angle." "We formed our line in the rear of the troops engaged and our orders were to move forward to their support," said Dawes. "The mud was half boot top deep and filled with the dead of the battle over whom we stumbled in the darkness. At 100 feet, the line stalled, unable to advance . . . Sometime in the night I suspected the enemies were retreating. I then ceased firing and my exhausted men lay down as best they could and some laid their heads upon the dead and fell asleep. The rebel works presented an awful spectacle . . . crowded with dead and wounded, lying in some cases upon each other and several inches of mud and water."[2]

During those bloody days, Ordnance Sergeant Jerome Watrous was detailed to take a train of thirty wagons loaded with Federal wounded to Fredericksburg for medical treatment. He called the run of ten to twelve miles "the most sorrowful experience" of his four years of service. Orders were to keep moving and make the trip as fast as possible, both because the army was expected to move at any hour, and because the ammunition hauled back on the return journey was greatly needed. "The roads were rough, stony and full of ruts, and in places it was necessary to go through fields and woods when fence rails and small trees had to be passed over. The joltings . . . kept that train loaded with hundreds of wounded, mangled human beings groaning, crying and loudly demanding help. . . . Not less than a dozen men died on that journey."

At Fredericksburg, the wounded were quickly unloaded with the help citizens and a contingent of volunteers from New York led by a man who seemed to be "here, there, and everywhere at about the same minute, giving orders, speaking words of encouragement, offering a swallow of wine to this one and something stronger to the man who needed it . . . " At one point the New Yorker walked to the wagons being reloaded with ammunition destined for the front. The western soldier and New Yorker shook hands. Watrous never forgot meeting Theodore Roosevelt, a New York merchant whose son would one day make quite a a name for himself.[3]

When the fighting around Spotsylvania died out, the armies slid east and south toward the North Anna River, where General Lee had erected another massive set of entrenchments in the hope of stopping Grant's relentless drive southward. For the Western men, the fighting there raged for an hour with tremendous fury. "We came near being driven into the river, but the enemy has lost vigor in attack. Their men are getting so they will not fight except in rifle pits," observed a Wisconsin soldier. Dawes, as exhausted and tired of war as anyone else, took stock of his position in a May 24 letter. "I have had not full night's sleep since May 7th when I took command of the regiment," he wrote. "Day after day, and night after night we have marched fought and dug entrenchments. I have not changed my clothing since May 3rd." The fighting and marching was not about to end anytime soon. More fighting awaited along the Cold Harbor line outside Richmond north of the James River. Unwilling to lay siege to the Southern capital, Grant shifted portions of his army south across the James River on massive pontoon bridges to encircle and capture the vital logistical city of Petersburg, Virginia.

In early June an order reached brigade headquarters releasing the 2nd Wisconsin to go home. They were being mustered out of service. The 2nd was the first of the four original regiments to leave the brigade. Two companies of soldiers who enlisted in the 2nd after 1861 (or reenlisted) were to be mustered into the 6th Wisconsin. Even for these tough veterans who had seen it all, the event was a sad goodbye. The brigade formed ranks together for the last time on June 11, 1864. The small line of 2nd Wisconsin men faced right and began marching to the landing for transport to the North. The blue regimental banner was about used up, the flag staff shattered by musket balls, and the colors "unfurled at the first Bull Run, now in tattered streamers." There were 800 men in the ranks when the 2nd joined the 6th and 7th Wisconsin and 19th Indiana at Washington, D. C. in 1861. Now, three years later, fewer than 200 remained—"a little body of bronzed veterans," was how one eyewitness described them. The band struck up "When Johnny Comes Marching Home," and those watching lifted their hats and offered three loud cheers as the 2nd Wisconsin marched away from the Army of the Potomac for the last time.[4]

There were other changes. Battles losses, illnesses, and desertions had thinned nearly every regiment in the army. The 19th Indiana was consolidated with the 20th Indiana. A short time later, the 24th Michigan was sent to Fortress Monroe and then to Baltimore to take charge of camps of drafted men. The regiment would later stop at a draft rendezvous in Springfield, Illinois, where it served as part of the honor guard for the burial of Abraham Lincoln in 1865.

The Iron Brigade also witnessed the explosion of a large mine outside Petersburg in the opening phase of the disastrous Battle of the Crater on July 30, 1864. The mine was an ingenious attempt to tunnel under and then blast open a segment of the Confederate line. Private William Ray of the 7th Wisconsin recorded what he saw that morning:

> Half past 4:00 arrived and with it the shaking of the ground awakened me. I rocked to and fro, looked at the ground to see the crack that might engulf me . . . the mine had burst. There were . . . parts of things

whirling and whizzing in the area. It was a grand sight. . . . Just as soon
as the thing burst, hundreds of pieces of artillery and different kinds
and thousands of small arms belched forth Death and Destruction
into the enemy's lines. I fired as fast as I could . . . Five minutes after
the fort blew up, our men piled over and into the fort and we see rebs
coming in. Oh how our boys cursed and damned them and damned
the officers for not reinforcing our brave fellows when the rebs would
charge on them. There is something wrong says the boys. The boys
yell too much commissary allowed meaning of this the officers was
too drunk on commissary whiskey. For last night when our brigade
ammunition train came up with ammunition they brought a barrel of
whiskey. I supposed think that it would been needed to ensure
success. But the rank and file did not get a smell.

During the last half of 1864, the Westerners were engaged at Globe
Tavern, Boynton Plank Road and Weldon Railroad, and then in early
February of 1865 in the cold fighting along Hatcher's Run. It was at Weldon
Railroad that James "Mickey" Sullivan of the 6th Wisconsin suffered his
fifth service-related injury. His first wound was in 1861 when he was struck
by a ramrod fired accidentally by a rear-rank 7th Wisconsin man during a
parade ground Washington's Birthday salute; at South Mountain in
September 1862 a bullet severed his middle toe; a slug drilled his shoulder at
Gettysburg in July 1863, and he lost a finger in an accident laying logs to
corduroy a roadway in early 1864. This time, a shell burst over his head and
knocked him unconscious. He awoke to find two of his friends pouring
water from their canteens on him. One of the soldiers pulled a sliver of
metal from the back of Sullivan's neck. The private admitted, "my head felt
as though a band of iron was tightening about it."

As Sullivan was waking up, another more pressing matter captured the
attention of the Western soldiers: every time the Confederates were driven
back, an officer on a white horse rallied them, despite the efforts of Union
"sharpshooters with their telescope rifles" who tried to "give him a quietus
but could not succeed." The Western boys talked it over and brought up
Jared Williams of Ontario, a noted marksman of Company K, and explained
the situation. Williams carefully put the powder from two cartridges in his
gun and patched his ball with part of his shirt tail. When all was ready, he
leveled his musket on a rail post, waited a few long moments, and fired.

"The Reb tumbled out of his saddle, and the horse dashed off behind the woods," Sullivan wrote with no little pride.[5]

For a time during those long months, the 6th and 7th Wisconsin were alone in the brigade, the ranks of the two regiments swelled by drafted and bounty men. The 91st New York, a heavy artillery organization converted to infantry, arrived in March 1865. The three regiments numbered almost 3,000 men.

On April 1, 1865, General Phil Sheridan and elements of the Fifth Corps overran the enemy at Five Forks, Virginia. The attack severed the Army of Northern Virginia's last supply line, and signaled loudly the beginning of the end of the Richmond-Petersburg siege. General Grant ordered an all-out offensive, and the Confederate lines began to crumble. The Southern army pulled out and moved inland heading west, destination unknown. The old veterans of the Iron Brigade were not actively involved in the final days of fighting. On April 9, a Baraboo soldier in the 6th Wisconsin wrote of the final day: "We saw an officer come riding down the lines, his horse wet and covered with lather. As he passed along we saw the boys' caps went up in the air—the shout rang with cheers. . . . As he came in front of us, he shouted, 'Gen. Lee and army had surrendered to Gen. Grant.' Cheer—Oh, no! We yelled for joy for we know the war was ended."

A few days later, paroled North and South Carolina soldiers walked past the camp of the 6th Wisconsin on their way home. Some of the Black Hats went out on the road to shake hands with their old foes and wish them "God speed" and a safe return to their homes. Just before they passed from view, one ragged Confederate called back with a smile: "You all kick up a row with Johnny Bull and we alls will help you." The Black Hats waved back and nodded in agreement, knowing the Johnnies would be there if again needed.[6]

A few weeks later on May 23, 1865, the Army of the Potomac marched for the last time in the Grand Review of the armies in Washington. Hour after hour the columns of blue filled Pennsylvania Avenue. Henry Morrow of the 24th Michigan, now Brevet Brigadier General Morrow, led the First Brigade of Crawford's Division of the Fifth Corps. He left his Michigan regiment at Springfield, Illinois, and came east to command the famed Iron Brigade. Marching behind him were some of the old veterans of the 6th and 7th Wisconsin. Dennis Dailey, who captured General James Archer's sword at Gettysburg, commanded the old "Calico 6th," and in the ranks were two companies from his old 2nd Wisconsin. The 7th Wisconsin was led by

Hollon Richardson, long since reconciled with his father-in-law, Colonel William Robinson. Also in the ranks of the passing soldiers were veterans of the 19th Indiana, now merged with the 20th Indiana. In the artillery train behind the Fifth Corps rolled Battery B, 4th U.S. Artillery.

A few weeks later, the 6th and 7th Wisconsin and 20th Indiana were ordered to Louisville, Kentucky. The 7th Wisconsin mustered out July 3, 1865, and the 6th Wisconsin eleven days later. The 20th Indiana mustered out July 12, 1865. The 24th Michigan, which served as the escort for President Lincoln's funeral at Springfield, Illinois, was sent home to Detroit and was mustered out June 30.

After the fighting ended, when the final tally was made, the Iron Brigade of the West held a place of melancholy honor: during the four years of the war, 1,131 soldiers from its five original regiments had been killed or died of wounds. It was the highest proportion of casualties of any brigade in the Union armies. Two additional footnotes emphasized the loss: Battery B lost more men killed and wounded than any other Union artillery battery during 1861-1865, and the 2nd Wisconsin, even though it served only three years, suffered the highest percentage of loss of any regiment in the Union armies.[7]

Other immediate matters were even more disconcerting. The returning veterans discovered much had changed while they had been away. Some returned disabled or wasted by disease that would take them before their time. Some were addicted to the alcohol and opium used to ease the pain of wounds and surgery. A few were troubled by nightmares and emotions they were unable to control. Wives and children were running shops and farms. Younger brothers and sisters had grown up. Parents were grayer, more frail, or dead. As they quickly discovered, the old way of life lacked the intensity of their days in the army; an inner sense of restlessness and yearning filled many Western hearts. What the future held was anyone's guess.

There was also a vast shift in the nation's social order. The young farmers and clerks who went off to become soldiers had tramped across hundreds of miles of the country, visited major cities, and fought in some of the world's largest battles. The immigrant's son who marched away a private returned—because of intelligence and ability—as an officer in charge of thousands of men. He now held a position of respect in his old hometown and could marry up into the more established classes. Ability trumped class lines.

The social order of the young nation had turned upside down. It was all new, and things would never be the same again.

Chapter 31

The Trust Imposed Upon Them

*G*ettysburg cast a long shadow over Iron Brigade veterans the rest of their waking days. It came to them in haunted dreams, aching old wounds, and troubled memories of lost friends. If there was a certain pride in having been on that bloody field with the famous Iron Brigade of the West, there was also a nagging concern that the final result might not have been worth the terrible cost. Immediately after the war, the restoration of the Union seemed enough. The veterans came to understand with the passing years what martyred President Abraham Lincoln meant when he described a "new birth of freedom" in his brief cemetery dedication at Gettysburg in November 1863. With that simple phrase, the veterans understood that the war not only restored the Union, but ended slavery. It was those accomplishments—a restored, permanent Union and an end to human bondage—that gave their years of hard war duty a higher moral standing.

The Wisconsin, Indiana, and Michigan veterans, however, came to believe with the passing of years that their service at Gettysburg was overlooked and largely forgotten. They were far from the large old soldier reunions at New York, Philadelphia, Boston, and Washington. The story of a Western brigade in an army of Easterners received scant attention as the reunion movement surged and membership in the Grand Army of the Republic grew to record numbers. However, the old men who once were young soldiers of an Iron Brigade of the West were convinced no unit did better service at Gettysburg than theirs. There would not have been a prolonged battle at Gettysburg had it not been for the vigorous delaying action waged on July 1, 1863, explained one veteran.

"Where has the firmness of the Iron Brigade at Gettysburg been surpassed in history?" asked Rufus Dawes in a letter from Marietta, Ohio, to an 1884 reunion of his Lemonweir Minute Men at Mauston. "Two thousand muskets were carried into battle and for four long hours these men breasted the billows of rebellion until twelve hundred were shot down under the colors. Then, with colors flying and unbroken front, they retired to the Cemetery Hill. But that four hours time saved our army the Cemetery Hill, and that enabled it to save the nation."

Others pointed to a letter from General Sol Meredith that explained the Iron Brigade, as "the first on the field . . . had to meet the first shock of a desperate attack of a far superior force, and nobly did it do its duty." Sentiments penned by former Private James Sullivan were typical of the concerns felt by old Black Hats about how their service was being overlooked. In writing of the successful charge of his 6th Wisconsin on the unfinished railroad cut, he lamented that the "steady, cool, straight-forward advance against a greatly superior force [was] forgotten by all, except the few veterans and cripples, and the wives and mothers who lost all they held dear."[1]

The men had a point. The bloody delaying action kept the Confederates from seizing Gettysburg until late on July 1. By that time, the Southern army was disorganized and exhausted, and unable to either halt the Union army's concentration on the Cemetery Hill, Culp's Hill, and Cemetery Ridge, or mount an attack to drive them off. And it was that ground that formed the backbone of the strong Union position on July 2 and 3. The Western men knew well and appreciated the role played by Union cavalry under John Buford. Despite being outnumbered, the cavalrymen fought dismounted and slowed the Confederate advance until the infantry could arrive. The Iron Brigade's quick and sharp repulse of two brigades late that morning alerted Confederates that they were facing infantry from the Army of the Potomac.

The disciplined advance of the 2nd, 7th Wisconsin, 19th Indiana, and 24th Michigan knocked James Archer's Brigade out of action quickly and captured the Confederate general. The 6th Wisconsin's quick attack on the railroad cut, with the help of the 95th New York and 14th Brooklyn, stabilized the first Union position and knocked Davis's Brigade out of the day's fighting.

It was not until near mid-afternoon, when almost two-thirds of the Confederate army was up and facing only elements of the First and Eleventh Corps that the Union line on McPherson's Ridge and then Seminary Ridge finally gave way after some of the heaviest infantry fighting of the Civil War. If the Union brigades were driven in retreat to the rally point on Cemetery Hill, the Confederates were so disorganized and exhausted by their victory that they could not take full advantage of what they had earned that day.

Long afterward, nagging questions remained to be answered. Did the Iron Brigade and regiments of the First Corps defend McPherson's acreage and the Seminary high ground too long because of a breakdown in communication? Colonel Charles Wainwright wrote in his journal there was confusion in the middle afternoon because of a misunderstanding that the order received directed them to hold Seminary Ridge "at all hazards" instead of Cemetery Ridge. With a certain tone of the prejudiced American-born, he blamed it on a German staff officer carrying the order. "What with the aide's broken English and our being on this [Seminary] hill and not knowing that there was a cemetery, I thought it was the Seminary Hill we were to hold." Rufus Dawes said when he led his 6th Wisconsin survivors through the shot-swept streets of Gettysburg, he was unaware of where the Union army was gathering. "We knew nothing about a Cemetery Hill. We could see only that the on-coming lines of the enemy were encircling us in a horseshoe."[2]

Another question hotly discussed had to do with General John Reynolds, who had been killed in the early minutes of the infantry fighting. Could he have successfully fought the delaying action and brought off his brigades with fewer casualties? Artilleryman James Stewart believed that was the case. "I can assure you that the news of his death was terrible to me, as I had thought he had no superior as a corps commander in the army." First Corps artillery commander Wainwright called Reynolds' death "our greatest misfortune." Not that the retreat could have been avoided, given the Union was outnumbered two to one by the Confederates, continued Wainwright, but because under Reynolds the retreat "would have been done in better order, with half loss to ourselves and much more to the enemy."

Other officers immediately after the battle whispered that Reynolds had assumed too much authority in his decision to fight west of Gettysburg. He should not, they said, have endangered himself by leading regiments into action, or should have fought a controlled delaying action, or should have withdrawn to the higher ground south and east of town. Of course, hindsight makes everything clear. Reynolds' on-the-spot decision to fight at Gettysburg became one of the shining moments of the battle. Army of the Potomac officers began circulating a petition within months of the general's death to raise a statue of him at Gettysburg, and the survivors of the Iron Brigade never doubted their heroic fight of July 1, 1863, was worth all the deaths and suffering. To them, Gettysburg became the grand epic of the American Civil War, the centerpiece of their years of service, and the "gallant Reynolds" the fallen knight of the Union.[3]

The cost of the first day at Gettysburg to the Iron Brigade regiments was frightful. The survivors tried to explain the intensity of the fighting, but were often unable to find the right words that captured their experience. Often, as was the case of William Harris of the 2nd Wisconsin and Charles McConnell of the 24th Michigan, they tried to capture it by examining their losses. In an October 8, 1895, address to the St. Paul, Minnesota, chapter of the Military Order of the Loyal Legion, a patriotic group organized by Union officers, Harris compared the loss of the Iron Brigade's 24th Michigan in its face to face infantry battle against the 26th North Carolina. The Michigan regiment entered the battle with 496 men and the North Carolina unit with 800. At the end of the day, the 24th Michigan counted 99 men in the ranks (a loss of 80 percent) against 92 (88.5 percent) for the Confederate regiment. He called it "a most notable incident of opposing valor." Harris also tried to set the losses against the backdrop of history. The Iron Brigade's loss of 64 percent, he said, compared with a loss of 27 percent for the entire Army of the Potomac at Gettysburg; 36.7 percent for the Light Brigade at Balaklava; and 14 percent for both sides at Waterloo.[4]

Charles McConnell called the fighting July 1, 1863—"with the opposing lines narrowing to a space of a hundred feet or less"—the key to the Union victory. "The first day's battle of Gettysburg has never been given proper appreciation by students of the war, or by the public generally," he wrote in an article in a veteran's newspaper. "This is probably because it was a decided Union defeat, whereas the subsequent days' battles were Confederate defeats, and negatively Union victories." He said he watched from Culp's Hill the mass charge of the Confederates on the third day —'a spectacularly, unmilitary, worse than useless slaughter of brave men predestined to defeat, astonishing in a General of Lee's caliber"—and said it did not begin to compare with the clash between Pettigrew's Brigade and the Iron Brigade in the first day's battle of Gettysburg. "There was nothing spectacular about that fight. It was cold-blooded, grim determination, give and take, until both commands were nearly annihilated. It was the most desperate fighting of the entire war, I venture to say, known to be such by all who participated in it." McConnell continued: "But in future years . . . the public appreciation will grow and intensify, and the title to greatest reverence and honor will be, 'He fought at Gettysburg,' and in an exalted degree, 'He fought in the Iron Brigade at Gettysburg'—First Brigade, First Division, First Corps—first in heroism always!"[5]

The official numbers of Gettysburg, as expected, vary from account to account, but do not hide the horrific details of the fighting.[6] In the 2nd Wisconsin, for example, the toll was three of four men in the ranks; the 6th Wisconsin and 7th Wisconsin lost one of every two; the 19th Indiana lost three of four, and the largest and newest regiment—the 24th Michigan—lost four of every five—the highest toll of any Federal regiment in the three days of Gettysburg. The Iron Brigade of the West carried 1,883 men into the battle and by the end of July 1, 1863, only 671 were reported in the ranks—a percentage loss of more than 64.3. In fact, that final tally of 671 survivors may be too high. A brigade quartermaster reported later that he issued rations to only 500 men that grim night on Culp's Hill.[7]

On December 28, 1878, William Dudley of the 19th Indiana, who lost a leg at Gettysburg, sent a belated report to Adjutant General E. D. Townsend on "the part borne by General Meredith's brigade at Gettysburg." The next year, he had 100 copies of his report "privately printed" and sent to survivors of his brigade. It is a matter of regret, Dudley wrote, "that General S. Meredith, our gallant and well beloved Commander, is not alive to prepare this important document himself, still the report may, I think, be said to be historically correct in its narration of the events of that decisive battle."

Of fourteen field officers, Dudley pointed out, nine were killed or wounded. Individual acts of heroism and gallantry "were the rule, and not the exception, among the officers and men. . . . All did their part manfully and well in this engagement, fully sustaining the reputation for steadiness and fearless devotion to duty, earned upon many hard fought fields, and the fear losses sustained by the brigade, on this one day, attest with what fidelity they discharged the trust imposed upon them."[8]

Chapter 32

The Chance of a Lifetime

F rank A. Haskell learned to soldier with the Iron Brigade. The former Vermont native and Madison, Wisconsin, lawyer returned to Gettysburg in November 1863 as an aide to General John Gibbon of the Second Corps. The two officers represented the Army of the Potomac at the dedication of a new soldier cemetery on the battlefield. At the time, Gibbon was stationed at Cleveland, Ohio, recovering from his Gettysburg wound and conducting light duty commanding a camp of drafted men. Their joint service began when Gibbon became the second commander of the Iron Brigade in May 1862; both were credited for turning the frontier volunteer regiments into an efficient fighting unit. When the general moved on to higher command, he took Haskell, the brigade adjutant, with him.[1] Gibbon and Haskell played key roles in the Second Corps' repulse of the Confederate charge on July 3, 1863, and both officers were anxious to once again see and examine the sprawling battlefield.

Haskell remained in Gettysburg with the wounded Gibbon after the Army of the Potomac left to pursue the retreating Confederate army. A few days after the battle he found Charles Fairchild among the new arrivals. An old friend from Madison, Charles was in town to care for his wounded brother, Colonel Lucius Fairchild of the 2nd Wisconsin. Fairchild, his brother said, was on the mend despite amputation of an arm in a community that was now "one vast hospital." Public buildings, churches, houses, barns, and sheds were full of "sick and wounded. Every open window shows a cot

Wisconsin Historical Society 25110

Lieutenant Frank Haskell
Adjutant, 6th Wisconsin Infantry

Frank Haskell was promoted to brigade adjutant by John Gibbon and when with Gibbon as an aide. His description of Pickett's Charge and Gettysburg became a classic when it was published long after his death at Cold Harbor in 1864 while colonel of the 36th Wisconsin.

and sometimes two or three. . . . But our victory has been the greatest of the war and all are happy."

The colonel was recuperating at the home of Reverend Charles F. Schaeffer of the Lutheran Theological Seminary, where he was carried by stretcher-bearers during the battle. "The family of Dr. Schaeffer, consisting of Mrs. S., & two daughters, are thorough practical Christians and as kind and attentive as possible," Charles Fairchild wrote home July 6, 1863. "Lushe [Lucius] occupies their back parlor—above—as large as one of the parlors at the University. His windows look out upon a pleasant garden. He is as jolly as a king & and when one don't look at the odd network of adhesive plaster that represents an army, seems perfectly well." From the window of his parlor room, the wounded colonel looked down upon the spot where his amputated arm had been buried in a tin box by Reverend Schaeffer immediately after the operation.[2]

Haskell rode into Gettysburg unsure of what he would find. "How different from the time we were there before," he wrote home on November 20, 1863. "The sights and sounds were all changed. Then it was sultry July—now it is somber November. – The leaves and harvests were then green and luxuriant—now they were yellow and sere, - then the sound of hostile cannon shook the earth—now the voices of women and children filled the air."

Haskell and Gibbon carried with them to display at a reception the Tiffany presentation flag given to the Iron Brigade by a group of Wisconsin, Michigan, and Indiana citizens. It was brought from Washington by W. Yates Selleck, Wisconsin's state agent. Haskell called it "the most magnificent flag I ever saw." The banner was made of "very heavy blue silk, with yellow silk fringe" and included the names of the five regiments and the brigade' battles: Gainesville, Bull Run, Antietam, South Mountain, Fredericksburg, and Gettysburg. "That Brigade is known to everybody and the flag was much noticed," Haskell wrote home with pride.

As for the Gettysburg observance, Haskell found the ceremonies and President Lincoln's remarks of little interest and did not even describe them. According to Gibbon, he and Haskell toured the battlefield after listening to the start of the main oration, but returned to the grounds in time to hear what he described as "Mr. Lincoln's touching speech."[3]

While the ceremonies concerned Haskell not at all, the same could not be said about the soldier cemetery. The combatants were buried hastily in the fields where they fell, he wrote, and if the bodies had not been interred and reburied the "places of their graves would soon be unknown, and the plow would have obliterated them." He continued:

> But what so appropriate for the soldier's rest as the spot where he died nobly fighting the enemies of the country—where perhaps the shout of victory went up with his spirit to Heaven—where his companions in arms, his survivors, had lovingly wrapped him in his blanket, and wet with brave men's tears, had covered him with the earth his blood had consecrated. . . . But no—these things were not to be. The skeletons of these brave men must be handled like the bones of so many horses, for a price, and wedged in rows like herrings in a box, on a spot where there was no fighting—where none of them fell!
>
> It may be all right, but I do not see it . . . but as it is now . . . we have instead a common, badly arranged grave yard, in which names, and graves, if designated at all, are as likely to be wrong as right. But read the newspapers—Every body says this is splendid, this making the 'Soldiers' Cemetery,' and I suppose it is.[4]

Frank Haskell was killed on June 3, 1864, leading the 36th Wisconsin near Cold Harbor, Virginia. His own burial site was in Portage, Wisconsin—far from his native Vermont or the field on which he fell.[5]

As the years after the battle passed, other Iron Brigade veterans also began to return to Gettysburg. Lucius Fairchild came in 1869 and was photographed with a group visiting the still incomplete national monument. After losing his arm in the battle six years earlier, he returned to Wisconsin a war hero, but rarely spoke of the injury. He didn't need to. His empty pinned left sleeve was a constant reminder to those who came in contact with him.

While his stump was healing in the months after the battle, he was bothered by phantom pain from the elbow, forearm, wrist, and hand of his missing arm. Troubled by an itch, he would absently scratch "only to find nothing there." The missing arm, he told friends and family, was "tired of being so constantly in the same position." Acting on a superstition that such discomfort was caused when an amputated limb was cramped or crooked, he had friends at Gettysburg disinter the tin box containing his arm from the garden near the Lutheran Seminary Building and sent to him by express. The pain gradually disappeared and Fairchild later admitted he was never sure whether the relief came from natural healing or the rearrangement of his amputated arm.[6]

Alexander Ivey of the 7th Wisconsin returned in 1885 amid troubled memories. He was in Pennsylvania getting fitted for a new artificial leg when he decided to journey to Gettysburg, where "twenty-two years and four months before, lost my leg in a little unpleasantness that occurred . . . on July 1st, 1863." He found the building where his leg was amputated and the yard in which the limb was buried. The site was now a lumberyard.

Wounded with the Iron Brigade Guard in the charge on the railroad cut, Ivey was carried to the town in an ambulance with a friend who died on the way. "My health was good, but suffering terribly with my broken leg, and I was, as you may suppose, exceedingly anxious for some surgeon to take it off; for I felt sure it was fractured too badly to be saved. . . . I was laid on a dissecting table . . . and when I awoke from the effects of the chloroform administered, I found I was to return to my friends a cripple for life." It was then, he realized, the true effects of war: "What we were liable to suffer for

Steve Victor

Colonel William W. Robinson
7th Wisconsin Volunteers

William Robinson (second from left) and other Iron Brigade veterans posed in front of the Iron Brigade monument at Gettysburg during the 25th anniversary of the battle in 1888. Robinson commanded the Iron Brigade after Sol Meredith was wounded.

the zeal and love we have for the dear old flag and our believed country and which we willingly sacrificed without grumbling, knowing that we only did our duty as every patriot and lover of his country ought to do, that it may live."[7]

Rufus Dawes of the 6th Wisconsin, Hollon Richardson, and his father-in-law, Colonel William W. Robinson of the 7th Wisconsin, joined Fairchild and other Wisconsin dignitaries at Gettysburg in the dedication of Wisconsin monuments June 30, 1888 on the battle's 25th anniversary. The delegation was gathering near a makeshift stand when a surprise visitor arrived: Confederate Lt. General James Longstreet. The Wisconsin men quickly gathered around the old general with greetings and handshakes.

"General, this looks very different from the scene of twenty-five years ago," offered Dawes.

"Yes, sir," replied Longstreet. "It reminds me of a camp meeting."

"Well, we'll soon be one," said one of the Wisconsin men.

"We are one now, sah, I think," said the general.[8]

The official notice of the event recommended that all living veterans of the Wisconsin Gettysburg regiments, "or of other organizations, and the patriotic citizens of the state, with their wives, sons and daughters, should, if they can afford the time and expense, join in the pilgrimage to this shrine of American liberty and be present at the dedication service. They will miss the chance of a lifetime if they do not." The excursion rail fare from Chicago to Washington and back were posted at $17.50 with three days in Gettysburg, one at Antietam, and two more in Washington.[9]

Hollon Richardson brought home to Chippewa Falls his own special souvenir of the day—an oak sapling. In 1900, when he moved to Keyport, Washington, he took the tree with him and planted it on the land where he and his family lived for the next sixteen years. The property was later acquired by the government and became the Keyport Naval Undersea Warfare Center; Richardson's home is formally Quarters 133. In 1960, a plaque was attached to the trunk of the large tree. It reads as follows:

> The Gettysburg Oak
> Transplanted from the famous Pennsylvania
> Battlefield by Civil War Hero Brigadier
> General Hollon Richardson of the 7th
> Wisconsin Vol. Infantry, who lived here from
> 1900 until his death December 24, 1916 at age 81.

Chapter 33

Glorious Remembrance

Gettysburg forever touched Charles McConnell, the young Irish immigrant who fought with the 24th Michigan of the Iron Brigade of the West. Somehow he escaped wounds and capture during his years in service. Like so many, he came to regard July 1, 1863, as one of the most significant days of his life. Immediately after the war, McConnell was more concerned about how to make a living and what his future might hold; there was little time to contemplate what was now the past. He moved to Chicago and became a wholesale druggist and over the years his friends watched him make and lose several fortunes. A careful observer, even in the latter stages of McConnell's life, could see the same erect carriage, steady eyes, and intelligence of the 21-year-old Detroit printer who enlisted in 1862.

By the time of Gettysburg he was a corporal, and he fired one of the last shots by his regiment in its epic confrontation with the 26th North Carolina. The ball felled a Confederate color bearer. He said he was one of only eight of the fifty-four men in his company still on their feet, and soon all were on the run for Gettysburg and the Union rally point. McConnell was promoted to color sergeant and flag bearer of the Michigan regiment on September 1, 1863.[1]

On February 11, 1865, outside Petersburg, Virginia, the 24th Michigan was ordered from the front to Baltimore and ultimately to Camp Butler, a draft rendezvous near Springfield, Illinois. One of its last duties was as part of the honor guard for the burial of assassinated President Abraham

Charles McConnell and officers
24th Michigan Infantry

Men of the 24th Michigan sit for a portrait. Charles McConnell (center) and Robert Gibbons (second from right) were two Detroit printers who enlisted as corporals July 24, 1862. McConnell was one of nearly 4,000 Irish immigrants who joined Michigan regiments.

Lincoln. A detachment of soldiers from the 24th Michigan met the train bearing the late president's body and escorted the coffin to the Illinois State House. The rest of the regiment was brought from Camp Butler by train May 4 and was given the place of honor at the head of the military escort, directly behind the hearse. The regiment marched "at slow time, company front, reversed arms," recalled one Black Hat. "The day was very warm and it was rather hard work." Lincoln was buried with great ceremony in Oak Ridge Cemetery. Military guards, including members of the Michigan regiment, were posted nearby until a permanent tomb and reinforced vault doors were installed over the next few weeks.[2] McConnell's regiment mustered out at Detroit June 30, 1865.

As the years passed, successful in business, McConnell began to return to his days as a young soldier and seek out old comrades. Although he did

Lucius Fairchild, Edward Bragg, and John Gibbon
Milwaukee 1880

Program of the 1900 Iron Brigade Association Reunion

These three officers of the Iron Brigade sat for a portrait during an 1880 soldier reunion in Milwaukee. Fairchild is on the left (note his empty sleeve), Bragg is standing, and Gibbon is on the right. It was at this reunion that veterans formed an Iron Brigade Association.

not attend Michigan Day at Gettysburg June 12, 1889, he became active in the Iron Brigade Association, an organization formed by veterans of the five regiments during a national reunion at Milwaukee in 1880. As a sign of his growing interest in his service and the occurrence of a Grand Army of the Republic reunion at Chicago, McConnell proposed and organized a gala 1900 "Reunion and Banquet of The Iron Brigade" at the Chicago Athletic Association on Monday evening, August 27, 1900—the night before the anniversary of the brigade's first major battle at Gainesville in 1862. The program listed "Sgt. Charles H. McConnell" as toastmaster and invited as a special guest was President William McKinley, who was detained in Washington and unable to attend. Other dignitaries on hand included governors and assorted Congressmen as well as former Iron Brigade Commander Edward S. Bragg of Wisconsin and Charles G. Dawes, representing his late father, Rufus Dawes of the 6th Wisconsin. The special embossed program for the evening carried the words to "The Song of the Iron Brigade," which was song with great enthusiasm by "Comrade Oscar B. Knight of Chicago" to the tune "Baby Mine." One verse read:

> And on Gettysburg's red field
> To the shock of battle steeled,
> Was the signet of their valor
> In the blood of hundred sealed,
> Dying steadfast by the banner which they bore

The song was "Written for Charles H. McConnell."

The evening included a dinner of boiled salmon, filet of beef, pineapple frappe and "roast spring chicken." It ended with the singing of "America."[3]

With the passing of the years, McConnell became very proud of his days in the Iron Brigade and the fighting he and his comrades had done at Gettysburg. In an effort to seek information on the 26th North Carolina, he penned and mailed a latter to Colonel A. M. Waddell of Wilmington, North Carolina. He directed McConnell to Colonel W. H. S. Burgwyn, whose brother, Colonel Harry K. Burgwyn, was killed leading the North Carolina regiment at Gettysburg against the 24th Michigan. Letters were exchanged and McConnell and his wife traveled to Richmond, Virginia, where Burgwyn met him. During the conversation, McConnell told how he fired one of the last shots by his company that brought down a color bearer of the 26th North Carolina. "Then you are the man who shot Colonel John R.

Program of the 1900 Iron Brigade Association Reunion

Iron Brigade Reunion Headquarters
Chicago 1900

This elaborate store front façade marked the headquarters for the 1900 reunion of the Iron Brigade Association organized in Chicago by Charles McConnell of the 24th Michigan, who made a fortune as a wholesale druggist.

Lane," replied Burgwyn with a smile. When McConnell expressed a "burning desire to know the man he almost mortally wounded," Burgwyn arranged a trip to North Carolina, where McConnell finally grasped the hand of the man he shot down four decades earlier. "Yes, I have come all the way from Chicago and brought my wife, for no other purpose than to grasp the hand of the gallant man I tried to kill and thought then that I had succeeded," McConnell told a reporter for the *Raleigh Post*.

The two old veterans talked about the fighting that had nearly annihilated the 24th Michigan and the 26th North Carolina. "The battle was nearing its close at Gettysburg and only 8 men of the 54 in our company of the 24th Michigan Regiment were left," remembered McConnell. "Our

Chicago Public Library 72-719

Charles McConnell
Gettysburg Monument of the 24th Michigan

Posing at the 24th Michigan monument at Gettysburg during the 40-year anniversary on July 4, 1903. The monument is close to where McConnell shot and wounded Lieutenant Colonel James Lane of the 26th North Carolina on July 1, 1863.

ammunition was exhausted but I had one cartridge left which was to be the last shot we fired in that engagement. As I loaded my rifle my lieutenant commander said, 'Charles, see that splendid color bearer, cannot you knock him over?' 'I have my last cartridge and I am going to try,' I replied, as I rested my rifle against a small tree and took careful aim at the man, who was waving his colors and shouting to his men. I fired, saw him fall and then hastened to join my comrades retreating through Gettysburg to Culp's Hill."[4]

Lane stepped forward and put his hand on McConnell's shoulder. "He is the man who shot me," said Lane, confirming the shot with corroborating details. "It was just as the battle ended and I had turned to cheer on my handful of men and waving our colors that the ball struck me." The old colonel raised his long black hair to display what the reporter described as "the ugly scar on his neck just below the base of the brain, where the well-nigh ball had pierced." The next two days were spent touring the area, including the old camp where the 26th North Carolina was organized and where Lane entered service as a private. The party also stopped at the state library to see the painting of the three colonels of the regiment: Zebulon Vance, who left the regiment in 1862 to become North Carolina governor; Harry King Burgwyn, killed on July 1; and John R. Lane. It was all very pleasant except for one incident when Lane's grandmother refused to allow McConnell into her home.[5]

On July 4, 1903, on the 40th anniversary of Gettysburg, McConnell, Lane, and W. H. S. Burgwyn met again on the battlefield where they and others posed for a camera in front of the monument to the 24th Michigan. McConnell also had one solo picture taken that shows his right leg lifted to the base of the monument, hat firmly on his head, and his eyes looking off to where the 26th North Carolina formed to begin its charge. Lane gave an emotional address to a gathering of Confederates. Year by year, he noted, the relentless temper of war was giving way to brotherhood and peace. "Your valor is coming to be regarded as the common heritage of the American nation," he told the aging veterans. As an example of the growing affection among veterans of both sides, Lane mentioned his own wounding at Gettysburg and pulled McConnell, standing nearby, to his side. "And this is the man that shot me," Lane told the crowd. McConnell responded with grace: "I thank God that I did not kill the gallant commander of the regiment whose list of casualties was greater than any other regiment in the Southern Army."

Old Foes Meet at Gettysburg
The 40th Anniversary July 4, 1903

Old foes stand near the monument of the 24th Michigan. They are, from left,
Lieutenant Colonel James Lane of the 26th North Carolina, W. H. S. Burgwyn,
and Charles McConnell of the 24th Michigan. Burwgyn's brother was the
colonel of the 26th North Carolina and was killed in the fighting. McConnell
seriously wounded Lane at the end of the fight, who assumed command after
the colonel fell.

The gathering ended, and the men parted. It was their last meeting. Lane died on December 31, 1908.[6]

In 1910, McConnell attended a small reunion of the Iron Brigade at the Milwaukee Soldiers Home. The twenty-one men were arranged in three rows for a photograph, one sitting on the ground, the second seated, and the third standing. In the last row, standing on the right side was Jerome Watrous, late of the 6th Wisconsin, well remembered for bringing up his train of ammunition at Gettysburg. McConnell was seated in the middle and over his left shoulder stood a veteran wearing what appears to be an old soldier coat, buttoned at the top, and the brigade's famous black hat, cocked at a rakish angle.

Iron Brigade Reunion 1910
Milwaukee

Veterans of the Iron Brigade met in reunion at the Milwaukee Soldiers' Home in 1910 and sat for this group photograph. Charles McConnell of the 24th Michigan is seated third from the right. Brigade Adjutant Jerome Watrous is standing on the far right. *Chicago Public Library 72.726*

Interior of the Iron Brigade Tent
50th Anniversary of Gettysburg

Veterans and visitors inside the Iron Brigade Reunion tent erected at the 50th anniversary of Gettysburg by Charles McConnell of the 24th Michigan. The tent called attention not only the service of his regiment, but the opposing 26th North Carolina and Pettigrew's Confederate Brigade as well.

A few months later, McConnell was appointed as an Illinois delegate to a committee preparing the 50th anniversary commemoration in Gettysburg for 1913. It would be the largest combined gathering of Civil War veterans since the war. More than 50,000 old soldiers attended, most of them staying in a large camp on the old battlefield. The encampment covered some 280 acres. More than 2,000 army cooks manned 173 field kitchens to provide rations. The reunion was scheduled for July 1-4, but first veterans trickled in as early as June 25.[7]

One of the highlights was a huge Iron Brigade tent erected in the camp grounds and paid for by Charles McConnell. Singled out for special attention at one session were large placards on each side of the stage for the "24th Michigan of the Iron Brigade" and the "26th North Carolina of Pettigrew's Brigade." The displays labeled the two brigades as "First at Gettysburg." A large American flag provided a stunning backdrop. It was in this tent that old veterans of the Iron Brigade met and embraced the equally aged veterans of the 26th North Carolina in "great reunion," recalled Watrous. The men gathered hear speeches and listened to entertainers such as John Pattee of Michigan, a veteran of the 24th Michigan now billed as "Colonel John A. Pattee" and his band, "Old Soldier Fiddlers of the Blue and Gray." The group included Pattee and two Union and two Confederate veterans. Everyone agreed it was a great success.

More than 400 survivors of the Iron Brigade registered at the tent. Meetings were held twice a day during the reunion, and 1,200 to 1,400 attended each session. A surviving photograph shows McConnell on the stage talking to a Confederate veteran who had ridden his horse inside the tent.[8]

George Fink of the 6th Wisconsin, who fought the battle as a 20-year-old newlywed was there, as was another member of his regiment named Levi L. Tongue of Hillsboro, a former county sheriff from back home in Vernon County. Jerome Watrous enjoyed himself immensely, taking notes for his newspaper stories as he talked with the old soldiers. George Eustice of the 7th Wisconsin, who fought beside Citizen John Burns a half-century before, bought souvenirs to take home to Gilroy, California. They included a commemorative badge, reunion book, and a chair whose wooden arms were made from a tree containing bullets fired during the battle.[9]

Many of the Gettysburg veterans attended, but so many others were sorely missed. Rufus Dawes had died in 1899 in Marietta, Ohio, of what some called "Soldier's Heart" caused by his war days. Gettysburg brigade

Stage at the Iron Brigade Tent, 50th Anniversary of Gettysburg. This photograph shows the stage inside the Iron Brigade Headquarters Tent at the 50th anniversary reunion at Gettysburg in 1913. Charles McConnell of the 24th Michigan (on stage in dark coat) poses with two visitors on horseback who appear to be Confederate veterans. *Chicago Public Library72-793-1*

Commander Sol Meredith found an early grave in Indiana in 1875. John Callis of the 7th Wisconsin died in 1898 of the effects of the rebel bullet lodged in his lung. J. P. "Mickey" Sullivan of the 6th Wisconsin died at Ontario, Wisconsin, in 1906 of old age and his lingering war wounds. Lucius Fairchild of the 2nd Wisconsin was placed in a grave with his amputated arm

Hollon Richardson of the 7th Wisconsin
Gettysburg 50th Anniversary Reunion 1913

He returned to the Gettysburg battlefield in 1913 for the 50th Anniversary Reunion. His father-in-law, Colonel William W. Robinson, who commanded the Iron Brigade during the fighting, had died a decade earlier in Seattle, Washington. *Steve Victor*

in Madison in 1896. After a long illness, Clayton Rogers—the lieutenant who arrested a general—was buried in 1900 at Hayward, Wisconsin, by a small community that deeply mourned his passing. Henry Morrow was interred with military honors in a grave in his wife's hometown at Niles, Michigan. Colonel Samuel Williams had been shot dead in the Wilderness in early May 1864, leaving behind a wife and six children. Colonel William W. Robinson died on April 27, 1903, at Seattle, Washington. He was 86.[10]

The next year, President McConnell issued a call for another Reunion of the Iron Brigade Association to be held September 1, 1914, at Detroit. Among those featured were to be Pattee and his fiddlers, "Major R. H. Hendershot, 'The Drummer Boy of the Rappahannock' and his son," as well as "Capt. Jack Crawford, the poet Scout," and various vocalists to "sing the old war songs that used to rouse us to enthusiasm in the days that tried our souls—and haven't lost their power to do so again, fifty years later! Some of them now draw tears, of which we are not ashamed."

"Come on boys," McConnell's letter urged, "bring your families! First care will be taken of such, and if there is any room left the citizens generally are welcome. Let this most probably last reunion of the Iron Brigade be its greatest." And it was the last major meeting of veterans. The association met on and off until the middle of the 1920s, but only a thinning handful of surviving Black Hats were able to attend.[11]

McConnell also planned to build a monument at Gettysburg for the Iron Brigade with the right face memorial for the 24th Michigan and the left face for the 26th North Carolina. In a letter to Colonel Burgwyn he promised $150,000 for the memorial. Unfortunately, McConnell died on March 18, 1916, without adding the provision to his will. He was 75. His obituary reported that he was a man who had made and lost several fortunes. No mention was made of his service at Gettysburg.[12]

In March 1939, as the world was gearing up for another more terrible war, newspapers in Wisconsin, Indiana, and Michigan published the obituary of the Iron Brigade. The last known survivor of the famous brigade—William Riley of the 6th Wisconsin—had died at the Soldier Home in Milwaukee. A handful of editorials praised the service of the brigade, and a feature article appeared in a few papers.

Twenty months later, in November of 1940, Josiah E. Cass of Eau Claire stepped forward and claimed to be the last of the surviving Black Hats. He said he was fifteen at the time of his enlistment in the 7th Wisconsin in 1864, and quoted an examining officer as telling him, "I think you are lying to me. I don't think you are 18 years old. But I think you'll make a darn good solider. Go in and sign up."[13]

Cass told *The Milwaukee Journal* in an interview printed November 24, 1940, that he was probably overlooked as an Iron Brigade survivor because he never joined the Grand Army of the Republic or any other patriotic organizations. "There were too many parades," he said, "and I didn't care for them." He died a few months later.

An Unknown. July 1, 1997

*W*hat may be the last body of a fallen soldier recovered from the battlefield at Gettysburg was buried July 1, 1997, with a military color guard, the playing of "Taps," and a final fired salute. The remains were discovered in 1996 in a washout after a rain on the edge of the railroad cut west of town. It was the same area where the Iron Brigade of the West and other regiments fought on July 1, 1863.

The skeletal fragments—parts of a skull, lower jaw and teeth, shoulder blade, backbone, pelvis, ribs, arms, a lower leg, and a foot—were of a man in his 20s who died of a gunshot wound to the head. It was not determined whether he was a Federal or Confederate. The skull fracture, however, was indicative of a smoothbore wound of the type of musket carried by several Confederate companies during the July 1 fighting—including those who comprised the 2nd Mississippi. Underwear buttons (but no brass military buttons) were found nearby, which indicates that his uniform may have been stripped from his body.

The fallen soldier was buried in the unknown section of the Soldiers' National Cemetery. In attendance were the widows of two Civil War soldiers: Daisy Anderson, 96, of Denver, Colorado, and Alberta Martin, 90, of Elba, Alabama. Mrs. Anderson's husband, Robert Ball Johnson, served in the 125th U.S. Colored Troops after fleeing slavery. Mrs. Martin's husband was William Jasper Martin of the Confederate 4th Alabama Infantry, Army of Northern Virginia.

Pulitzer Prize-winning historian and author James McPherson, one of the speakers at the event, explained that it did not really matter whether the fallen soldier fought for the Union or Confederacy. "His death in the fighting at the Railroad Cut one hundred and thirty-four years ago," spoke McPherson, "abolished that distinction between enemies." The end of the Civil War in 1865, he concluded, "made all soldiers Americans again, whether they had worn the blue or the gray."[1]

Appendix 1

Regiments in the Iron Brigade

The First Army Corps disbanded January 23, 1864. Its units were absorbed into the First Brigade, Fourth Division, Fifth Army Corps. The Fourth Division became the Third Division August 24, 1864.

2nd Wisconsin (October 1861 to June 11 1864)

Became Wisconsin Independent Battalion on June 11, 1864, and served as division provost until November 30, 1864, when it was merged into the 6th Wisconsin as Companies G and H.

6th Wisconsin (October 1861 to July 1865)

7th Wisconsin (October 1861 to July 1865.)

19th Indiana (October 1861 to October 18, 1864.)

The 7th Indiana merged into the 19th Indiana on September 23, 1864, and the 19th merged into 20th Indiana on October 18, 1864, and left the brigade.

24th Michigan (October 8, 1862 to February 10, 1865.)

Battery B, 4th U.S. Artillery (October 1861 to April 1865)

Accepted volunteers from the 2nd, 6th, 7th Wisconsin, 19th Indiana and 23rd and 35th New York in January 1862. Assigned First Corps Artillery Brigade 1863. All volunteers had been returned to regiments by August 1864).

167th Pennsylvania Infantry (July 18, 1864 to August 1863)

Organized November 11 to December 6, 1862. Mustered out August 12, 1863.

1st New York Sharpshooters (August 1863 to 1864)

(Four companies raised, A, B, D and H).

7th Indiana (August 1863 to September 1864)

Mustered September 13, 1861. Mustered out September 20, 1864. Veterans merged into 19th Indiana on September 23, 1864.

76th New York Infantry (January 1865 to February 1865)

143rd Pennsylvania Infantry (August 25, 1864 to February 10, 1865)

Organized October 18, 1862, mustered out June 12, 1865.

149th Pennsylvania Infantry (August 25, 1864 to February 10, 1865)

Organized August 1862, mustered out June 24, 1865.

150th Pennsylvania Infantry (August 25, 1864 to February 10, 1865)

Organized September 4, 1862, mustered out June 23, 1865.

91st New York Infantry (March 3, 1865 to May 1865)

Mustered September 12, 1861, mustered out July 3, 1865.

Appendix 2

Iron Brigade Counties

Company	The 2nd Wisconsin	County
A	Citizen Guard	Dodge
B	La Crosse Light Guards	La Crosse
C	Grant County Grays	Grant
D	Janesville Volunteers	Rock
E	Oshkosh Volunteers	Winnebago
F	Belle City Rifles	Racine
G	Portage City Guards	Columbia
H	Randall Guards	Dane
I	Miner's Guards	Iowa
K	Wisconsin Rifles	Milwaukee
K*		Dane and Milwaukee

*Replaced original Company K in January 1862 after the original was detached and converted to heavy artillery.

The 6th Wisconsin		
Company		County
A	Sauk County Riflemen	Sauk
B	Prescott Guards	Pierce
C	Prairie du Chien Volunteers	Crawford
D	Montgomery Guards	Milwaukee
E	Bragg's Rifles	Fond du Lac
F	Citizens' Corps	Milwaukee
G	Beloit Star Rifles	Rock
H	Buffalo County Rifles	Buffalo
I	Anderson Guards	Juneau and Dane
K	Lemonweir Minute Men	Juneau

The 7th Wisconsin		
Company		County
A	Lodi Guards	Chippewa/Columbia
B	Columbia County Cadets	Columbia
C	Platteville Guards	Grant
D	Stoughton Light Guard	Dane
E	Marquette County Sharp Shooters	Marquette
F	Lancaster Union Guards	Grant
G	Grand Rapids Union Guards	Wood
H	Badger State Guards	Grant
I	Northwestern Tigers	Dodge/Waushara
K	Badger Rifles	Rock

The 19th Indiana		
Company		County
A	Union Guards	Madison
B	Richmond City Greys	Wayne
C	Winchester Greys	Randolph
D	The Invincibles	Marion
E	Delaware Greys	Delaware
F	Meredith Guards	Marion
G	Elkhart County Guards	Elkhart
H	Edinburgh Guards	Johnson
I	Spencer Greys	Owen
K	Selma Legion	Delaware

The 24th Michigan		
A-K	No known company names	Wayne County

Appendix 3

List of names registered at the Iron Brigade Headquarters Tent
at Gettysburg Celebration, July 1 to 4, 1913

2nd Wisconsin Infantry, Iron Brigade

Philo B Wright, Co. C, Grand Rapids, Mich.
Frederick Pettigrew, Co. C, Hampton, Neb.
Geo H. Otis, Co. I, Monona, Ia.
Henry Burghardt, Co. I, Union, Ia.
Geo. Williams, Co. I, Miffin, Wis.
Geo. Jencks, Co. I, Mineral Point, Wis.
John T. Metcalf, Co. G, U.S. Soldiers Home, Washington, D.C.
Lucien Wilkins, No. 412, Co. G, Enid, Okla.
Frank Wilkins, Co. H, 645 H. St. Washington, D.C.
L.K. Lockman, Co. B, 631 S. 11th St. La Crosse, Wis.
E. Markle, Co. B, R.F.D. La Crosse, Wis.
J.B. Rand, Co. B, 839 Princeton, Portland, Ore.
T.B. Rand, Co. B, 111 E. 72nd, Portland, Ore.
Alexander F. Lee, Co. D, Janesville, Wis.
Newton Biddle, Co. H.
S.A. Nickols, Vol. G, Tipton, Calif.
E.K. Bucham, Co. H, 2624 Ricker Ave. Evart, Wash.
Geo. L. Powers, Co. A, Puyallup, Wash.
Daniel Schunall, Co. B, Beloit, Wis.
Edward Moscrip, Co. E, Harrisburg, S.D.
George Folmady, Co. G, P.O. Box 6, Minneiska, Wabasna Co. Minn.
R.H. Branton, Co. A, Minneapolis, Minn.
Wm. H. Scofbonrow, Co. I, Monroe, Wis.
Rudolf Stoll, Sharon, Walworth Co. Wis.
Chauncey Bartholemew, Pasaic, N.J.
A.E. Haven, Co. B, Faribault, Minn.

Jos. Bock, Co. C, Lancaster, Wis.
Wm. Frawley, Co. C, Lancaster, Wis.
G.H. Easterbrook, Co. B, National Home, Wis.
A.E. Baker, Co. H, Evansville, Wis.
F.H. Liscum, Co. C, Geneseo, Kans.
Hugh Evans, B. B. #2, Amherst, Wis.
Lafayette Pursley, B. B. #2, Farmland, Ind.
Christian Schlosser, Co. I, Ottawa, Ill.
William H. Dow, Co. I, 3132 Cedar Ave. Minneapolis, Minn.
Sidney Wells, Co. H, Lodi, Wis.
W.H. Harris, Co. B, Minneapolis, Minn.
G.M. Woodward, La Crosse, Wis.
Fred. J. Pischel, Leader of Band, 1440 Warner Ave. Chicago
Lewis A. Briggs, Co. E, Appleton, Wis.
Ed. Lorrie, Wilmot, Wis.
J.E. Northup, Co. H, Marshalltown, Ia.

6th Wisconsin Infantry

B.H. Krebs, Co. E, Muskegon, Mich.
J.A. Watrous, Co. E, Milwaukee, Wis.
C. Morton, Co. G, Evart, Mich.
John F. Buherer, Co. F, Wisconsin
Loring B.T. Winslow, Co. I, Janesville, Wis.
John Davidson, Junction City, Kans.
Lyman D. Holford, Co. C, Tulare, Cal.
Ferdinand Martin, Co. H, Trempealeau, Wis.
George K. Clements, Co. B, Gilroy, Cal.
E.E. Moran, Co. B, San Diego, Cal.
Theodore Huntington, Co. D, Newcastle, Cal.
H.L. Childs, 2723 Warren Ave. Chicago
Eli. Rockwell, Co. I.
S.R.W. Faulkner, Co. C, Cadott, Wis.
Andrew Gallup, Co. K, Sharon, Wis.
Albert H. Rolfe, Co. K, La Forge, Wis.
Cyrus Spooner, Co. K, Monroe, Wis.
Christian F. Beltz, Co. F, Aberdeen, Wash.
Isaac Merssman, Co. F, Alpha, Minn.
Edward Lind, Co. I, 818 North 43 St. Seattle, Wash.
Franklin Wilcox, Co. K, Mauston, Wis.
Alfred R. Withrow, Co. C, National Home, Milwaukee
J.H. Kocher, Co. I, R. 5-6, East Jordan, Mich.

7th Wisconsin Infantry, Iron Brigade

Albert C. Morse, Co. F, Lancaster, Wis.
A.D. Rood, Co. K, Paw Paw, Mich.
John Blackburn, Co. F, Lancaster, Wis.
Richard Huffill, Co. F, Fennimore, Wis.
Benj. F. Moore, Co. H, Janesville, Wis.
A.S. Eayes, Co. D, Lincoln, Neb.
Curtis Chandler, Carter, Nebr.
John Draggs, Co. H, Fennimore, Wis.
Washington Russell, Co. H, Fennimore, Wis.
E. Whitmore, Co. H, Lancaster, Wis.
John W. Bruce, Co. K, Wis. Vets. Home.
George Eustis, Co. F, Gilroy, Cal.
Ed. W. Parker, Co. A, Sutherland, Ia.
Hollon Richardson, Co. C, Keyport, Wash.
Horace Ripley, Co. B, Deerfield, Mo.
Henry Bucham, Co. B, Neligh, Nebr.
John Walrod, Co. A, Lents, Ore.
Philip Brother, Co. F, Neilsville, Wis.
W.G. Henman, Co. E, Marshfield, Wis.
Eben B. Dunlap, Co. A, Cambria, Wis.
S.C. Waterman, Co. I, Plainfield, Wis.
H.C. Perkins, Co. I, Hay Springs, Nebr.
Philip H. Walker, Co. D, Claremont, Mo.
John Harrison, Co. E, Comfrey, Minn.
John Geargeson, Co. A, Tamarack, Minn.
Joseph Heathcock, Co. H, Mineral Point, Wis.
John Cavanaugh, Co. C, Spokane, Wash.
Julius A. Englike, Co. B, Columbus, Wis.

19th Indiana Infantry, Iron Brigade

John M.F. Spitler, Co. G, Dimondale, Mich.
H.C. Marsh, Hospital Steward, Muncie, Ind.
David White, Co. D, La Fayette, Ind.
A.J. Wood, Co. F, Ridgeville, Ind.
Julius Waldschmidt, Co. G, Vinton, Ia.
Wm. Everett, Co. D, South Bend, Ind.
F.B. Leonard, R. "11", Oklahoma City, Okla.
T.C. Leonard, Chautauqua, Kans.
A.I. Wood, Co. C, Ridgeville, Ind.
David R. Fort, Co. B, Indianapolis, Ind.
Henry Kirby, Co. C.

Patterson McKinney, Co. B, Converse, Ind.

W.H. Murray, Co. K, Selma, Ind.

Jesse E. Jones, Co. B, Richmond, Ind.

Joseph B. Bennett, Co. B, Richmond, Ind.

Saml. A. De Kover, Co. K, Selma, Ind.

John W. Knight, Co. K, Parker, Ind.

Ezra Hackman, Co. K, Rossville, Ill.

John W. Poland, Co. K, Muncie, Ind.

Lafayette Pursley, Farmland, Ind.

24th Michigan Infantry

Charles H. McConnell, Co. B, 122 N. State St. Chicago

John A. Pattee, Co. K, 1492 Broadway, New York

Henry R. Bird, Co. B, 217 F. St. N.W. Washington, D.C.

James R. Lewis, Co. G, Belleville, Mich.

Augustus Hussey, Co. I, 6340 Drexel Ave. Chicago

Asa Joy, Co. C. Plymouth, Mich.

Samuel T. Hendricks, Co. G, Salina, Kans.

J.N. Bartlett, Co. D, Trenton, Mich.

William Hamilton, Co. G, Jackson, Mich.

William Hamilton, Co. G, Ovid, Clinton Co. Mich.

Edwin Martin, Co. S [Co. G. in records], 232 East 9th St. Traverse City, Mich.

Ignaz Holton, Co. A, 1542 Townsend Ave. Detroit, Mich.

John R. Brown, Co. K, Flat Rock, Mich.

Samuel Brown, Co. G, 112 Greeley St. Detroit, Mich.

John Proctor, Co. E, Corbett, N.C.

Oscar S. Phelps, Co. K, Pensacola, Fla.

George R. Walsh, Co. C, 164 N. State St. Rockford, Ill.

Richard Conner, Co. B, Detroit, Mich.

George L. Packard, Co. D, R. 3, Greenville, Mich.

Steven D. Smith, Hospital Dept. Olympia, Wash.

S.R. Kingsley, Co. D, Romulus, Mich.

Isaac L. Greusel, Co. D, Detroit, Mich.

Robert C. Bird, Co. D, Romulus, Mich.

Charles E. Maynard, Co. K, Plymouth, Wis.

Patrick Gasley, Co. K, Smiths Creek, Mich.

Charles Gasley, Co. K, Smiths Creek, Mich.

M.S. Weed, Co. C, Plymouth, Mich.

Patrick B. Gorman, St. Cloud, Minn.

H.W. Hughes, Co. C, Harrison, Mich.

Aldrich Townsend, Co. D, East Jordan, Mich.

Geo. W. Haigh, Co. D, Mankato, Mich.

Walter Niles, Co. A, Croswell, Mich.

Chas. Rills, Co. H, Caro, Mich..
C.D. Durfee, Co. C, Joplin, Mo.
Henry Brown, Co. B, 3078 N. Bates, Saginaw, Mich.
Frederick DeLosh, Co. B, National Home, Wis.
James O. Palmer, Co. D, Greenville, Mich.
John Nolett, Co. H, Bay City, Mich.
Albert O. Williams, Co. K, Toledo, Oh.
John Malcho, Co. H, Detroit, Mich.
Geo. A. McDonnell, Co. A, Detroit, Mich.
S.F. Smith, Flat Rock, Mich.

Battery B, 4th U.S. Artillery

Jack Cook, 1123 Park Pl. N-E, Washington, D.C.
James Davidson, Capt. U.S.A.
Mrs. Jas. Davidson, Passaic, N.J.
C.E. Harris, 1723 West 5th St, Duluth, Minn.

26th North Carolina Infantry, Pettigrew's Brigade, Army of Northern Virginia (CSA)

C.A. Trente, Lenoir, N.C.
I.A. Lineback, 26th N. Car. Troops.
G.T. Mickey, " " " "
David C. McPhearson, Alamont Co., Burlington, N.C.
G.P. Arawell, Co. H, Carthage, N.C.
J.T. Henler, Co. K, R.F.D. #1, Wadesboro, N.C.
S.A. Benton, Co. K, Wadesboro, N.C.
Wm. Gulledge, Co. H, McOlums, N.C.
John Stewart McCain, 26th Regt. N.C. Vol.
Maxhaw Jackson Grayes, Co. B, Wilson company.
Thos. Purnett, Co. G, Faison, N.C.
C.A. Tunte, Co. F, Lenoir, N.C.
John Q. Carter, Co. G, Ore Hill, Chatham Co. N.C.
E.W. Flake, Co. K, Poketon, N.C.
John R. Jarman, Co. K, Wadesboro, N.C.
Jesse Gaddy, Co. K, Rock River, N.C.

Other North Carolina and Confederate Soldiers

A.H. Gibboney, Wytheville, Va.
J.Q. Siles, Puxico, Mo.
Dr. J.A. Pierin, Co. E. 11th N.C. Inf, Corbett, N.C.
J.H. Rose, Co. K. 47th N.C, Inf. Burlington, N.C.

P.H. Boone, Co. K. 47th N.C. Inf, Burlington, N.C.

J. McGarrison, Co. K. 47th N.C. Inf, Burlington, N.C.

A.J. Glover, Co. A. 47th N.C. Inf, Bailey, N.C.

H.H. High, Co. D. 47th N.C. Inf, Bailey, N.C.

W.E. Kyle, Pettigrew's Brigade, Fayetteville, N.C.

A.D. McGill, Ransom's Brigade, Fayetteville, N.C.

A.H. Hevnor, Co. F, W. Va.

William Reed, McConnellsburg, Fulton County, Pa.

Wm. Love, Co. K, 47th N.C, Pettigrew Brigade

Dr. J. A. Pisiny, Co. E, 11th N.C, Pettigrew Brigade

W.W. Boswell, 3rd N.C., Pettigrew Brigade, Burlington, N.C.

James Malone, 15 N.C., Pettigrew Brigade Graham, N.C.

I.N. White, Co. F, 11th N. Car., Hertford, N.C.

Wm. A. Lamb, 22nd N.C. Co. I, Bloomingdale, Ind.

F.M. Hinton, Co. E, 50th N.C., O'Neil, N.C.

J.W. Wooter, Co. H, 1st N.C., Newbern, N.C.

S.R. Street, Co. K, 2nd N.C., Newbern, N.C.

Allen A. Perry, Co. C, 52nd N.C., Hertford, N.C.

John C. McInnis, Co. I, 52nd N.C., Largo, Fla.

A.E. McNeil, Co. G, 24th N.C., Fayetteville, N.C.

J.A. Dwaim, Co. G, 47th N.C., Greensboro, N.C.

D.C. Waddell, Co. G, 11th N.C., Greensboro, N.C.

M.N. Bissett, Co. A, 4th N.C., Bailey, N.C.

Miscellaneous Registration

J.M. Stone, Co. C, 67th N.Y. Inf., Woodbury, Mich.

John A. Booker, Co. D, 21st Va.

Geo. E. Albee, Capt. U.S.A.

Edward White, Co. D, 13th Pa. Cav., Hollidaysburg, Pa.

John B. Mallott, Co. A, 3d Del., Milford.

Henry Nately, Co. G, 29th Wis., Saginaw, Mich.

D.L. Brink, 9th Michigan, Weedsport,

George W. Sharp, Co. H, 23rd N.J., Moorestown, N.J.

James B.O. Holback, Co. L, 147th Pa., McKeesport, Pa.

C.S. Smith, Co. D, 67th Pa., Tylersburg, Pa.

Wm. H. Good, Co. E, 147th Pa., Pittsburgh, Pa.

Ellis Pugh, 137th P.V., Philadelphia, Pa.

Esaac Wolfe, K, 13 Pa., Cav. Kerrmoor, Pa.

Andrew Strong

W.A. Lourman, Co. D, 1st Mich. Cav., Elsie, Mich.

Noah N. Webster, Co. F, 2500 Webster St, Berkley, Calif.

Isaac P. Simkins, 24th N.J.V. Inf, Penns Grove, N.J.

Wm. Myers, Co. 121 N.Y, Little Falls, N.Y.

Benjamin Conlin, 54 P.V. Penn. Inf, Camden, N.J.
Fred Graff, 26 N.Y. Inf, 83g MC. 9 N.Y. 1 Utica, New York
Jacob J. Gilder, Co. G, 13th N.Y., Danville, N.Y.
John J. Williams, Co. R. R. No. 1, Hornell, N.Y.
George P. Holt, Co. G, 47 N.Y.V., New Haven, Conn.
John Scott Davison, Passaic, N.J.
Mrs. H.W. Tooker, Passaic, N.J.
Helen M. Davison, " "
Capt. J.W. Crawford, 56 West 104th St, N.Y.
Mrs. E. L. Cox, 56 West 104th St., N.Y.
Isaac Baty, Co. A. 7th Vt., Concord, N.H.
Mrs. Isaac Baty, 7th Ind. Bat.
Hiram D. Kittie, 120th N.Y.S.V.
Charles Van Streenbergh, Kingstron, Ulster Co. N.Y.
C.H. Barrows, whose uncle served in 6th Wis.
Jacob A. Drew, Co. F, Lancaster, Wis.
T.S. Smith, Co. H, 7th N.Y., Seattle, Wash.
Gen. George P. Scriven, Chief U.S. Signal Corps Washington, D.C.
Wm. Mitchell, Capt. General Staff U.S. Army Milwaukee, Wis.
Augela F. Small, Washington, D.C.
Mildred Curran,   "   "
Frank B. Rockwood, Chicago
Charles A. Miller, Co. F, 3rd Regt. Mich., Vt.
James V. Wood, Co. University Place, Nebr.

A copy of this registry list is sent to every name thereon as a Souvenir of the glorious reunion of the Blue and Gray on the Battle Field of Gettysburg, on the Fiftieth Anniversary of the battle.

Fraternally,

Charles McConnell, Prest. Iron Brigade Association for the Gettysburg Reunion, No. 122 North State Street, Chicago.

Notes

Chapter 1

1. *Janesville*, Wis., *Daily Gazette*, June 28, 1861; Nathaniel Rollins, diary, Wisconsin Historical Society.

2. Long afterward, Wisconsin veterans established a "Survivors Association of the Battle of Bull Run, July 21, 1861." Sherman refused to take a role. It was organized in 1895 and met several times, but never attracted a large following. For a full and excellent account of the 2nd Wisconsin at Bull Run see Alan Gaff, *If This is War* (Dayton, Ohio: 1991).

3. Jerome A. Watrous, *Appleton*, Wis., *Crescent*, August 20, 1861.[3]

4. *Mineral Point Tribune*, October 22, 1861; [Jerome Watrous], "Gen. John Gibbon," *Milwaukee Sunday Telegraph*, December 7, 1879; J.O. Johnson, "Army Reminiscences," *Milwaukee Sunday Telegraph*, November 30, 1884.

5. John Gibbon, *Personal Recollections of the Civil War* (New York: 1928), 37

6. Lance J. Herdegen, *The Men Stood Like Iron: How the Iron Brigade Won Its Name* (Bloomington & Indianapolis: 1992).

7. McClellan told the story to John Callis of the 7th Wisconsin October 8, 1868, at a reception for the general at the Continental Hotel in Philadelphia. The version cited appeared in the program for the 1900 reunion of the Iron Brigade Association in Chicago.

8. Tom Clemens, "'Black Hats' off to the original 'Iron Brigade,'" *Columbiad*, Vol. 1, Number 1, Spring 1997, 46-58.

9. *Cincinnati*, Ohio, *Daily Commercial*, September 22, 1862. "The cat is out of the bag. The game is ended. Wisconsin, Indiana and Michigan have been wearing a mask. It is indeed a sad, sad exposure," wrote S.E. Chandler of the 24th New York to a Washington newspaper in claiming his brigade was "the old original Iron

Brigade." In copying the letter, Editor Jerome Watrous of *The Milwaukee Sunday Telegraph*, late of the 6th Wisconsin, admitted with a written smirk July 5, 1885 that there "was a brigade in the Potomac army whose name sounded a little like 'Iron Brigade,' but the spelling was markedly different. It was known as the 'I-run-brigade'."

10. Hugh Perkins to "Dear friend Herbert" September 21, 1862. The Perkins letters were printed in *The Christian Science Monitor*, April 6, 1983, and April 7, 1983. He served in the 7th Wisconsin.

11. Rufus R. Dawes, *Service With The Sixth Wisconsin Volunteers* (Marietta, Ohio: 1890), 43.

Chapter 2

1. Clayton E. Rogers, "Shooting a Deserter," *Milwaukee Sunday Telegraph*, May 24, 1885; [Howard J. Huntington], *Milwaukee Sunday Telegraph*, March 1, 1885; E.R. Reed, "Shooting a Deserter," *Milwaukee Sunday Telegraph,* April 12, 1885; James P. Woods court-martial record, cited Alan Gaff, *On Many of Bloody Field* (Bloomington and Indianapolis, Indiana: 1996), 248-249.

2. John A. Kress, "At Gettysburg," St. Louis *Missouri Republican,* December 4, 1886.

3. Frank Wilkeson, "Coffee Boilers," *Milwaukee Sunday Telegraph*, August 1885; Rufus Dawes to Mary Beman Gates August 6, 1863, Rufus Dawes Papers, Wisconsin Historical Society; Dawes, *Service,* 197.

4. Jerome A. Watrous, "Three of a Kind—Reminiscences," *Milwaukee Sunday Telegraph,* April 6, 1882.

Chapter 3

1. Rufus Dawes to Mary Beman Gates April 13, 1863; Dawes, *Service,* 132, 118. Dawes wrote: "General Hooker was much admired in the army. He was grand in his personal appearance and military bearing but his assignment to the command did not restore confidence to the country."

2. Dawes, *Service,* 125, 132; O.B. Curtis, *History of the Twenty-Fourth Michigan of the Iron Brigade* (Detroit: 1891), The order sent to the First Division detailing the shape of the badges and coloring can be found in the regimental papers of the 7th Wisconsin Infantry, Wisconsin Historical Society.

3. Edward S. Bragg to his wife May 22, 1863, Edward Bragg Papers, Wisconsin Historical Society; Dawes, *Service,* 142. Bragg was colonel of the 6th Wisconsin Infantry.

4. George H. Otis, *Second Wisconsin Infantry*, Alan D. Gaff, editor (Dayton, Ohio: 1984) 83. The Otis history was serialized in 11 parts in 1880 issues of the *Milwaukee Sunday Telegram*, Walker S. Rouse to *Oshkosh*, Wis, *Northwestern*, June 11, 1863, cited in Mark R. Karweick, editor, *Ever Ready, A History of the Oshkosh Volunteers – Co. E, 2d Regiment of Wisconsin Volunteer Infantry, 1861-1865*, unpublished manuscript.

Chapter 4

1. James P. Sullivan, "Old Company K," *Milwaukee Sunday Telegraph*, May 16, 1886.
2. Dawes, *Service*, 45, 314; Jerome A. Watrous, *Milwaukee Sunday Telegraph*, September 27, 1885.
3. James P. Sullivan, "Old Company K," *Milwaukee Sunday Telegraph*, May 16, 1886; Also see William J.K. Beaudot and Lance J. Herdegen, editors, *An Irishman in the Iron Brigade: The Civil War Memoirs of James P. Sullivan, Sergt., Company K, 6th Wisconsin Volunteers* (New York: 1993).
4. Rufus Dawes to Mary Gates June 12, 1863; Dawes, *Service*, 151; Mary Frances (Dawes) Beech, "Mary Beman Gates Dawes," Walton Ferris, compiler, *Dawes-Gates Ancestral Lines, a Memorial Volume Containing the American Ancestry of Mary Beman Gates-Dawes*, vol. 2 (Privately printed, 1931): "A Memoir, Rufus R. Dawes," (New York, 1900).
5. Dawes, *Service*, 129; Rufus Dawes to Mary Gates May 30, 1863; Dawes, *Service*, 146.
6. James E. Northup to his father June 23, 1863, cited in *Drifting to an Unknown Future: The Civil War Letters of James E. Northup and Samuel W. Northup*, Robert C. Steensma, editor (Sioux Falls, South Dakota: 2000), 69.

Chapter 5

1. Dawes, *Service*, 136.
2. J[ames] P. Sullivan, "Charge of the Iron Brigade at Fitzhugh's Crossing," *Milwaukee Sunday Telegraph*, September 30, 1883; Sullivan, *Irishman*, 74-79.
3. Sullivan, *Irishman*, 76-77. Hancock was shot and killed November 27, 1864, by a Confederate guard while a prisoner at Salisbury, North Carolina.
4. Dawes *Service* 136.
5. Earl Rogers, "Fitz-Hugh Crossing," *Milwaukee Sunday Telegraph*, August 7, 1887.
6. Edward Bragg to Rufus Dawes, no date; Sullivan, *Telegraph*, September 30, 1883.

7. Walter Rouse to the *Oshkosh* Wis., *Northwestern,* "Camp near White Oak Chapel, Va., May 15, 1863."

8. Philip Cheek and Mair Pointon, *History of the Sauk County Riflemen, Known as Company "A" Sixth Wisconsin Veteran Volunteer Infantry, 1861-1865* (No publisher: 1909), 64-65. The private was Bodley Jones of Baraboo, Company A, 6th Wisconsin. Trumbull enlisted May 10, 1861 from Lemonweir and was killed in action April 29, 1863.

9. Cheek and Pointon, *Sauk County,* 64-64.

10. Timothy Webster, letter, to a friend, May 9, 1863, Navarro College's Pearce Civil War Collection; Cheek and Pointon, *Sauk County,* 64-64.

11. Sullivan, *Telegraph,* September 30, 1883; Bragg to Dawes, no date.

12. Rogers, *Telegraph,* August 7, 1887. Conklin enlisted June 1, 1861, and Ruby the same date. Ruby had also been wounded at Antietam. Stedman also enlisted June 1, 1861, and was wounded at Antietam. He died July 17, 1863, of wounds received at Gettysburg. *Roster of Wisconsin Volunteers, War of the Rebellion, 1861-1865,* Vol. 1 (Madison, Wisconsin: 1886) 529, 531, 532.

13. *Wisconsin Newspaper Volumes* (10 vols.), Contemporary newspaper clippings organized by regiment and containing letters of Wisconsin soldiers from *Milwaukee Daily News, Milwaukee Sentinel, Wisconsin State Journal,* Madison; *Beloit Free Press; Janesville Daily Gazette, Mauston Star; Home Intelligencer,* Mineral Point, and others. Wisconsin Historical Society, Vol. 8, 408; Thomas Walterman, *There Stands "Old Rock:" Rock County, Wisconsin, and the War to Preserve the Union* (Friendship, Wisconsin: Rock County Historical Society, 2001), 254

14. Cheek and Pointon, *Sauk County,* 64-65, 212.

15. Kress, *Republican,* December 4, 1886.

16. Cheek and Pointon, *Sauk County,* 65.

Chapter 6

1. James M. McPherson, "To Conquer a Peace? Lee's Goals in the Gettysburg Campaign," *Civil War Times.* March/April 2007.

2. Ed. E. Bryant, "Our Troops!," *Milwaukee Sunday Telegraph,* October 26, 1879; Curtis, *Twenty-fourth,* 466. The quotation is from Phil Cheek of the 6th Wisconsin to a Grand Army of the Republic meeting in Detroit.

3. Jerome Watrous, "Of One Day's Work," *Milwaukee Telegraph,* October 28, 1893; Dawes, *Service,* 101; Lucius Shattuck to his brother, October, 17, 1862, Lucius Shattuck Papers University of Michigan Historical Library, Ann Arbor. The feeling against the Michigan regiment was also fueled by a rumor the men enlisted for bounty money. Of course, it was not true.

4. Alan T. Nolan, *The Iron Brigade* (Macmillan, 1961), 20-21, 223- 224.

5. Lucius Shattuck to family June 21, 1863.

Chapter 7

1. Lance J. Herdegen and Sharon Murphy, *Four Years with the Iron Brigade: The Civil War Journal of William Ray, Seventh Wisconsin* (New York: Da Capo, 2001), 184-185; Rufus Dawes to Mary Gates, June 15, 1863, June 18, 1863, June 21, 1863; Adolphus Shepard to his mother, June 11, 1863. Shepard was a member of the 24th Michigan and was killed in action serving with Battery B of the 4th U.S. Artillery.

2. Grayson, [Loyd G. Harris], "Fredrick City to Gettysburg," *Milwaukee Sunday Telegraph*, January 25, 1885.

3. General Order No. 24, Order Book First Brigade, First Division, First Army Corps, 7th Wisconsin Records, National Archives.

4. Dawes, *Service*, 183; Kress, *Republican*, December 4, 1886; Sullivan, *Irishman*, 77, 78, 95-97, 102.

5. Grayson [Loyd G Harris], "Asleep At His Post," *Milwaukee Sunday Telegraph*, June 6, 1880; Rufus Dawes to Mary Gates June 24, 1863; Dawes, *Service*, 155-156.

6. Curtis, *Twenty-fourth*, 150.

7. Dawes, *Service*, 158.

8. Rufus Dawes to Mary Gates, June 18, 22, 24, 27, 1863; Dawes, *Service* 157; Ray, *Iron Brigade*, 184.

9. Lucius Lamont Shattuck to family June 24, 1863; Charles Walker *Diary*, Institute for Civil War Studies; Ray, *Iron Brigade*, June 30, 1863; Amos Rood, memoir, Wisconsin Historical Society. Rood, who enlisted at Milwaukee, wrote the memoir between 1889 and 1892 and recopied it with added remarks in 1918 based on the diaries he kept during his service. Inside Walker's journal book was a thin pamphlet from one of the Christian societies. It concerned a matter close to the soldier heart—letters from home: "Keep him posted in all the village gossip, the lectures, the courtings, the Sleigh rides, and the singing school. . . . Tell him every sweet and brave and pleasant and funny story you can think of. Show him that you clearly apprehend that all this warfare means peace, and that a dastardly peace would pave the way for speedy, incessant and more appearing warfare."

10. Augustus Buell, "The Story of a Cannoneer," *National Tribune* (October 10, 1889, through April 3, 1890, with additional articles on May 15, May 22 and June 12, 1890; Augustus Buell, *The Cannoneer: Story of a Private Soldier* (Washington: 1890), 62. Buell's account has been questioned. Milton W. Hamilton, "Augustus C. Buell, Fraudulent Historian," *Pennsylvania Magazine of History and Biography 80* (1956) 478-492, documented Buell, in fact, was never carried on the Battery B rolls and did not enlist until August 21, 1863, six weeks after Gettysburg, and then joined the 20th New York Cavalry. Author Silas Felton has since shown Buell's account included solid information and received written support by veterans who were in the battery. Felton concluded Buell's articles were probably based on extensive oral interviews with Charles Henry Moore, a regular army soldier who served with the battery and

was present at Gettysburg. To support Felton's conclusion was the fact that Buell published his account in a popular nationally read "old soldier" newspaper *The National Tribune.* A fraudulent account would have quickly been uncovered. In addition, many minor details of Buell's account are also supported by several obscure Wisconsin sources. See Silas Felton, "Pursing the Elusive Cannoneer," *The Gettysburg Magazine*, Volume 9, 33-39, and Silas Felton, "Postscript To: Pursuing the Elusive 'Cannoneer," *The Gettysburg Magazine*, Volume 19, 53-56. The private was Frank Nobels, Stoughton Light Guard, Company D, 7th Wisconsin. He enlisted from Rutland in August 10, 1861, and served in the battery from June 8, 1862 until January 1864. *Wisconsin Roster* 553.

11. Kress, *Republican*, December 4, 1886. Kress was an aide to General James Wadsworth.

12. Walker Diary; Ray, *Iron Brigade*, 191; James P. Sullivan, *Mauston* [Wis], *Star*, March 22, 1883.

13. J[erome]. A. Watrous, "How They Celebrated: A July Fourth Story," *Milwaukee Telegraph*, July 2, 1892.

14. Jerome A. Watrous, "Old Days in Washington," *Milwaukee Telegraph*, January 14, 1890.

15. Charles S. Wainwright, *A Diary of Battle: The Personal Journals of Colonel Charles S. Wainwright, 1861-1865,* Allen Nevins, editor (New York: 1962) 232.

Chapter 8

1. Curtis, *Twenty-fourth,* 24-51

2. Wainwright, *Diary*, 206.

3. Jerome Watrous, *Milwaukee Sunday Telegraph*, September 7, 1884.

4. Adolphus Shepherd to Mother, Sisters and Brothers, February 15, 1863 and April 21, 1863.

5. John Cook, manuscript, "Cook's Time in the Army," John Cook Papers, Wisconsin Historical Society.

6. Buell, *Cannoneer*, 30-31; Edward Bragg to J.S. Driggs, May 15, 1898; "Where he lost it," *Milwaukee Sunday Telegraph*, July 11, 1880. Driggs was a Battery B volunteer. The article quotes Gibbon as saying in a July 1, 1880, letter, from Fort Snelling, Minnesota, where he was stationed, that James Stewart confirmed Tartar lost his tail about "ten feet from where Captain Smead, Fifth Artillery, was killed."

Chapter 9

1. Charles A. Stevens, *Berdan's U.S. Sharpshooters in the Army of the Potomac, 1861-1865* (St. Paul, Minnesota: 1892), 277-278. Stevens' brother was George H. Stevens, lieutenant colonel of the 2nd Wisconsin, who was killed at Gettysburg.

2. Gibbon, *Recollections,* 37. "A great deal of the prejudice against me as a regular officer was removed when the men came to compare their own soldier appearance and way of doing duty with other commands, and although there were still some malcontents, who chafed under the restraints of a wholesome discipline and would have chaffed under any, they were gradually reduced in number and influence.":

3. Michael H. Fitch, *Echoes of the Civil War as I Hear Them* (New York: 1905), 330.

4. Dawes to Mary Gates, August 6, 1863; Dawes, *Service*, 197.

5. Otis Howard, "The Campaign and Battle of Gettysburg," *Battles & Leaders of the Civil War,* Vol. 5, Peter Cozzens, editor. (Chicago: 2005), 323-324. The article first appeared in the July 1876 issue of the *Atlantic Monthly.*

6. Curtis, *Twenty-fourth,* 155; [James P. Sullivan], "Mickey, of Company K,*"* *Milwaukee Sunday Telegraph*, December 20, 1884; *The War of the Rebellion: A Compilation of the Official Records of the Union and Confederate Armies*, Series 1, Volume 27, Part 3, 416-417; A study concerning ammunition issued to the First Corps determined the 8,700 soldiers expended an average of about 68 rounds per man. Dean S. Thomas, *Ready . . . Aim . . . Fire . . . Small Arms Ammunition in the Battle of Gettysburg* (Biglerville, Pennsylvania, 1981), 13.

7. *Milwaukee Sentinel,* August 17, 1861, January 20 and January 27, 1862. The Austrian Lorenz was the second most common imported shoulder arm used by both sides in the Civil War. It was designed by Lieutenant Joseph Lorenz and introduced in 1854. It was generally regarded a sound weapon. The Union reported purchases of 226,924 pieces, and the Confederacy as many as 100,000.

8. [James P. Sullivan] Mickey, of Company K, "The Charge of the Iron Brigade at Gettysburg," February 13, 1883, *Mauston*, Wis., *Star.*

9, Ray, *Iron Brigade,* February 16, 1862, and June 19, 1862. "We got everything pertaining to the new guns, which are as follows. First a brass Stopple, a very pretty one, a good wormer and a good screwdriver and wrench. They are in one piece."

10. For a full description see Howard Michael Madaus, "The Uniform of the Iron Brigde at Gettysburg July 1, 1863," Appendix III, Lance J. Herdegen and William J.K. Beaudot, *In The Bloody Railroad Cut at Gettysburg* (Dayton, Ohio: 1990).

11. R. K. Beecham, *Gettysburg: The Pivotal Battle of the Civil War* (Chicago: 1911), 120. Beecham was with the 2nd Wisconsin.

12. Earl M. Rogers, "The 2nd, of Fifty-sixth—Which?" *Milwaukee Sunday Telegraph,* June 22, 1884. Rogers quotes his brother, Clayton, an aide to Wadsworth, as saying the gap was "one mile" due to Meredith's "delay in giving orders…"

13. Sullivan, *Star,* "Mickey, of Company Co. K" February 13, 1863; "Grayson" [Loyd Harris] *Milwaukee Sunday Telegraph*, February 15, 1885; George Fairfield Diary, July 1, 1863, George Fairfield Papers, Wisconsin Historical Society.

Chapter 10

1. [Jerome A. Watrous], "A Badger Traveler," *Milwaukee Sunday Telegraph,* December 22, 1878; *Soldiers and Citizens Album of Biographical Record, Vol. II* (Chicago, 1888), 578-82; Hollon Richardson family records.

2. Edward J. Nichols, *Toward Gettysburg: A Biography of General John F. Reynolds* (College Station, Pennsylvania:1958); 75-76, 220-223; Edward P. Adams to his father from Washington, July 3, 1863, Edward R. Adams Papers, Carroll University Institute for Civil War Studies; Wainwright, *Diary,* 227.

3. Credit for withdrawing the pickets is given to Lieutenant Clayton Rogers of the 6th Wisconsin, an aide to General Abner Doubleday. See Lance J. Herdegen, "The Lieutenant Who Arrested a General," *Gettysburg Magazine* (January 1991), 25-32.

4. Wainwright, *Diary,* 218; Beecham, *Gettysburg,* 120

5. For a full description of Reynolds' career, see Nichols, *Toward Gettysburg;* Lance J. Herdegen, "John F. Reynolds and the Iron Brigade," *Giants in Their Tall Black Hats: Essays on the Iron Brigade,* Alan T. Nolan and Sharon Eggleston Vipond, editors (Bloomington, Indiana: 1998), 101-112; Beecham, *Gettysburg,* 71.

Chapter 11

1. Watrous, *Telegraph,* September 26, 1896; [Harris], *Telegraph,* March 11, 1883; *Janesville* Wis. *Daily Gazette,* July 10, 1862.

2. [Harris], Telegraph, December 20, 1884; George Fairfield Diary, George Fairfield Papers, Wisconsin Historical Society; Rufus R. Dawes to John B. Bachelder, March 18, 1868; Dawes, *Service,* 164; John W. Bruce, "Lieutenant Bruce Relates His Experiences at Gettysburg After Being Shot Through the Body," *Milwaukee Sunday Telegraph,* January 23, 1881; Rufus R. Dawes, "Align on the Colors," *Milwaukee Sunday Telegraph,* April 27, 1890. The *Telegraph* account was written earlier, but Editor Jerome A. Watrous held the copy apparently to reproduce sketches of the maneuver that Dawes sent with the article. Bruce was a second lieutenant with Company K, 7th Wisconsin.

3. This flag has been restored and is held by the Wisconsin Veterans Museum in Madison.

4. One Wisconsin orator called the flags "sacred colors" and priceless relics—symbols of sacrifice and bravery as well as Wisconsin's "power and grandeur." But Jerome Watrous, who served his four years in the 6th Wisconsin, was the most eloquent. He spoke for all the Badger veterans when he was called to make the dedication address for a new Grand Army of the Republic Hall in the state capitol building where the soiled, shot-ripped banners were to be displayed. "Through our dim eyes, we can see these old flags as they appeared in our camps of instruction, as

they went with us upon great reviews, as they went with us in long marches, as they went into battles with us, and were a constant inspiration," he told the gathering. "It was in those days when we were boys or young men that we first began to understand what those flags, what our beautiful national emblem, means. It was in those early days in our experience in the war that we learned to love the stars and stripes, all of the stars, all of the stripes—everything about the dear old flag of our regiment; our flag, wherever it might be. There was a thrill whenever we saw it; it was a great part of us when the war ended." The old soldiers "love the old flags," Watrous said. "We followed them in victory and in defeat; we were with them in great demonstrations; we marched under them after the great victory had been won." Jerome Watrous, "Program for the Dedication of Grand Army memorial in the Capitol, Madison, Wisconsin, June 14, 1918," Wisconsin Veterans Museum, Madison.

5. Dawes, *Telegraph*, April 27, 1890; [Harris] *Telegraph*, February 15, 1885; Sullivan, *Telegraph*, December 8, 1884.

6. James P. Sullivan, *Mauston*, Wis. *Star*, February 13, 1883; Otis, *2nd Wisconsin*, 83-84; Cheek and Pointon, *Sauk County*, 70.

7. Edward Bragg of the 6th Wisconsin made the comment in a speech to an Army of the Potomac reunion at Chicago. The copy of the address was not dated. Edward Bragg Papers, Wisconsin Historical Society.

8. Jerome Watrous, in the August 15, 1880, edition of The *Milwaukee Sunday Telegraph*, wrote of the McClellan incident and added: "This news had the effect to bring out as hearty cheers as that army ever indulged in. It is doubtful any army commander in our late war was more popular with his men than George B. McClellan, and yet when he became a candidate for president—the candidate of a party that said the war was a failure, his old soldiers did not give him their united votes." Sullivan, *Telegraph*, December 20, 1884.

Chapter 12

1. Earl M. Rogers, "The 2nd, of Fifty-sixth—Which," *Milwaukee Sunday Telegraph*, June 22, 1884. Rogers quoted his brother, Clayton, an aide to Wadsworth, as saying the distance was "one mile" and was caused by Sol Meredith's "delay in giving orders…"

2. Henry Heth, "Why Lee Lost At Gettysburg," *Battles and Leaders of the Civil War, Vol. 5*, Peter Cozzens, editor, Chicago: 2002), 364-373. The article first appeared in the September 22, 1877, issue of the *Philadelphia Weekly Times*. Heth's account of going to Gettysburg to seek shoes has been discredited.

3. The troopers were not, as is often claimed, using the multi-shot repeating Spencer carbine, but were carrying single-shot, breech loading carbines made by Sharps, Burnside, Smith and others. They were able to fire two or three times faster

than a muzzle-loaded weapon, but the effective range was short—only 200 to 300 yards.

4. Charles H. Veil, *The Memoirs of Charles Henry Veil*, Herman J. Viola, editor (New York: 1993), 28-30.

5. George Meade, *The Life and Letters of George Gordon Meade*, Volume II, editor George Gordon Meade (New York: 1913), 35-36; Edwin B. Coddington, *The Gettysburg Campaign* (New York: 1968), 267.

6. Cornelius Wheeler, Reminiscences of the Battle of Gettysburg," *2nd Wisconsin*, 283-284. Legate enlisted April 22, 1861, and was promoted to sergeant major April 1, 1863. *Wisconsin Roster*, 371. Williams enlisted April 22, 1861, *Wisconsin Roster*, 372.

7. Michael E. Stevens, editor, *Glory: Robert Beecham's Civil War from the Iron Brigade to the Black Regiments* (Madison, Wisconsin: 1998), 71-72. Beecham's memoir first appeared in the *National Tribune*, a weekly published at Washington, D.C., and aimed at veterans. It was serialized between August 14 and December 18, 1902, under the title "Adventures of an Iron Brigade Man."

Chapter 13

1. Including a stint at Prairieville Academy, now Carroll University in Waukesha, Wisconsin.

2. See Sam Ross, *The Empty Sleeve: A Biography of Lucius Fairchild* (Madison: The State Historical Society of Wisconsin for the Wisconsin Civil War Centennial Commission, 1964)

3. For a detailed description of the march of Archer's Brigade's to Gettysburg and the subsequent fighting along Willoughby Run see Marc and Beth Storch, "What A Deadly Trap We Were In," *Gettysburg Magazine*, January/1992, 13-27.

4. Lysander Cutler to Gov. Andrew Curtain of Pennsylvania, November 5, 1863, Copy, Gettysburg College Civil War Institute.

5. E. R. Reed, "A Private's Story," The *Milwaukee Sunday Telegraph*, June 12, 1887; Beecham, *Gettysburg*, 62. Reed had been captured at First Bull Run and returned to the army several months later.

6. "The 19th Indiana at Gettysburg: The Thrilling Story of a Great Regiment in a Great Battle. Deathless Glory of its Color Bearers," Indiana State Library; Howard Michael Madaus and Richard H. Zeitlin, *The Flags of the Iron Brigade* (Madison, Wisconsin: 1997) 32-33.

7. George H. Otis, *The Second Wisconsin Infantry*, Alan D. Gaff, editor (Dayton, Ohio: 1984), *Beecham, Gettysburg*, 72

8. Reed, *Telegraph*, June 12, 1887; Helmes survived the war.

9. Cheek and Pointon, *Sauk County*, 73; Lucius Fairchild, unfinished manuscript, Lucius Fairchild Papers, Wisconsin Historical Society; Jerome A.

Watrous, *Richard Epps and Other Stories* (Milwaukee: 1906), 10; C. Tevis, *The History of the Fighting 14th [Brooklyn]* (Brooklyn: 1911), 132.

10. There is a sorrowful postscript to Reynolds' death. While preparing the general's body, the family discovered a ring with the inscription "Dear Kate." It was a name the general had never mentioned. As his body lay in the parlor of his sister's home in Philadelphia, a young woman in black came to the front door. My name, she said, was Catherine Mary "Kate" Hewitt. She told the family how she and Reynolds had met in California three years earlier and planned to marry after the war. She had followed him when he was transferred to the U.S. Military Academy at West Point and had attended the Academy of the Sacred Heart in Torresdale, Pennsylvania. The couple had decided, she said, that if anything happened to him during the war, she would forsake the world and enter a convent. "Kate" soon entered the Sisters of Charity Catholic Convent at Emmitsburg, Maryland. She remained in touch with the Reynolds family until 1868, when she left the convent. Veil, *Memoirs*, 29; Coddington, *Gettysburg*, 269; Steve Sanders, "Enduring Tales of Gettysburg: The Death of Reynolds," *Gettysburg Magazine*, No. 14 January/1996, 27-36: Charles Veil to D. McCopnaughy, April 7, 1864, Gettysburg College Civil War Institute, copy Gettysburg National Military Park Library; Cornelius Wheeler, "Reminiscences of the Battle of Gettysburg," Otis, *Second Wisconsin*, 282; W.B. Murphy to Rufus Dawes, June 20, 1892; Nichols, *Toward Gettysburg*, 211-212. Also see Kent Gramm, *Gettysburg: A Meditation on War and Values* (Bloomington and Indianapolis: 1999).

11. "Alexander Hughes, A Sketch of a Wisconsin Solider Who Has Won a High Place in Dakota," *Milwaukee Sunday Telegraph,* May 20, 1887; Rood, memoir, 60. Hughes enlisted May 24, 1861, at Otsego. He mustered out September 1, 1864, his term expired. *Wisconsin Roster* 546. Hughes was a prominent attorney when the article was written.

12. Mansfield's Report, OR 43, 273-274; Robinson's Report, OR Series 1, 43, 279; Morrow's report, OR 43, 267; 19th at Gettysburg; Andrew Wood Pension file, cited, Gaff, *Bloody Fields*, 256; Ray, *Iron Brigade*, 191.

13. John B. Callis to John Bachelder, *The Bachelder Papers: Gettysburg in Their Own Words*, Vol. I, David L. and Audrey J. Ladd, editors (Dayton, Ohio, 1994); "Dick Hutfill and the Flag," *Lancaster Herald*, reprinted in the *Milwaukee Sunday Telegraph*. No date. Huftill enlisted August 19, 1861, and was mustered out September 1, 1864, term expired. Webster Cook, Beetown, enlisted August 19, 1861. He was wounded in 1864 and mustered out July 3, 1865. *Wisconsin Roster,* 559, 561.

14. Madaus and Zeitlin, *Flags*, 9-12.

15. William Lowry Morse, *Grandad and The Civil War*, printed privately for the Morse Family and friends, 1994. 39, 121-123. Morse was in Company F of the 7th Wisconsin. Philander Bracket Wright, the color bearer of the 2nd Wisconsin, was Morse's cousin. Wright's information was taken from a Civil War memoir he wrote

and presented to family members in 1921. He enlisted from Tafton April 22, 1861, and had previously been wounded at Gainesville. He was discharged May 25, 1864, disability. *Wisconsin Rosters*, 356.

16. Lucius Fairchild, unpublished and undated manuscript, Fairchild Papers; Morse, *Grandad*, 122-123; Madaus and Zeitlin, *Flags*, 31-32; Reed, *Telegraph*, June 12, 1887. Davison mustered out June 23, 1864, term expired, and Brisbois was absent wounded when the regiment mustered out. *Wisconsin Rosters*, 368, 365.

17. Daniel Burton enlisted at Potosi May 20, 1861. He previously had been wounded at First Bull Run. Otto Ludwig enlisted at Lancaster April 20, 1861. *Wisconsin Rosters*, 354-5.

18. Morse, *Grandad*, 122-123; Beecham, *Gettysburg*, 69.

19. Reed, *Telegraph*, June 12, 1887; Rood, memoir, 62.

Chapter 14

1. *Confederate Veteran*, 1900, 65; John W. Busey and David G. Martin, *Regimental Strengths and Losses, at Gettysburg* (Hightown, New Jersey: 1986), 291.

2. Maloney enlisted at Madison May 22, 1861. He was killed later July 1, 1863. Wisconsin *Roster*, 366; Beecham, *Glory*, 72-73; "Osseo," "The Surrender of Gen. Archer," *Milwaukee Sunday Telegraph*, February 4, 1883.

3. William H. Harries, "The Sword of General James J. Archer," *Confederate Veteran*, July, 1911. Harries, an officer with the 2nd Wisconsin, reported in 1911 the sword was in the possession of Dailey's widow who was living at Council Bluff, Iowa; D.B. Daily [sic] to Bachelder, March 24, 1890.

4. Beecham, *Gettysburg* 1911, 67. In his earlier account of Gettysburg, "Adventures of an Iron Brigade Man," written around 1900 for *the National Tribune*, a weekly paper aimed at veterans, Beecham was more careful about his criticism of Dailey, who was still alive at the time. He did not mention Dow's earlier encounter with Archer. Dailey's own memory was that when "the sullen General was subdued," he approached: "General Archer appealed to me for protection from Maloney. I then requested him to give me his sword and belt, which he did with great reluctance, saying that courtesy permitted him to retain his side arms." Dennis B. Dailey to Abner Doubleday, March 24, 1891, *The Bachelder Papers: Gettysburg in Their Own Words*, David L. and Audrey J. Ladd, editors (Dayton, Ohio: Morningside. 1995), Vol. II, 1807. Archer was imprisoned at Johnson's Island in Ohio. He was exchanged and returned to the Army of Northern Virginia in August 1864. Always frail and suffering from ill-health, he sickened and died on October 24, 1864.

5. Rufus R. Dawes to John Krauth, April 20, 1885. Krauth was secretary of the Gettysburg Association.

6. "Grayson" [Loyd G. Harris], "The Iron Brigade Guard at Gettysburg," *Milwaukee Sunday Telegraph*, March 22, 1885.

7. Sullivan, *Telegraph*, December 20, 1884; [Albert V. Young], "A Pilgrimage," *Milwaukee Sunday Telegraph*, April 22, 1888; [Jerome A. Watrous] "Some Premonitions," *Milwaukee Sunday Telegraph*, July 27, 1895.

8. Rufus R. Dawes to John B. Bachelder, March 18, 1868; Earl Rogers to Jerome Watrous, undated; Dawes, *Telegraph*, April 27, 1890.

9. Captain J.W. Pierce, *New York at Gettysburg*, Vol. III, 990-994, 1004.

10. Dawes, *Telegraph*, April 27, 1890; [Harris], *Telegraph*, March 22, 1885; Fairfield Diary, July 1, 1863; George Fairfield to Jerome A. Watrous, undated; Dawes, *Service*, 166; R.L. Murray, *First on the Field: Cortland's 76th and Oswego's 147th New York State Volunteer Regiments at Gettysburg* (Wolcott, New York:1998) 27.

11. Lance J. Herdegen, "The Iron Brigade and John Reynolds," *Giants in Their Tall Black Hats: Essays on the Iron Brigade*, Alan T. Nolan and Sharon Eggleston Vipond, editors (Bloomington and Indianapolis: 1988), 101.

12. OR Series 1, 27, 246. The report of Abner Doubleday.

13. Dawes, *Telegraph*, April 27, 1890.

14. [Young], *Telegraph*, April 22, 1888.

15. Dawes, *Telegraph*, April 27, 1890; Dawes, *Service*, 167. The injured and confused animal had a bullet lodged under her skin behind the left shoulder blade and Dawes said later: "Woe to the man who felt it, as her temper had been spoiled."

16, Dawes, *Telegraph*, April 27, 1890; Dawes, *Service*, 167; [Jerome A. Watrous], "Gettysburg," *Milwaukee Sunday Telegraph*, November 26, 1879.

Chapter 15

1. Dawes, *Telegraph*, April 27, 1890; [Harris], *Telegraph*, March 22, 1885; Sullivan, *Telegraph*, December 20, 1884.

2. Sullivan, *Telegraph*, December 20, 1884, Rufus Dawes to Bachelder, March 18, 1868; [Young] *Telegraph*, April 22, 1888; [Harris] *Telegraph*, March 22, 1885.

3. Sullivan, *Telegraph*, December 20, 1884.

4. Sullivan, *Telegraph*, May 9, 1886.

5. Dawes, *Service*, 29.

6. Around Polleys was a color guard containing Corporals William Day of Patch Creek, Company C; C. L. Jones of Mauston, Company I; Charles Mead of Newark, Company G; Francis Deleglise of Appleton, Company E; Milo G. Sage of Delafield, Company B; Arland F. Windsor of Summit, Company K, and Clarence E. Bullard of Menomonie, Company B. Dawes, *Service*, 131. Regimental General Order 23 named Polleys, Company H, as color bearer, and Regimental General Order No. 11, March 25, 1863, listed the members of the color guards. The National flag carried by the 6th Wisconsin has been restored and is held by the Wisconsin Veterans Museum in Madison.

7. [Harris] *Telegraph*, March 22, 1885. Harris was bitter against the 95th New York and 14th Brooklyn, for not joining the charge: "The Ninety-fifth N.Y. did rally and re-form their regiment and deserve great praise for it, but they never joined the left of the 6th. That place was occupied by the 'Iron Brigade Guard.'... They failed to respond and the 'truth of history' compels me to state that 6th, with the brigade guard, charged, singly and alone."

8. [Harris] *Telegraph*, March 22, 1885. Earl M. Rogers to Jerome Watrous, undated; Dawes, *Service*, 168.

9. Rufus R. Dawes, "Sketches of War History," *Military Order of the Loyal Legion of the United States, Commandery of the State of ohio, War Papers*, Vol. 3 Reprinted in Rufus R. Dawes, *Service with the Sixth Wisconsin Volunteers* (Dayton, Ohio: Morningside, 1984), 351; Dawes, *Telegraph*, April 27, 1890.

10. Schildt was knocked out of active service for several months, but would again join his German Company F as captain near the end of the war. Born in Prussia in 1820, his family moved to Brunswick and he saw six years of service with the Brunswick Army. He migrated in 1847 to Canada and finally to New York State and then in 1858 or 1859 to Iowa County in Wisconsin where he took up farming. Henry, at age 41, with several small children to care for, moved his family to Mazomanie in Dane County and enlisted as a private in the German Milwaukee Citizens' Corps, Company F of the 6th Wisconsin Infantry. His son, Andrew, enlisted in the 6thWisconsin in early 1864. He told the enlisting officer he was 15 and a farmer, but in truth he was five months shy of his 15th birthday. He served all the major battles of 1864 and 1865 and mustered out with his regiment—a 16-year-old veteran. Young Schildt did not return home. From 1866 to 1872, he worked as a cowhand in Texas, and then moved on mining camps in Nevada and California. In 1882, he was living on the Blackfoot reservation in Montana Territory where he courted a young Blackfoot girl named Nellie. The family history says the two were "married by a Methodist minister when he was on a buffalo hunt with a party of hunters from Fort Benton, Montana." The couple had seven children. Andrew Schildt died October 21, 1925 and was buried at his ranch home west of Browning, Montana. His father was buried at Mazomanie, Wisconsin.

11. George Fairfield to Jerome Watrous, undated; Frank Wallar to Earl Rogers in *Milwaukee Sunday Telegraph*, March 22, 1885.

12. William Remington, *Milwaukee Sunday Telegraph*, April 29, 1883. His account was dated December 17, 1882; Cornelius Okey, *Milwaukee Sunday Telegraph*, April 29, 1883.

13. John O. Johnson, "One Rebel Flag," *Milwaukee Sunday Telegraph*, July 17, 1887.

14. Lewis Eggleston of Shiocton came into the regiment as a drummer, but soon assumed soldier duties. His friend, David Anderson of Minneapolis, was

remembered as a "rough-looking man with a shaggy head of hair." He was nicknamed "Rocky Mountain" for his pre-war travels.

15. Earl Rogers, *Milwaukee Sunday Telegraph*, July 29, 1883; Cheek and Pointon, *Sauk County*, 47. Pointon and Cheek wrote in their history of the Sauk County Riflemen that Wallar told them: "Bodley Jones of A Company had made for the flag in the charge and had captured it and had it in his possession when killed. I grabbed it as Jones fell and carried it back and surrendered it to our proper officers, and I got the medal of honor for the capture. But if he had not been killed he and not I would have the medal."

16. Earl Rogers to Jerome Watrous, undated.

17. W.B. Murphy to Dr. F.A. Dearborn, Nashua, N.H., June 29, 1900, Edward S. Bragg Papers, Wisconsin Historical Society. "I was about fifty paces East of the cut, and on the side toward Gettysburg, and I and my color guard were about ten paces south of the railroad. There was no cut there at all; the ditch was not more than two feet deep where I passed over the railroad. Our regiment stopped in the railroad for protection," Murphy wrote.

18. Wallar, *Telegraph*, July 29, 1883. Wallar was presented a Congressional Medal of Honor in 1864 for capturing the flag.

19. [Harris] *Telegraph*, March 22, 1883; Dawes, *Service*, 169. I.F. Kelly to Rufus Dawes, August 2, 1892

20, George Fairfield to Jerome Watrous, undated; Joseph Marston, *Milwaukee Sunday Telegraph*, April 24, 1881

21. Sullivan, *Telegraph*, December 20, 1885. The target of the thrown sword was probably A.H. Belo of the 55th North Carolina. "One officer, seeing me, threw his sword at me and said: 'Kill that officer, and we will capture that command.' One of my men, however, picked him off and we were able to get out of the railroad cut after a severe struggle," Belo wrote. Belo, *Confederate Veteran*, 165-168. The article was based on a talk by Belo before the Sterling Price Camp at Dallas, Texas, January 20, 1900.

22. Dawes, *Service*, 173. Dawes said about 1,000 dropped muskets lay in the bottom of the railroad cut and that the 95th New York "took prisoners, as did also the 14th Brooklyn."

23. Dawes, *Service*, 168. Rufus Dawes to Aug. Gaylord, Adjutant General, State of Wisconsin, July 19, 1863: William W. Dudley, 19th Indiana, in his "official report" on the Iron Brigade at Gettysburg, listed 22 soldiers in the Brigade Guard as wounded, including the two officers. William W. Dudley, *The Iron Brigade at Gettysburg: 1878, Official Report of the Part borne by the 1st Brigade, 1st Division, 1st Army Corps* (Cincinnati, Ohio, privately printed, 1879), 15.

24. John Kellogg, letters, to John B. Bachelder, November 1, 1865, and March 31, 1868. Earl Rogers, letter, to Jerome Watrous.

25. Sullivan, *Telegraph*, December 20, 1884.

Chapter 16

1. John A. Blair, letter, October 31, 1890, to Dawes, W.A. Murphy to Rufus Dawes. Dawes wrote: "Adjutant E.P. Brooks buckled on one of the captured swords, and he still retains it, but the other six were given to a wounded man and delivered to our chief surgeon, A.W. Preston. The enemy, when they took the town, captured and hospital and the swords. No discredit to the doctor is implied, as his hands were full of work with wounded men." Dawes, *Service*, 170.

2. [Jerome Watrous] "Talking over Old Times," *Milwaukee Sunday Telegraph*, November 25, 1883

3. Marston, *Telegraph*, April 24, 1881; R.W. Leavell to Captain J.H. Marston, May 12, 1881.

4. Jerome A. Watrous, "Soldier Stories," *Milwaukee Telegraph*, November 24, 1894.

5. Dawes, *Service*, 170-172; Sullivan, *Telegraph*, December 20, 1884; I.F. Kelly to Rufus Dawes, August 21, 1892. In his letter, Kelly told Dawes: "How you ever got through without being killed is more than I can understand, as you were always in front in every fight. . . . Always looking after the interests of your men and officers. Never asking them to go where you did not lead. Perfectly cool under fire. A brave leader of as noble a band of patriots as ever wore the blue and fought under the stars and stripes."

6. Wainwright, *Diary*, 232-233.

7. Clayton E. Rogers, "Gettysburg Scenes," *Milwaukee Sunday Telegraph*, May 14, 1887; Stanley E. Lathrop, *A Brief Memorial Tribute to Captain Clayton E. Rogers* (Hayward, Wisconsin, 1900), 1; James G. Adams, *History of Education in Sawyer County, Wisconsin* (McIntire, Iowa, 1902), 237; Dawes, *Service*, 113-114. Rogers, a squarely-built Wisconsin sawmill operator who, with his brother, Earl, enlisted in 1861, was a man of ability and promise. He was remembered in his soldier days as a man with an eye for showy horses and one who possessed "great energy" and "absolute fearless in battle." In disposition, he had what a friend described as stern "in manner of expression" that gave his words "pertinence and force." Rogers was born into a Quaker family at Mount Pleasant, Pennsylvania. He moved to Wisconsin with his brother in 1849 and built a sawmill on the Kickapoo River at Whitestown (now Ontario). With the firing on Fort Sumter, Rogers and his brother enlisted in a volunteer company. Clayton Rogers' worth was quickly recognized. He served on the staff of both General Abner Doubleday and Major General James Wadsworth.

8. James Stewart. "Battery B Fourth U.S. Artillery at Gettysburg," *Sketches of War History (Ohio)*, Vol. IV. 183-184.

9. Gibbon, *Recollections*, 83-84; Buell, *Cannoneer*, 34-35; Gibbon, *Telegraph*, December 5, 1880.

10. For a full description of artillery usage, see Jack Coggins, *Arms and Equipment of the Civil War* (Garden City, New York: 1962); Silas Felton, "The Iron Brigade Battery: An Irregular Regular Battery," *Giants in Tall Black Hat,* 142-159.

11. Sidney G. Cooke, "The First Day at Gettysburg," *War Talks in Kansas,* 280.

Chapter 17

1. Recollections of John L. Kendlehart written for his sisters, Mary and Sarah, February 1916. Privately held. He was 12 years old at the time of the battle. His father was David Kendlehart, president of the Gettysburg Town Council. Margaretta Kendlehart McCartney, "A Story of Early's Raid," *Gettysburg Compiler,* June 30, 1923.

2. Timothy H. Smith, *John Burns: The Hero of Gettysburg* (Gettysburg: 2000), 43-45.

3. For one of the best accounts of the 26th North Carolina see Rod Gragg, *Covered with Glory: The 26th North Carolina Infantry at Gettysburg* (New York: 2000), 110-116.

4. Jerome A. Watrous, "The Mule Train Charge at Gettysburg," *Milwaukee Sunday Telegraph,* July 30, 1882.

5. Albert O'Connor enlisted Company A, Lodi Guards, from West Point, Wisconsin, June 12, 1862. He was wounded at the Wilderness in 1864 and was mustered out with his company July 3, 1865. *Wisconsin Roster,* 542.

6. Jerome A. Watrous, "Major General Winfield S. Hancock, Memorial Meeting, March 3, 1886," *War Papers, Commandery of Wisconsin, Military Order of the loyal Legion of the United States, Vol. 1* (Milwaukee: 1891) 298-300; Watrous, "The Mule Train Charge at Gettysburg."

Chapter 18

1. Sullivan, *Telegraph,* December 20, 1884; [Albert V. Young], A Pilgrimage," *Milwaukee Sunday Telegraph,* April 22, 1888.

2. Curtis, Twenty-fourth, 225-227; Madaus and Zeitlin, *Iron Brigade Flags,* 34-35.

3. George C. Underwood, *History of the 26th Regiment of North Carolina Troops in the Great War, 1861-'65* (Goldsboro, North Carolina: 1901), 351. The report of Colonel Samuel Williams of the 19th Indiana in Alan D. Gaff, "Here Was Made Our Last and Hopeless Stand—The 'Lost' Gettysburg Reports of the 19th Indiana," *Gettysburg Magazine,* January/1990, 25-32; Curtis, *Twenty-fourth,* 182.

4. William W. Dudley, "Sgt. Mjr. Blanchard at Gettysburg," *Indiana Magazine of History,* June 1939, 215-216; Dudley's statement as printed in Ladd and Ladd, *Bachelder,* 328.

5. Dudley, "Blanchard at Gettysburg"; Madaus and Zeitlin, *Iron Brigade Flags*, 33-35.

6. Smith, *John Burns*, 50-67. One of the locations Burns fought was just east of the 7th Wisconsin monument. Smith's account is the best on Burns at Gettysburg and makes an effort to resolve the many conflicting details.

Chapter 19

1. *OR*, Series 1, Vol. 27, Part 2, 643

2. Watrous, *Telegraph*, July 30, 1882; Watrous, *War Papers*, 299-300.

3. Clayton E. Rogers, "Gettysburg Scenes," *Milwaukee Sunday Telegraph*, May 13, 1887.

4. Lt. James Rosengarten, ordnance officer for the I Corps, estimated 228, 000 rounds of small arms ammunition were expended. The 8,700 men of the First Corps fired about 86 rounds per man in the fighting, or 60 rounds carried to the field and 26 issued from the wagons. Rosengarten also said 9,000 rounds were issued from the Watrous train to the Third Division of the First Corps and 13,000 from the train to the Third Division, Eleventh Corps. *OR*, Series 1, Vol. 27, Pt. 1, 264-265. Some of the ammunition issued to the Iron Brigade regiments ultimately fell into the hands of the Confederates. An officer of the 26th North Carolina said in his report that his men collected ammunition from the enemy's dead as his men were very low on ammunition. *OR*, Series 1, Vol. 27, pt. 2, 642-644.

5. Watrous, *War Papers*, 299-300; Watrous, *Telegraph*, July 30, 1882.

Chapter 20

1. Walter Clark, editor, *Histories of the Several Regiments and Battalions from North Carolina*, 5 vols. (Goldsboro, North Carolina: 1901), vol. 5, 615, as cited in Roger Long, "A Gettysburg Encounter," *Gettysburg Magazine*, July 1992. The quotations are from a letter Callis wrote September 3, 1893, from Lancaster, Wisconsin.

2. The arriving Confederates were Pender's Division. Scales' Brigade was on the left, Perrin's Brigade in the Center, and Lane's Brigade on the right. Thomas' Brigade was in reserve.

3. Beecham, *Glory*, 75.

4. Stewart's Report, *OR*, Series 1, Vol. 27, Pt. 2, 566.

5. Buell, *Cannoneer*, 65. He was probably not present at Gettysburg so all quotes and events were second hand as told to him by men who were there. Silas Felton, "Pursuing the Elusive Cannoneer," *Gettysburg Magazine*, July 1993, 33-39.

6. Buell, *Cannoneer*, 67-71

7. I.F. Kelly to Rufus Dawes, August 2, 1892; Dawes, *Service*, 175; [Young], *Telegraph*, April 22, 1883.

8. Rogers, *Telegraph*, May 13, 1887.

9. Buell, *Cannoneer*, 73-75; Herdegen and Beaudot, *Railroad Cut*, 219; Stewart, "Fourth U.S. Artillery at Gettysburg" *War Papers*; Rufus R. Dawes to the *National Tribune*, December 5, 1889.

10. Cited in William DeLoss Love, *Wisconsin in the War of the Rebellion* (Chicago: 1866), 413.

11. See Ladd and Ladd, *Bachelder*, Vol. 1, 301. In writing about the incident, Correspondent Whitelaw Reid of the *Cincinnati Gazette* wrote Richardson "seized the colors of a retreating Pennsylvania regiment and strove to rally the men around their flag. It was in vain; none but troops that have been tried as by fire can be reformed under such a storm of death; but the captain, left alone and almost in the rebels' hands, held on to the flaunting colors of another regiment, that made him so conspicuous a target, and brought them safely off." See James G. Smart, editor, *A Radical View: The 'Agate' Dispatches of Whitelaw Reid, 1861-1865*, 2 vols (Memphis, Tennessee: 1976), Vol. 1, 31: Ray, *Iron Brigade*, 191.

12. Curtis, *Twenty-fourth*, 165.

13, Ray. *Iron Brigade*, 191.

14, *OR*, Series 1, Vol. 27, Pt. 1, 281; Henry Young letter to his father, July 11, 1863, Henry Young Papers, Wisconsin Historical Society; McDermott, who enlisted at Clinton, was wounded again at Petersburg in 1864. He mustered out with the regiment in July 1865. *Wisconsin Roster*, 573. Alexander Hughes was born in Canada and was an infant when his parents came to Wisconsin in 1846. He was only 14 when he enlisted in Company B, 7th Wisconsin. [Jerome A. Watrous], "Alexander Hughes," *The Milwaukee Sunday Telegraph*, March 20, 1887.The sapling flag staff is held by the Wisconsin Veterans Museum in Madison. Young said it was difficult if not impossible to tell who was dead or wounded or a prisoner "for men were falling thick and fast around us and there was no time to pick them up or even see who they were."

Chapter 21

1. Robert McClean, "A Boy in Gettysburg—1863," *Gettysburg Compiler,* June 30, 1909.

2. Sullivan, *Telegraph*, December 20, 1884.

3. Okey, *Telegraph*, April 29, 1883; *Soldiers' and Citizens Album*, 171, 723.

4. John C. Hall, Journal, July 2, 1863; Dawes, *Service*, 176n.

5. Sullivan, *Telegraph*, December 20, 1884.

6. Reed, *Telegraph*, June 12, 1887.

7. [Loyd G. Harris], "Advances of a Rebel Flag," *Milwaukee Sunday Telegraph*, January 29, 1880.

Chapter 22

1. Buell, *Cannoneer*, 73-74; Rood, memoir, 63; Dawes, *Service*, 177-179.

2. Beecham, *Glory*, 77.

3. Stewart, "Battery B, 4th U.S. Light Artillery at Gettysburg," Ohio War Papers; Buell, *Cannoneer*, 73-76.

4. Wainwright, *Diary*, 237.

5. John Callis, Letter, September 3, 1893; Beecham, *Glory*, 78; Curtis, *Twenty-fourth*, 184.

6. Ladd and Ladd, *Bachelder*, 1806-07; Gettysburg memoirs of Mary McAllister, Adams County, Pennsylvania, Historical Society.

7. Wainwright, *Diary*, 237.

8. Transcript of the Court-Martial of Brig. Gen. Thomas A. Rowley, Edmund L. Dana Papers, Wyoming Historical and Genealogical Society, Wilkes-Barre, Pennsylvania, Folder: 1864 B. A typed copy of the original is on file at the Gettysburg National Military Park. Dana served as Rowley's defense counsel during the proceedings. The original transcript was 14 double-sided pages, plus a three-page statement by Rowley.

9. Looking back on the incident, Dawes credited Rogers with helping save the position on Cemetery Hill. "History now shows us that the whole fate of the battle turned on rallying those troops on Cemetery Hill and Culp's Hill, and forming them at once in line of battle." [Rufus Dawes]. Gallant Officer," *Milwaukee Sunday Telegraph*, February 3, 1884.

10. Dawes, *Telegraph*, February 3, 1884; Rogers, *Telegraph*, May 13, 1887. Rowley was charged with drunkenness on duty on the battlefield, conduct prejudicial to good order and military discipline, conduct unbecoming an officer and a gentleman, and disobedience of orders. At his court-martial, he was found guilty of every accusation except the last. Secretary of War Edwin M. Stanton, however, refused to approve the sentence and instead reassigned the general to command the District of the Monongahela until the cessation of hostilities. Ezra J. Warner, *Generals in Blue* (Baton Rouge, Louisiana: 1964), 414.

Chapter 23

1. Dawes, *Service*, 179; I.F. Kelly to Rufus Dawes, August 2, 1892; George Fairfield to Jerome Watrous, undated.

2. Dawes, *Service*, 176-178.

3. Silas Felton, "The Iron Brigade Battery at Gettysburg," *Gettysburg Magazine*, July, 1994, 63.

4. The placing of the regiments is based on the 1898 Gettysburg Park Commission map; Rood, memoir, 63; Dawes, *Service*, 179.

5. Kenan was a lawyer and graduate of the University of North Carolina; Norman M. Shapiro, "John Benton Callis: Madison County's Republican Congressman," *The Huntsville Historical Review*, Spring-Summer 2004, Huntsville, Alabama. Callis was in ill-health and died September 24, 1898. Kenan died January 9, 1912.

6. Bruce, *Telegraph*, January 23, 1881.

7. Curtis, *Twenty-fourth*, 187.

8. Ray, *Iron Brigade*, 191.

9. George Neff, manuscript, cited Smith, *Twenty-fourth*, 150.

10. Sullivan, *Telegraph*, December 20, 1884. William Hancock enlisted from Mauston, June 25, 1861. He was later wounded and captured at Petersburg, Virginia, in 1864. Hancock died after being shot by a guard at the Salisbury, North Carolina prison on November 27, 1864. *Wisconsin Roster*, 534.

Chapter 24

1. Beecham, *Glory*, xviii. A full record of Beecham's service was included in Editor Michael Stevens' Introduction. The book was compiled from Beecham's *National Tribune* articles.

2. Beecham, *Glory*, 78-79.

3. The Iron Brigade's opponents were also in some disorganization. In Heth's Division (the general himself slightly wounded), Archer's and Davis' brigades were battered as well as Brockenbrough's Brigade. In Pettigrew's Division, two of four colonels were killed and wounded. The Twenty-sixth North Carolina carried 800 men into the fighting and there were 216 survivors. In Pender's Division, Perrin's Brigade counted 500 men killed and wounded, and Scales' Brigade suffered 545 killed, wounded and missing. Nolan, *Iron Brigade*, 253-254.

4. Ross, *Empty Sleeve*, 49-50,

5. Buell, *Cannoneer*, 77.

6. Buell, *Cannoneer*, 80-81.

7. Dawes, *Service*, 179.

Chapter 25

1. Levi Tongue to his wife, July 2, 1863.

2. Sullivan, *Telegraph*, December 28, 1884.

3. Sullivan, *Telegraph*, December 28, 1884; *Soldiers and Citizens Album*, 171.

4. Ray, *Iron Brigade*, July 2, 1863, 192-193.

5. Smith, *Twenty-fourth*, 147-148.

6. [Harris] *Telegraph*, October 26, 1864.

7. Buell, *The Cannoneer*, 80.

8. [Young] *Telegraph*, April 22, 1888.

9. Dawes, *Service*, 171-172; I.F. Kelly to Rufus Dawes, August 2, 1892.

10. Sullivan, *Telegraph*, December 28, 1884.

Chapter 26

1. Dawes, *Service* 182.

2. Sullivan, *Telegraph*, December 28, 1884; Neff, Manuscript, cited Smith, *Twenty-fourth*, 151.

3. Buell, *Cannoneer*, 91.

4. Buell, *Cannoneer*, 91-92; Felton, *Gettysburg Magazine*, 68-69. Blackley was a member of the 24th Michigan attached to the battery.

5. Sullivan, *Telegraph*, December 28, 1884.

6. Kress, *Republican*, December 4, 1886.

7. Sullivan, *Telegraph*, December 28, 1884; Sullivan, *Irishman*, 104.

8. Kress, *Rebublican*; Neff, manuscript, cited Smith, *Twenty-fourth*, 151.

9. Elisha Rice Reed, "General Lee at Gettysburg, Pa.," Elisha Reed Papers, Wisconsin Historical Society.

10. Smith, *Twenty-fourth*, 148; Curtis, *Twenty-fourth*, 190-192.

11. Ray, *Iron Brigade*, July 3, 1863, 193.

Chapter 27

1. Sullivan, *Telegraph*, February 13, 1883.

2. Ray, *Iron Brigade* 193-194.

3. Neff, Manuscript, cited Smith, *Iron Brigade*, 151-152.

4. Curtis, *Twenty-fourth*, 184; Watrous, *Richard Epps*, 102; Ray, *Iron Brigade*, 194; Sullivan, *Telegraph*, February 13, 1883; Sullivan, *Irishman*, 101-102. Killed were Captain John Ticknor of Company K and Lieutenant Orrin Chapman of Company C. Wounded officers included Howard F. Pruyn of Company A, William Remington of Company I, John Beeley of Company H and Loyd Harris of Company C.

5. Sullivan, *Telegraph*, December 28, 1884; Sullivan, *Irishman*, 102; Rufus Dawes to Mary Gates, July 4, 1863; Dawes *Service*, 159-160; *Soldiers' and Citizens' Album*, 171.

6. Sullivan, *Telegraph*, December 28, 1884; Sullivan, *Irishman*, 102; Sullivan Green, Letter, July 2, 1863, cited in Curtis, Twenty-fourth, 184.

7. Rufus Dawes to Mary Gates, July 4, 1863; Dawes *Service*, 159-160; Sullivan Green, Letter, July 4, 1863, as cited in Curtis, *Twenty-fourth*, 184.

8. Dawes, *Service*, 160.

9. Ray, *Iron Brigade*, 195; Jerome A. Watrous, untitled manuscript. A fifer in the 7th Wisconsin, Ludolph Longhenry, described it as a "serenade of pretty music."

Ludolph Longhenry Diary, June 4, 1863, Institute for Civil War Studies, Carroll University.

Chapter 28

1. Longhenry, Diary, July 5, 1863; Fairfield, Diary, July 5, 1863; Neff, Manuscript, cited Donald Smith, *The Twenty-Fourth Michigan of the Iron Brigade* (Harrisburg, Pennsylvania: Stackpole, 1962), 184; Otis, *Second Wisconsin,* 88; Curtis, *Twenty-fourth,* 193-194.

2. Rood, memoir, 68; *OR,* Series 1, Vol. 27, Part 1, 80, 84; Sullivan D. Green, Letter, July 5, 1863, cited Curtis, *Twenty-fourth,* 184-185.

3. Rood, memoir, 68.

4. Rufus Dawes to Mary Beman Gates, July 9, 1863; Dawes, *Service,* 184; Curtis, *Twenty-fourth,* 194.

5. McAllister Memoir, Adams County Historical Society.

6. Curtis, *Twenty-fourth,* 195.

7. Rood, memoir, 68; Longhenry, diary, July 14, 1863; John Hay, *Lincoln and the Civil War Letters and Dairies of John Hay,* ed. Tyler Dennett (New York, 1939), 667.

8. Rufus Dawes to Mary Beman Gates, July 14, 1863; Dawes, *Service,* 186; Curtis, *Twenty-fourth,* 194.

9. Dawes, *Service,* 187. John A. Kress, a staff officer of General James Wadsworth, in 1886, voiced the same conclusion. "After three days' fighting, marching and indescribably hard and exhausting work for the whole army, reserves included, it seemed as if we had just about reached the limit of human endurance and must have rest." He added, however, that he believed if U.S. Grant or Phil Sheridan had commanded the army at Gettysburg, Lee's army would never have been allowed to cross the Potomac River.

10. Beecham, "Adventures of an Iron Brigade Man," 1902.

11. George Fink to his brother, in *The Milwaukee Sentinel,* July 20, 1863.

12. Charles Dow to *Portage,* Wis. *Register,* August 1, 1863.

13, The Pennsylvanians joined the brigade July 16 as they were halted on the north bank of the Potomac. "The commanding general directs...the One hundred and sixth-seventh ... Pennsylvania Volunteers ... to the first Corps...." *OR,* Series 1, Part 45, 674-675.; Dawes, *Service,* 194; Nolan, *Iron Brigade* fn 367.

14. The flag is presently held by the Wisconsin Veterans Museum at Madison. See Madaus and Zeitlin, *Iron Brigade Flags,* and Iron Brigade correspondence, 1200 series, Wisconsin Historical Society.

15. State legislatures provided state agents whose duties attached them to regiments to serve soldier needs. Duties included distributing mail and goods sent from home, visiting hospitals to see the soldiers received adequate care, and helping to administer the state's new voting-in-the-field law. Democrats contended the

agents were in fact "political commissars" interested in "manufacturing Republican votes from camp and battlefield." Governor Lewis Harvey directed Selleck, of Milwaukee, be attached to the Washington area rather than regiments. Selleck was often praised for his work. The criticism of state agents is found in *Madison Daily Patriot*, September 9, November 8, 12, 1862. Frank L. Klement, *The Gettysburg Soldiers' Cemetery and Lincoln's Address*, "A Milwaukeean Witnesses Lincoln's Gettysburg Address: W. Yates Selleck and the Soldiers' Cemetery at Gettysburg," (Shippensburg, Pennsylvania: 1993) 122-123.

16. Dawes, letters of September 6, September 13, September 17 and September 18, 1863, to Mary Gates; Dawes, *Service*, 202-204; Charles Walker Diary, September 17, 1863; Cheek and Pointon, *Sauk County*, 80. Walker wrote: "The presentation came off this afternoon. The whole brigade was out and also Battery B. The presentation speech as made by Mr. Sellick [sic]. After that Col. Robinson made a speech. The regiments were all marched to their own quarters and the officers went and got drunk, some of them."

Chapter 29

1. See Nolan, *Iron Brigade*, 266-267, for a full listing of promotions and other changes in the brigade.

2. [Jerome Watrous], "Campfire Chats," Milwaukee Sunday Telegraph, December 28, 1884.

3. Charles Walker Diary.

4. Dawes, *Service*, 235.

5. Cheek and Pointon, *Sauk County*, 86-87; [Jerome A. Watrous], *The Milwaukee Telegraph*, February 25, 1899.

6. Dawes, *Service*, 237-238.

7. Dawes, *Service*, 239.

8. U.S. Grant attended a reunion of Civil War veterans in Milwaukee and Jerome Watrous "edged through a crowd and shook hands with him. I recalled the Culpepper incident, reviewing the 6th Wisconsin troops. He said, 'I remember it well. I was busier then than ever before or since. Gen. Lee and the Army of Northern Virginia made me think harder and oftener than anyone else ever would.'" *The Milwaukee Telegraph*, May 1, 1897.

Chapter 30

1. Dawes, *Service*, 261.

2. Dawes, *Service*, 267-268.

3. J.A. Watrous, *Richard Epps and Other Stories*, [Milwaukee: no date] 156-158. Roosevelt's son would also be a soldier of some reputation and would become president of the United States.

4. Earl Rogers Papers, Wisconsin Veterans Museum, Madison. Rogers enlisted as a private in the 6th Wisconsin and was a lieutenant when seriously wounded at Petersburg, Virginia, in 1864.

5. Williams enlisted February 1, 1862, from Ontario in Bad Ax County. He served until war's end. The standard load for a 58-caliber rifle-musket was 60 grains of musket black powder. Doubling the load to 120 grains would have flattened bullet trajectory dramatically. *Wisconsin Roster*, 536.

6. Cheek and Pointon, *Sauk County*, 170-172.

7. See *William F. Fox, Regimental Losses in the American Civil War*.

Chapter 31

1. Sol Meredith to Henry Morrow, no date; Sullivan, *Telegraph*, February 13, 1883.

2. Wainwright, *Diary*, 235; Dawes, *Service*, 176.

3. Stewart, *Battery B*, Ohio War Papers; Wainwright, *Diary*, 239; Joseph G. Rosengarten, "Reynolds, hero of the First Day, by one of his staff," *New York Times Magazine*, June 29, 1913; Thomas L. Livermore, *Gettysburg Papers*, Volume 1 (Dayton, Ohio: Morningside, 1995), 118; Samuel P. Bates, *The Battle of Gettysburg* (Philadelphia 1875), 475-476.

4. William H. Harries, *The Iron Brigade in the First Day's Battle of Gettysburg*, pamphlet, privately printed.

5. Charles H. McConnell, "First and Greatest Day's Battle of Gettysburg," Library, Gettysburg National Military Park.

6. A modern study shows that of the 1,883 men who marched to Gettysburg that morning, 1,212 or 65 percent were down or missing, most killed or wounded. The 24th Michigan had the largest number of casualties in any regiment at Gettysburg. It lost a total of 363—the highest of any Federal regiment in the three days at Gettysburg.

7. Dudley, *Iron Brigade*, 15. Busey and Martin, *Regimental Strength*, 265-66. The authors cite lower numbers, but rank the 24th Michigan as the Union regiment with the greatest total loss at Gettysburg (363); the Union regiment with the greatest number killed (67), and the regiment with the greatest wounded (210).

8. Dudley, *Iron Brigade*, 13-15 The figures carefully compiled after the war by Dudley show losses of 233 of 302 for the 2nd Wisconsin (77 percent); 167 of 344 for the 6th Wisconsin (48 percent); 178 of 343 for the 7th Wisconsin (51 percent); 210 of 288 for the 19th Indiana (72 percent), and 399 of 496 for the 24th Michigan (80 percent). The Brigade Guard carried 102 officers and men into the fighting and lost 22. One brigade general and two staff officers were also wounded.

	In Ranks	Killed	Wounded	Missing	Loss	Balance
2nd Wisconsin	302	27	153	53	233	69
6th Wisconsin	344	30	117	20	167	177
7th Wisconsin	343	26	109	43	178	165
19th Indiana	288	27	133	50	210	78
24th Michigan	496	79	237	83	399	97
Brigade Guard	102	—	22	—	22	??
Brig. Staff	8	—	3	—	3	??
Total	1,883	189	774	249	1,212	671

Chapter 32

1. See Herdegen, *Men Stood Like Iron*, for a full account of Gibbon and the Iron Brigade.

2. Ross, *Empty Sleeve*, 49-50.

3. Gibbon, *Recollections*, 184.

4. The full text of the letter is included in Byrne and Weaver, *Haskell of Gettysburg*, 232-236.

5. His body was returned to his brother at Portage, Wisconsin, and buried in the Silver Lake Cemetery. His long account of Gettysburg was privately printed by his brother Harvey circa 1881. In 1898, it was included in a history of the Dartmouth Class of 1854 and reprinted in 1908 by the Massachusetts Commandery of the Military Order of the Loyal Legion (and the same year by the Wisconsin History Commission).

6. Ross, *Empty Sleeve*, 52-53. The quotes are from various letters mentioning the phantom pain.

7. Alexander Ivey, "Visiting Gettysburg," *Milwaukee Sunday Telegraph*, December 6, 1885. Ivey, of Muscoda, enlisted September 10, 1861. He was promoted to corporal and sergeant before being wounded at Gettysburg July 1, 1863. He was mustered out for wounds May 14, 1864. *Wisconsin Roster* 552.

8. "It's Again a Tented Field," *New York Times*, June 30, 1888. The markers dedicated were for the 2nd, 3rd, 5th, 6th, 7th, 26th Wisconsin, and Company G of the 1st U.S. Sharpshooters.

9. "A Great Excursion," *Milwaukee Sunday Telegraph*, May 27, 1888.

Chapter 33

1. *Raleigh*, North Carolina, *Post*, May 3, 1903.

2. Alfred Noble, Diary, May 6, 1865, Bentley Historical Library, University of Michigan.

3. The program listed Charles Dawes on "What the Younger Generation Owes to the Iron Brigade," while Bragg spoke on "Gen. John Gibbon and his Children, The Iron Brigade." The invocation was given by Rt. Rev. Samuel Fallows, late colonel of the 49th Wisconsin. The Chicago *Register* reported August 27, 1900, that the handful of survivors of the famous Iron Brigade attracted "no little attention" despite the "many attractions incident to the formal opening of the encampment week…" Fort Worth *Star Telegram*, August 28, 1900.

4. The reporter described McConnell as "six feet tall, well-proportioned, with his hair and moustache almost white, stands perfectly erect and appears as agile as a youth." *Raleigh Post*, May 3, 1903.

5. The painting by G. Randall was completed in 1897. *Raleigh Post*, May 3, 1903. Vance commanded the regiment until 1862 when he became governor of North Carolina. Harry Burgwyn, who succeeded Vance as commander, was killed July 1, 1863 in the assault on Seminary Ridge at Gettysburg. Lane succeeded Burgwyn. Lane recovered from his Gettysburg wound, but was wounded three times afterward. He died December 31, 1908, and was buried at the Brush Creek Baptist Church near Silver City, North Carolina.

6. *Raleigh News & Observer*, July 5, 1903.

7. Veterans were provided a cot and bedding in a tent holding eight men. Meals were served from a kitchen. Despite temperatures near 100, only nine veterans died during the week long encampment.

8. Jerome A. Watrous, "The Most Famous Regiment," *Confederate Veteran*, no date. See Appendix 3 for a list of those who registered at the Iron Brigade tent.

9. Tongue was captured in 1864 and spent nearly four months at Andersonville, Georgia, and other Confederate prison camps before being released on March 5, 1865. He weighed 190 pounds on his enlistment and came out of the prison camps a skeletal seventy-three pounds. Tongue died March 9, 1918; George Eustice family records.

10. Troubled by his Gettysburg wound, Sol Meredith returned to Indiana in 1864 with what was called "general nervous prostration." He died in Indiana October 2, 1875.

Rogers resigned less than two weeks after Gettysburg and his arrest of General Rowley. He was superintendent of the Wisconsin Lumber Company mill at Hayward at the time of his death.

James "Mickey" Sullivan was wounded five times during his four years in the 6th Wisconsin. He never returned to Gettysburg. Sullivan farmed for a time near Hillsboro and then became a lawyer in Ontario, Wisconsin, painting his office a patriotic red, white and blue. He died October 22, 1906.

Lucius Fairchild served as Wisconsin secretary of state and served three terms as governor. Long active as a Republican stalwart, he was a major figure in the surging veterans' movement with its "bloody shirt" overtones campaigning against Democrats and former Confederates. He died May 23, 1896, and was buried with his Gettysburg arm in Madison.

Six months after Gettysburg, Rufus Dawes of the 6th Wisconsin married Mary Beman Gates of Marietta, Ohio. A victim of combat stress, he resigned in 1864 and returned to his native Ohio where he served a term in the Congress. Dawes returned to Gettysburg only once before dying in 1899.

After a lengthy recovery from his Gettysburg wound, John Callis stayed in the army and moved to Huntsville, Alabama, where he resigned his commission in 1868. He was elected to Congress as a Republican in 1868 and served one term. He did not stand for reelection and returned to Lancaster, Wisconsin.

Henry Morrow was wounded again at the Wilderness and a third time at Petersburg in 1864. He mustered out with his regiment in July 1865 and served for a time as the collector of the port at Detroit. He returned to the Regular Army and served at several locations. Morrow's final post was as colonel of the 21st U.S. Infantry at Hot Springs, Arkansas, where he died January 31, 1891.

Dennis Dailey, who took the sword of captured James Archer, died March 25, 1898, at Council Bluffs, Iowa. He was 57.

11. A copy of the invitation is found in the files at the Gettysburg National Military Park Library. The Iron Brigade Association's latest reunion came in 1997 as part of the 50th anniversary meeting of the Milwaukee Civil War Round Table. Two sons of Iron Brigade veterans, William H. Upham, son of William Upham of the 2nd Wisconsin, and James F. Sullivan, son of James P. Sullivan of the 6th Wisconsin. in 1990 turned operation of the association over to the Milwaukee Round Table. Brigade veterans in 1897 at Devil's Lake, Wis., gave full membership to their children and grandchildren.

12. Jerome A. Watrous, "The Most Famous Regiment"; Jerome Watrous, "Iron Brigade Held Meeting," *Fond du Lac*, Wisconsin, *Reporter*, September 11, 1916; *Fort Worth*, Texas, *Morning Register*, March 18, 1916. McConnell's obituary noted he "made and lost two fortunes aggregating nearly $1,000,000 and built a third after he was fifty years old and was $400,000 in debt. His last fortune was made in the 'cut rate drug business.'"

13. Cass enlisted in Company B from Gilmanton October 15, 1864, and mustered out with the regiment July 3, 1865. Riley, of Viroqua, enlisted June 1, 1861. He reenlisted as a veteran in 1864, but was sent to an insane asylum March 26, 1864. He was discharged May 11, 1864. *Wisconsin Roster, Vol I,* 545, 531.

Epilogue

1. *Gettysburg Times,* July 2, 1997.

Bibliography

Newspapers and Periodicals

Baraboo News-Republic, Baraboo, Wisconsin
Baraboo Republic, Baraboo, Wisconsin
Beloit Free Press, Beloit, Wisconsin
Beloit Journal, Beloit, Wisconsin
The Blackhat, Occasional Newsletter of the 6th Wisconsin Vols.
Chicago Chronicle
Chippewa Herald, Chippewa Falls, Wisconsin
Christian Science Monitor
Civil War Times Illustrated
Confederate Veteran
Evening Wisconsin, Milwaukee
Fond du Lac Reporter, Fond du Lac, Wisconsin
Gettysburg Compiler
Gettysburg Magazine
Grant County Herald, Lancaster, Wisconsin
La Crosse Morning Chronicle, La Crosse, Wisconsin
La Crosse Republican and Leader, La Crosse, Wisconsin
Mauston Star, Mauston, Wisconsin
Milwaukee Daily News
Milwaukee Free Press
Milwaukee History, Milwaukee County Historical Society
Milwaukee Journal
Milwaukee Sentinel
Milwaukee Sunday Telegraph/Milwaukee Telegraph
Mineral Point Tribune, Mineral Point, Wisconsin
Missouri Republican, St. Louis, Missouri
The National Tribune, Washington, D.C.
Prescott Journal, Prescott, Wisconsin
Vernon County Censor, Viroqua, Wisconsin
Wisconsin Magazine of History
Wisconsin Necrology [51 volumes of newspaper and similar obituaries].
Wisconsin State Historical Society

Wisconsin Newspaper Volumes. [Clippings from various Civil War era newspapers]. Wisconsin Historical Society

Official Records

Indiana at Gettysburg. Report of the Fiftieth Anniversary Commission. Indianapolis, 1913.

Revised United States Army Regulations of 1861. Washington, D.C.: United States Government Printing Office, 1863.

War of the Rebellion: Official Records of the Union and Confederate Armies. Washington, D.C. United States Government Printing Office, 1889-1900.

State, County and Local Histories

Adams, James G., *History of Education in Sawyer County, Wisconsin.* McIntire, Iowa: M.E. Granger, 1902.

Aderman, Ralph M., ed., Trading *Post to Metropolis, Milwaukee:* Milwaukee County Historical Society, 1987.

Bruce, William G. *History of Milwaukee, City and County.* (3 vols) Chicago: S. J. Clare Publishing Co., 1922.

Conard, Howard L., *History of Milwaukee From its First Settlement to the year 1895.* (3 vols). Chicago: American Biographical Publishing co., [1895].

Cozen, Kathleen Neils, *Immigrant Milwaukee, 1836-1860.* Cambridge: Harvard University Press, 1976.

Current, Richard N., *The History of Wisconsin . . . The Civil War Era 1848-1873.* Madison: Wisconsin Historical Society, 1976.

[Flower, Frank A.], *History of Milwaukee, Wisconsin.* Chicago: Western Historical Co., 1881.

History of Crawford and Richland Counties, Wisconsin. Springfield, Illinois: Union Publishing Company, 1884.

History of Vernon County, Wisconsin. Springfield, Illinois: Union Publishing Co., 18843.

Kessinger, Lawrance, *History of Buffalo County, Wisconsin.* Alma., Wis., 1888.

Koss, Rudolf, *Milwaukee.* Milwaukee, Wis., *The Milwaukee Herald,* 1871. [English translation for the Federal Writer's Project by Hans Ibsen].

Books, Articles, Memoirs, and Secondary Accounts

Aubery, Doc [Cullen B.], *Recollections of a Newsboy in the Army of the Potomac.* Milwaukee, 1900. [Contains the monograph, Echoes of the Marches of the Famous Iron Brigade, 1861-1865].

Bates, Samuel P., *The Battle of Gettysburg*. Philadelphia: T.H. David & Co., 1875.

Battles and Leaders of the Civil War, Vol. 5, Peter Cozzens, editor, Chicago: University of Illinois Press, 2005.

Beaudot, William J.K., and Herdegen, Lance J., *An Irishman in the Iron Brigade: The Civil War Memoirs of James P. Sullivan, Sergt., Company K, 6th Wisconsin Volunteers*, New York: Fordham University Press, 1993.

Beecham, R[obert] K., *Gettysburg: The Pivotal Battle of the Civil War*, Chicago: A.C. McClurg & Co., 1911.

—, edited by Michael E. Stevens, *As if it were Glory: Robert Beecham's Civil War from the Iron Brigade to the Black Regiments*, Madison, Wisconsin: Madison House, 1998.

Buell, Augustus, *The Cannoneer; Recollections of Service in the Army of the Potomac*. Washington, D.C.: *The National Tribune*, 1897.

Byrne, Frank L., and Andrew T. Weaver, eds., *Haskell of Gettysburg, His Life and Civil War Papers*, Madison: State Historical Society of Wisconsin, 1970.

Cheek, Philip, and Mair Pointon, *History of the Sauk County Riflemen, Known as Company "A" Sixth Wisconsin Veteran Volunteer Infantry, 1861-1865*. [N.P.], 1909.

Coddington, Edwin B., *The Gettysburg Campaign*. New York: Charles Scribner's Sons, 1968. [Revised and reprinted, Morningside Bookshop, 1979.

Curtis, O[rson] B., *History of the Twenty-Fourth Michigan of the Iron Brigade*. Detroit: Winn & Hammond, 1891.

Dawes, Rufus R., "Sketches of War History." *Military Order of the Loyal Legion of the United States, Commandery of the State of Ohio, War Papers, Vol. III*. [Reprinted in: *Service with the Sixth Wisconsin Volunteers*. Dayton, Ohio: Morningside Books, 1984.]

—. *Service with the Sixth Wisconsin Volunteers*, Marietta, Ohio: E.R. Alderman & Sons, 1890.

Doubleday, Abner, *Chancellorsville and Gettysburg*, New York: Charles Scribner's Sons, 1886.

Dougherty, *James J. Stone's Brigade and the Fight for the McPherson Farm: Battle of Gettysburg, July 1*, 1863. Conshohocken, Pennsylvania: Combined Publishing, 2001

Dudley, William W., *The Iron Brigade at Gettysburg*, 1878, Official Report of the Part Borne by the 1st Brigade, 1st Division, 1st Army Corps. Cincinnati, privately printed, 1879.

Dunn, Craig L., *Iron Men, Iron Will: The Nineteenth Indiana Regiment of the iron Brigade*, Indianapolis: Guild Press of Indiana, Inc. 1995.

Dyer, F.H., *A Compendium of the War of the Rebellion*. Des Moines, Iowa, 1908. [Reprinted Dayton, Ohio: Morningside Bookshop, 1987.]

Fitch, Michael H., *Echoes of the Civil War As I Hear Them*, New York: R.F. Fenno and Co., 1905.

Fox, William F., *Regimental Losses in the American Civil War*, Albany, New York: Albany Publishing Company, 1889.

Freeman, Douglas A., *Lee's Lieutenants*. (3 vols.) New York: Charles Scribner's Sons, 1942-1944.

Gaff, Alan D., *Brave Men's Tears: The Iron Brigade at Brawner Farm*, Dayton, Ohio: Morningside House, 1985.

—. *On Many a Bloody Field: Four Years in the Iron Brigade*, Bloomington, Indiana: Indiana University Press, 1997.

Gallagher, Gary W., editor, *The First Day at Gettysburg, Essays on Confederate and Union Leadership*, Kent, Ohio: Kent State University Press, 1992.

Gibbon, John, *Personal Recollections of the Civil War*. New York: G.P. Putnam's Sons, 1928.

Gottfried, Bradley, *The Maps of Gettysburg: An Atlas of the Gettysburg Campaign, June 3 – July 13, 1863*. Savas Beatie LLC, 2007.

Gragg, Rod, *Covered With Glory: The 26th North Carolina Infantry at the Battle of Gettysburg*, New York: HarperCollinsPublishers, 2000.

Haskell, Frank A., *The Battle of Gettysburg*, Madison: Wisconsin History Commission, 1908.

Hassler, Warren W., *Crisis at the Crossroads: The First Day at Gettysburg*. Tuscaloosa, Alabama: University of Alabama Press, 1970.

Herdegen, Lance J. and Sharon Murphy, *Four Years With the Iron Brigade: The Civil War Journal of William Ray, Seventh Wisconsin*, New York: DeCapo Press, 2001.

—, and William J.K. Beaudot, *In the Bloody Railroad Cut at Gettysburg*. Dayton, Ohio: Morningside House, 1990.

—. *The Men Stood Like Iron: How the Iron Brigade won its Name*. Bloomington, Indiana: Indiana University Press, 1997.

Johnson, Robert U. and Clarence C. Buel, eds., *Battles and Leaders of the Civil War*. (4 vols.) New York: The Century Co., 1884-1887.

Kellogg, John A., *Capture and Escape: A Narrative of Army and Prison Life*. Madison: Wisconsin History Commission, 1908.

Ladd, David L. and Audrey J Ladd, editors, *The Bachelder Papers: Gettysburg in their Own Words* (3 vols). Dayton, Ohio: Morningside, 1995.

Love, William D., *Wisconsin in the War of the Rebellion*. Chicago: Church & Goodman, 1866.

Livermore, Thomas L., *Numbers and Losses in the Civil War*, Bloomington: Indiana University Press, 1957.

Madaus, Howard Michael and Richard H. Zeitlin, *The Flags of the Iron Brigade*, Madison: Wisconsin Veterans Museum, 1998.

McLean, James L., *Cutler's Brigade at Gettysburg*. Baltimore: Butternut and Blue Press, 1987.

Meade, George G. and George G. Meade, Jr., *The Life and Letters of George Gordon Meade*, (2 vols.), George Gordon Meade III editor, New York: Charles Scribner's Sons, 1913.

Michigan at Gettysburg, Detroit: Michigan Monument Commission, 1889.

Military Order of the Loyal Legion of the United States, Commandery of the State of Wisconsin, *War Papers*, Vol. I. Milwaukee: Wisconsin Armitage & Allen, 1891.

Military Order of the Loyal Legion of the United States, Commandery of the State of Wisconsin, *War Papers*, Vol. II. Milwaukee: Armitage & Allen, 1896.

Military Order of the Loyal Legion of the United States, Commandery of the State of Wisconsin, Vol. III. Milwaukee: Armitage & Allen, 1903.

Nichols, Edward J., *Toward Gettysburg: A Biography of John F. Reynolds,* University Park: Pennsylvania State University Press, 1958.

Nolan, Alan T. and Sharon Vipond, eds., *Giants in Their Tall Black Hats: Essays on the Iron Brigade.* Bloomington, Indiana: Indiana University Press, 1998.

—. *The Iron Brigade,* New York: Macmillan, 1961.

Otis, George H., *The Second Wisconsin Infantry, with Letters and Recollections by Other Members of the Regiment,* ed. by Alan D. Gaff. Dayton, Ohio: Morningside Press, 1984. [Originally serialized in The *Milwaukee Sunday Telegraph* in 11 parts between July-December, 1880.]

Patridge, Jr., George Washington. ed. by Hugh L. Whitehouse, *Letters from the Iron Brigade,* Indianapolis: Guild Press of Indiana, 1994.

Pfanz, Harry W., *Gettysburg: The First Day,* Chapel Hill: University of North Carolina Press, 2001.

Quiner, E[dwin] B., *The Military History of Wisconsin.* Chicago: Clarke & Co., 1866.

Ross, Sam, *The Empty Sleeve: A Biography of Lucius Fairchild,* Madison: The State Historical Society of Wisconsin for the Wisconsin Civil War Centennial Commission, 1964.

Smith, Donald, *The Twenty-fourth Michigan of the Iron Brigade.* Harrisburg, Pennsylvania: Stackpole Company, 1962.

Smith, Timothy H., *John Burns: The Hero of Gettysburg.* Gettysburg: Thomas Publications, 2000.

—. *The Story of Lee's Headquarters.* Gettysburg: Thomas Publications, 1995.

Soldier' and Citizens' Album of Biographical Record. (2 vols.) Chicago: Grand Army Publishing Company, 1888.

Steensma, Robert C., editor, *The Civil War Letters of James E. Northup and Samuel W. Northup,* Sioux Falls, South Dakota: Augustana College, 2000.

Stine, J. H., *History of the Army of the Potomac.* Philadelphia: J.B. Rogers Printing Co., 1892.

Tevis, C., The *History of the Fighting 14th [Brooklyn].* New York: Brooklyn Eagle Press, 1911.

Veil, Charles H., *The Memoirs of Charles Henry Veil,* Herman J. Viola, editor, New York: Orion Books, 1993.

Venner, William Thomas, *The 19th Indiana Infantry at Gettysburg: Hoosiers' Courage,* Shippensburg, Pennsylvania: Burd Street Press, 1998.

Wainwright, Charles S., *A Diary of Battle: The Personal Journals of Colonel Charles S. Wainwright, 1861-1865,* Allan Nevins, ed. NY: Harcourt, Brace &World, 1962.

Walterman, Thomas, *There Stands "Old Rock:" Rock County, Wisconsin, and the War to Preserve the Union* (Friendship, Wisconsin: Rock County Historical Society, New past Press, 2001).

Washburn, William H., "Jerome A. Watrous: The Civil War Years." Madison, Wis., Wisconsin Veterans Museum. Unpublished manuscript.

Watrous, J[erome]. A. *Richard Epps and Other Stories.* Milwaukee, 1906.
Whitehouse, Hugh L., ed., *Letters from the Iron Brigade: George W. Partridge, Jr., 1839-1863.* Indianapolis: Guild Press of Indiana, 1994
Williams, T. P., *The Mississippi Brigade of Brig. Gen. Joseph R. Davis: A Geographical Account of Its Campaigns and a Biographical Account of Its Personalities, 1861-1865,* Dayton, Ohio: Morningside Press, 1999.

General Biographic Sources

Biographical Directory of the American Congress, 1774-1960. Washington, D.C., United States Governement Printing Office, 1961.
Dictionary of American Biography, (10 vols.) New York: Charles Scribner's Sons, 1946.
Dictionary of Wisconsin Biography. Madison: Wisconsin Historical Society, 1960.
Warner, Ezra J., *Generals in Blue: Lives of Union Commanders.* Baton Rouge: Louisiana State University Press, 1964.
Warner Ezra J., *Generals in Gray:* Lives of Confederate Commanders. Baton Rouge: Louisiana State University Press, 1959.

Ordnance and Technical Manuals

Coggins, Jack, *Arms and Equipment of the Civil War.* Garden City, New York: Doubleday & Co., 1962.
Confederate States Ordnance Bureau, *Field Manual.* Richmond, Virginia: Ritchie & Dunnavant, 1862.
Coppee, Henry, *Field Manual of Evolutions of the Line.* Philadelphia: J.B. Lippincott & Co., 1862.
Gibbon, John, *The Artillerist's Manual,* New York: D. Van Nostrand, 1860.
Fuller, Claud E., *Springfield Muzzle-Loading Shoulder Arms.* New York: Francis Bannerman Sons, 1930.
Hardee, W. J., *Rifle and Light Infantry Tactics.* (2 vols.) Philadelphia: J. B. Lippincott & Co., 1861.
McClellan, George B., *Manual of Bayonet Exercise.* Philadelphia: J. B. Lippincott & Co., 1862.
Reilly, Robert M., *United States Military Small Arms, 1816-1865,* Eagle Press, 1970.
Thomas, Dean S., *Ready . . . Aim . . . Fire.* Bilgerville, Pennsylvania: Osborn Printing Co., 1981.
U.S. Infantry Tactics. Philadelphia: J.B. Lippincott & Co., 1863.

Index

Academy of the Sacred Heart, 284(n)

"Adventures of an Iron Brigade Man," 175

Alabama Military Units, *4th Infantry*, 260; *13th Infantry*, 101

Albee, George E., 272

Anderson, Daisy, 260

Anderson, Pvt. David, 116, 287(n)

Andersonville Prison, Georgia, 300(n)

Antietam, Battle of, 11-12, 15, 17-18, 41-42, 71, 92, 105, 117, 126, 148

Arawell, G.P., 271

Archer, Brig. Gen. James J., 89-90, 101-102, 163-164, 204, 228

Archer's Brigade, 92, 94, 96-97, 103, 107, 124, 127-128, 131-132, 191, 232 283(n), 294(n)

Army of Northern Virginia, 19, 39, 19, 128, 176, 207, 219, 228

Army of the Potomac, 4, 10, 13, 17-18, 20, 26, 37, 39, 42, 47, 52, 70, 78-79, 94, 107, 126, 139, 192, 197, 202-204, 206-207, 211, 215, 218, 221, 223, 228, 234, 237

Army of Virginia, 10

Baker, A. E., 268

Barlow, Gen. Francis C., and his brigade, 131

Barrows, C. H., 273

Bartholemew, Chauncey, 267

Bartlett, J. N., 270

Bartlett, Dr. O. F., 156

Baty, Isaac, 273

Beauregard, Gen. P. G. T., 3

Beecham, Pvt. Robert, 102, 163, 175-176, 207, 285(n)

Beeley, Lt. John, 157, 159, 173, 295(n)

Belo, Pvt. A. H., 288(n)

Beltz, Christian F., 268

Bennett, Joseph B., 270

Benton, S. A., 271

Biddle, Newton, 267

Bird, Henry R., 270

Bird, Robert C., 270

Bissett, Pvt. John, *photo*, 8

Bissett, M. N., 272

"Black Hat Brigade," see Iron Brigade

Blackburn, John, 269

Blackley, Pvt. Lyman W., 189

Blair, Governor Austin, 51

Blair, Maj. John, 118-121

Blanchard, Sgt. Maj. Asa, 138-139

Bock, Joseph, 268

Booker, John A., 272

Boone, P. H., 272

Boswell, W. W., 272

Boughton, Pvt. Lewis, 113

Boynton Plank Road, battle of, 227

Bragg, Col. Edward S., 31-32, 34, 37, 76, 105, 214, 217, 246, 275(n) 282(n) 300(n); *photo*, 245

Branton, R. H., 267

Brian, Pvt. Jonathan, 99

Briggs, Lewis A., 268

Brink, D. L., 272

Brisbois, Cpl. Paul V., 98, 285(n)

Brockenbrough's Brigade, 128, 132, 191, 294(n)

Brooks, Adjutant Edward, 110, 118, 123, 289(n)

Brother, Philip, 269

Brown, H. J., 25, 33

Brown, Henry, 271

Brown, John R., 132, 270

Brown, Samuel, 270

Bruce, Lt. John W., 172-173, 269, 281(n)

Bryan, Sgt. Jonathan, 102

Bucham, E. K., 267

Bucham, Henry, 269

Buchanan, James, 70

Buckles, Pvt. A. J., 92, 96-97, 138

Buell, Pvt. Augustus, 278(n)-279(n)

Buford, Gen. John, 50, 62-63, 78, 81-83, 232

Buherer, John F., 268

Bull Run, First Battle of, 3-4, 18, 73, 88, 283(n)-285(n)

Bull Run, Second battle of, 10, 15, 18, 71

Bullard, Pvt. Clarence E., 286(n)

Burghardt, Henry, 267

Burgwyn Jr., Col. Henry K., 132, 137-138, 246, 249, 300(n)

Burgwyn, Col. W. H. S., 246, 249-250, 256

Burns, John, 129-130, 139, 141, 253, 291(n); photo, 140

Burnside, Gen. Ambrose, 17-18, 70, 78

Burton, Pvt. Daniel, 98, 285(n)

Callis, Lt. Col. John, 96-97, 141, 147, 152, 163, 168, 171, 173, 176, 255, 274(n), 291(n), 294(n), 301(n); *photo*, 169

Campbell, Lt. William S., 217

Carter, John Q., 271

Cass, Josiah E., 256-257, 302(n)

Cass, Senator Lewis, 52

"Cast Iron Brigade," 11

Cavanaugh, John, 269

Cemetery Hill, 128, 146, 161-162, 165, 167, 175-177, 183, 232-233

Cemetery Ridge, 183, 187, 191, 201, 232

Chambersburg Pike, 69, 82-83, 89, 104-105, 107, 109, 112, 119, 122, 124-125, 127, 132, 145, 150, 163

Chancellorsville Campaign, 12-13, 15, 20-21, 29-33, 35-37, 39, 42, 59, 71, 127, 178

Chandler, Curtis, 269

Chandler, S. E., 274(n)

Chapman, Lt. Orrin, 49, 112, 295(n)

Cheek, Pvt. Phil, 106, 277(n)

Chicago Athletic Association, 246

Childs, H. L., 268

Christ Lutheran Church, 163

Clarey, Pvt. Patrick, 180-182

Clements, George K., 268

Clifford, Pvt. Burr M., 139

Cold Harbor, battle of, 191, 226, 240

Conklin, Pvt. Charles, 34, 277(n)

Conlin, Benjamin, 273

Conner, Richard, 270

Converse, Capt. Rollin, 149

Cook, Jack, 271

Cook, Pvt. Webster, 97, 284(n)

Copway, George, 221

Crater, battle of the, 175, 226

Crawford, Cpl. Charles, 110

Crawford, Capt. J. W., 273

Culp's Hill, 167-168, 171, 173, 176-178, 232, 234; *July 1*, 179-180, 182, 235; *July 2*, 183, 185; *July 3*, 187-192; *July 4*, 196, 198

Cunningham, Sgt. Burlington, 92, 96, 138

Cutler, Col. Lysander, 8, 54; biography, 27-28; Fredericksburg, Battle of, 70; railroad cut, 120; commands brigade, 209, 214;

Wilderness, battle of, 23; Spotsylvania Court House, battle of, 224; *photo*, 90

Cutler's Brigade, 65, 76, 81, 83, 89, 94, 105, 107-108, 124, 127

Dailey, Lt. Dennis, 102, 163-164, 204, 228, 285(n), 301(n)

Dana, Edmund L., 293(n)

Daniel's Brigade, 171

Davidson, Lt. James, 148-149, 271

Davidson, John, 268

Davis' (Joe) Brigade, 89-90, 94, 107-108, 114, 117, 119, 124, 127-128, 191, 199, 233, 294(n)

Davis, Color Sgt. Christopher, 116

Davis, Jefferson, 89

Davis, Brig. Gen. Joe, 89, 191

Davison, Lt. James, 125

Davison, John S., 273

Davison, Cpl. Rasselas, 98

Dawes, Charles G., 25, 246

Dawes, Lt. Col. Rufus, 22-23, 25, 40, 46-47, 78, 214, 217-218, 246, 275(n), 281(n), 288(n)-289(n), 293(n), 301(n); Hooker is appointed to command army, 18; Chancellorsville, 32-34; march to Pennsylvania, 48; march from Marsh Creek, 76; arrives on field, 103-105; Chambersburg Pike, 107-108; railroad cut, 108, 110, 112-115, 118-119, 121, 123; flag of the 2nd Mississippi, 121-124, 197, 199; McPherson's Ridge, 149; retreat through Gettysburg, 161; chaos in town, 162; arrives at Cemetery Hill, 165; Culp's Hill, 168, 179, 185; the truth of the day, 178; July 4, 196, 198; departs Gettysburg, 203, 206; meets and marries Mary Gates,

217; impression of Grant, 219; members from Indian tribes, 221; Wilderness, battle of, 223; Spotsylvania Court House, battle of, 224-225; Gettysburg's long shadow, 232-233; returns to the battlefield, 242; death of, 253; *photo*, 24, 103

Day, Cpl. William, 286(n)

De Kover, Samuel A., 270

Delaware Military, *3rd Infantry*, 272

Deleglise, Cpl. Francis, 112, 156, 180, 286(n)

DeLosh, Frederick, 271

Devil's Den, 183

Devin, Col. Thomas and his brigade, 63, 125

Dickey, Lt. Gilbert, 141

Doubleday, Maj. Gen. Abner, 102, 104, 125, 213, 281(n), 289(n); arrives on field, 62, 83; Chambersburg Pike, 107; biography, 127; railroad cut, 128; retreat through Gettysburg, 162-163; Thomas Rowley, 165; arrives on Cemetery Hill, 167; replaced as commander of First Corps, 182

Dow, Pvt. Charles, 102, 285(n)

Dow, William H., 268

Draggs, John, 269

Drew, Jacob A., 273

Druen, Sgt. W. H., 77

Dudley, Lt. Col. William, 97, 138, 235

Dunlap, Eban B., 269

Dunn, Pvt. Harry, 112

Durfee, C. D., 271

Dwaim, J. A., 272

Early, Maj. Gen. Jubal and his division, 129-131, 180, 183

East, Lt. Crockett, 139

Easterbrook, G. H., 268

Eayes, A. S., 269

Edwards, Capt. A. M., 152, 167

Eggleston, Pvt. Lewis, 114-116, 287(n)

Englike, Julius A., 269

Eustice, George, 253, 269

Evans, Hugh, 268

Evans, Sgt. William, 123, 158-159, 197

Everett, William, 269

Ewell, Lt. Gen. Richard S. and his corps, 130-131, 161, 171-172, 176, 183, 187, 223

Fairchild, Col. Lucius, 239, 285(n), 301(n); arrives on field, 85; biography, 87, 89; McPherson's Ridge, 92; wounded, 97, 125, 158, 176-177, 237; amputated arm, 162; leaves the brigade, 214; returns to the battlefield, 240; death of, 255 *photo*, 88, 245

Fairfield, Sgt. George, 114

Faulkner, S. R. W., 268

Fink, George, 253

"Fitzhugh's Crossing," 29, 33

Five Forks, battle of, 228

Flake, E. W., 271

Flanigan, Lt. Col. Mark, 52, 96

Fletcher, Pvt. Oliver, 61

Folmady, George, 267

Fort Brown, Texas, 52

Fort Leavenworth, Kansas, 52, 54

Fort Monroe, Virginia, 5

Fort Snelling, Minnesota, 9

Fort Sumter, South Carolina, 1, 21, 26, 49, 52, 59, 70, 110, 127

Fort, David R., 270

Foust, Pvt. Peter L., *photo*, 60

Frawley, William, 268

Fredericksburg Campaign, 13, 15, 17-19, 29, 33, 68, 70-71

Gaddy, Jesse, 271

Gainesville, battle of, 15, 90

Gallup, Andrew, 268

Gasley, Charles, 270

Gasley, Patrick, 270

Gates, Mary B., *photo*, 217

Geargeson, John, 269

Georgia Military, *25th Infantry*, 180

Gettysburg, Pennsylvania, chaos in town, 146, 149, 152, 155; retreat through town, 156-157, 159; July 1 aftermath, 182

Gibbon, Brig. Gen. John, 9-12, 27, 52, 54, 126-127, 238-239, 300(n); assumes command of the brigade, 7; his opinion of the brigade, 59; Pickett's Charge, 191; commands brigade, 237; *photo*, 6, 245

Gibboney, A. H., 272

Gibbons, Pvt. Robert, *photo*, 244

Gilder, Jacob J., 273

Globe Tavern, battle of, 227

Glover, A. J., 272

Good, William H., 272

Goodwin, Pvt. John, 113

Gordon Jr., Capt. Alexander, 35

Gordon, Gen. John B., 193

Gorman, Patrick B., 270

Graff, Fred, 273

Grand Army of the Republic, 231, 246, 257, 277(n), 281(n)

Grand Review, 228

Grant, Gen. Ulysses S., 203, 218-219, 223-224, 226, 228, 296(n)-297(n)

Grayes, Maxhaw J., 271

Greene, Brig. Gen. George S., 185

Greusel, Isaac L., 270

Grignon, Robert, 221

Gulledge, William, 271

Hackman, Ezra, 270
Haigh, George W., 271
Hall, Lt. James, 65, 83, 98, 103, 105, 124
Hall, Dr. John C., 156
Hamilton, William, 270
Hancock, Cpl. William, 173, 276(n)
Hancock, Maj. Gen. Winfield S., 144, 146, 167
Hancock, Pvt. William, 30, 185, 195, 294(n)
Harland, Pvt. John, 116
Harries, Pvt. William H., 285(n)
Harris, C. E., 271
Harris, Lt. Loyd, 47, 49, 104-105, 158-159, 173, 182, 295(n); march to Pennsylvania, 43-44, 46; march from Marsh Creek, 78; railroad cut, 109, 112, 114, 119; retreat through Gettysburg, 157; *photo*, 44
Harris, W. H., 268
Harris, William, 234
Harrisburg, Pennsylvania, 198
Harrison, John, 269
Harvey, Governor Lewis, 297(n)
Haskell, Frank A., 7, 12, 191, 237, 239-240, *photo*, 238
Hatcher's Run, battle of, 227
Hauser, Maj. John, 76, 114
Haven, A. E., 268
Heathcock, Joseph, 269
Helmes, Pvt. Virgil, 92
Hendricks, Samuel T., 270
Henler, J. T., 271
Henman, W. G., 269
Heth, Maj. Gen. Henry and his division, 81-82, 128, 131, 282(n), 294(n)
Hevnor, A. H., 272
Hewitt, Catherine M., 284(n)

High, H. H., 272
Hill, Gen. Ambrose P., and his corps, 81-82, 99, 161, 190, 223
Hinton, F. M., 272
Hofmann, Col. John W., 90
Holback, James B.O., 272
Holford, Lyman D., 268
Holt, George P., 273
Holton, Ignaz, 270
Hooker, Maj. Gen. Joseph, 10, 17-20, 42, 47, 70-71, 275(n)
Howard, Maj. Gen. Oliver O. and his corps, 62, 82-83, 128, 130-131, 133, 145-146, 157, 162-163, 175-176, 178, 195-196, 233, 291(n)
Huftill, Pvt. Dick, 97, 269, 284(n)
Hughes, Pvt. Alexander, 96, 152, 284(n), 292(n)
Hughes, H.W., 271
Huntington, Theodore, 268
Hussey, Augustus, 270
Hyatt, Capt. John, 124
Indiana Military Units, *7th Battery*, 273; *7th Infantry*, 27, 65, 179, 223, 261-262; *19th Infantry*, 12, 26, 41, 54, 60, 70, 197, 214, 224, 262, 290(n), 298(n)-299(n); arrives in Wash. D.C., 4, 5; Volunteer Infantry, 13; Solomon Meredith, 27; march to Pennsylvania, 48; weapons, 64; arrives on field, 66, 92; march from Marsh Creek, 76; nickname, 76; McPherson's Ridge, 96-97, 130-132, 137-139, 147; moves to Culp's Hill, 168; Culp's Hill, 176; does not Veteran Reserve Corps, 216; Wilderness, battle of, 223; consolidated into 20th Indiana, 226; merged with 20th Indiana, 229; mustered out, 229; Gettysburg's long shadow,

232; losses at Gettysburg, 235; organization, 261, 266; 50 Year Gettysburg Celebration, 269; *20th Infantry*, 226, 229, 261; *Delaware Greys*, 266; *Edinburgh Guards*, 266; *Elkhart County Guards*, 266; *The Invincibles*, 266; *Meredith Guards*, 266; *Richmond City Greys*, 41, 266; *Selma Legion*, 266; *Spencer Greys*, 266; *Union Guards*, 266; *Winchester Greys*, 266

Iron Brigade of the West, 6, 9-11, 26, 127, 257, 274(n), 291(n), 294(n), 300(n); early history, 5, 77; McClellan names the brigade, 11-12; Meredith assumes command, 12, 27; firing squad for Pvt. Woods, 13-16; the march north begins, 17; Chancellorsville campaign, 21, 29, 31, 34, 36-37; march to Pennsylvania, 39-40, 42-43, 48, 57; first brigade, first division, first corps, 42; arrives at Gettysburg, 50, 62-63, 67, 73, 81, 83, 92; opinion of Reynolds, 70; march from Marsh Creek, 76; McPherson's Ridge, 85, 96, 99, 101, 130-133, 135, 143, 147-148; first volley at Gettysburg, 94; capture of Archer, 102; arrives at Gettysburg, 103; Chambersburg Pike, 107; Railroad Cut, 124; Gen. Meredith wounded, 139; Robinson commands, 147; Lutheran Theological Seminary, 150; Iron Brigade completely wrecked, 153; retreat through Gettysburg, 155, 162; arrives on Cemetery Hill, 167; moves to Culp's Hill, 167, 168; Culp's Hill, July 1, 178, 179; Culp's Hill, July 2, 182; July 3, 188, 191; July 4, 196, 197-198; Culp's Hill, July 5, 201; departs Gettysburg, 202-203, 206; survivors belief in a turning point, 207; 167th Pennsylvania, 208-209; what to become of it? 208; greatest days behind it, 209; wholesale shuffling, 213; Meredith retires out, 214; post Gettysburg, 214, 218; reenlistments, 215; merged into Fifth Corps, 218; Grand Review, 219, 228; Wilderness, battle of, 223-224; Spotsylvania Court House, battle of, 224; Crater, battle of, 226; Boynton Plank Road, battle of, 227; Globe Tavern, battle of, 227; Hatcher's Run, battle of, 227; Weldon Railroad, battle of, 227; total casualties, 229; Gettysburg's long shadow, 231-235; losses at Gettysburg, 234; John Gibbon commands, 237; veterans return to the battlefield, 240, 243, 245; 1910 reunion, 251, 253-255; 1914 reunion, 256; last survivor, 256; monument at Gettysburg, 256; 1997 body found, 259; *photo*, 60, 64, 210

Iron Brigade Association, 245-247, 301(n), 274(n)

Iron Brigade Guard, 78, 102, 104-105, 107-110, 112, 124, 241, 287(n)-288(n), 298(n)-299(n)

Iverson, Gen. Alfred, 131

Ivey, Alexander, 241

Jackson, Maj. Gen. Thomas J. "Stonewall," 10, 18-20, 87, 101, 132

Jarmin, John R., 271

Jencks, George, 267

Johnson, Maj. Gen. Edward and his division, 183, 185, 187

Johnson, Pvt. John O., 116

Johnson, Robert B., 260

Johnson's Island Prison, Ohio, 285(n)

Jones, Pvt. Bodley, 277(n)-288(n)

Jones, Pvt. C.L., 286(n)

Jones, Cpl. Charles, 113

Jones, Pvt. Enoch, 123

Jones, Jesse E., 270

Joy, Asa, 270

Keeler, Pvt. Charles, *photo*, 9

Kellogg, Pvt. Charles, 35

Kellogg, Pvt. John, 120

Kelly, Pvt. Isaiah F., 123-124, 149, 167, 185

Kelly, Pvt. James, 113

Kenan, Col. Thomas S., 171

Kendlehart, Pvt. David, 130, 290(n)

Kern, Clara, 217

Kerr, Capt. Thomas, 32

Keyt, Pvt. George M., 122, 123

King, Pvt. Frank, 104, 112, 122-123

King, Gen. Rufus, 5, 7, 10, 74

Kingsley, S.R., 270

Kirby, Henry, 270

Kittie, Hiram D., 273

Knight, John W., 270

Knight, Oscar B., 246

Kocher, J. H., 269

Krebs, B. H., 268

Kress, John A., 190-192, 296(n)

Kyle, W. E., 272

Lamb, William A., 272

Lane, Gen. James H., 132, 300(n)

Lane, Col. John R. and his brigade, 132, 137-138, 147, 246, 248-251, 291(n)

Leavell, Capt. R.W., 122

Lee, Alexander F., 267

Lee, Gen. Robert E., 5, 18-20, 39, 42, 62-63, 78, 81, 99, 102, 128, 172, 175-176, 187, 190-191, 193, 197, 199, 204, 206-207, 213, 219, 223-225, 228, 297(n)

Lee, Sgt. Alexander, 99

Lefler, Pvt. Amos, 114, *photo*, 113

Legate, Pvt. George, 85, 177, 283(n)

Leonard, F. B., 269

Leonard, T. C., 270

Lewis, James R., 270

Lincoln, President Abraham, 1, 3, 14, 18, 26, 40, 49-51, 55, 70-71, 79, 121, 206, 214, 218-219, 229, 231, 239, 244

Lind, Pvt. Edward, 113, 268

Lineback, I.A., 271

Liscum, F.H., 268

Little Round Top, 183

Lockman, L.K., 267

Longhenry, Pvt. Ludolph, 295(n)

Longstreet, Lt. Gen. James, and his corps, 82, 183, 187, 190, 242

Lorenz, Lt. Joseph, 280(n)

Lorrie, Edward, 268

Lourman, W.A., 273

Love, William, 272

Ludwig, Pvt. Otto W., 98

Lutheran Theological Seminary, 102, 125, 150, 152, 157, 169, 171, 177, 181, 192, 233, 239-240

Lythson, Frederick, *photo*, 2

Macy, Capt. William W., 96, 138-139

Maher, Cpl. Jimmy, 189

Mahoney, Pvt. Patrick, 102

Maine Military Units, *2nd Battery*, 65, 81, 103, 105, 124; *5th Battery*, 148

Malcho, John, 271

Mallott, John B., 272

Malone, James, 272

Mangan, Sgt. Michael, 156, 198
Mansfield, Lt. Col. John, 214
Markel, E., 267
Marsh, H. C., 269
Marston, Pvt. Dick, 46-47
Marston, Capt. Joseph, 112, 119, 122, *photo*, 116
Marten, Lt. Benjamin T., 104
Martin, Alberta, 260
Martin, Edwin, 270
Martin, Ferdinand, 268
Martin, William, 260
Maynard, Charles E., 270
McAllister, Mary, 163-164, 203-204
McCain, John S., 271
McClellan, Gen. George B., 4-6, 10-12, 18-19, 24, 42, 70, 78-79, 211, 218-219
McConnell, Charles H., 234-235, 246, 270, 300(n)-301(n); returns to the battlefield, 243; veterans return to the battlefield, 246; plans another reunion, 247-249; 1903 Reunion, 250; 1910 reunion, 251-254, 256; monument at Gettysburg, 256; *photo*, 244, 248
McDermott, Sgt. Daniel, 152, 292(n)
McDonnell, George A., 271
McDowell, Gen. Irvin, 3-5, 18, 42
McGarrison, J., 272
McGill, A. D., 272
McInnis, John C., 272
McKinley, President William, 246
McKinney, Patterson, 270
McLean, Pvt. Jim, 113
McNeil, A. E., 272
McPhearson, David C., 271
McPherson's Ridge, 69, 83-98, 123-124, 127-128, 130-133, 135, 137-141, 143-144, 147, 149, 168, 175-176, 202, 233
Mead, Cpl. Charles W., 123-124, 286(n)
Meade, Maj. Gen. George G., 47-48, 70-71, 78, 82-83, 148, 183, 192-193, 199, 201-204, 206, 213, 218, 223
Meredith, Gen. Solomon, 26, 40, 67, 104-105, 124, 127, 235, 241, 300(n); promoted to command the brigade, 12; march to Pennsylvania, 44, 46-47; arrives at Gettysburg, 65; orders for Dawes, 103; wounded, 139, 176; leaves the brigade, 214; Gettysburg's long shadow, 232; death of, 255; *photo*, 27
Merssman, Isaac, 268
Metcalf, John T., 267
Michigan Military Units, *1st Cavalry*, 273; *3rd Infantry*, 273; *9th Infantry*, 272; *24th Infantry*, 25-26, 63, 71, 139, 163, 172-173, 180-181, 188, 196, 203, 208, 214, 216, 228, 247, 266, 278(n), 298(n)-299(n); Chancellorsville Campaign, 30-31, 33-34, 37; joins brigade, 41; formation of, 51; march to Pennsylvania, 59; weapons, 64; arrives at Gettysburg, 66; march from Marsh Creek, 76; nickname, 76; McPherson's Ridge, 96, 130-133, 135, 137, 47; Lutheran Theological Seminary, 152; retreat through Gettysburg, 157, 164; arrives on Cemetery Hill, 167; moves to Culp's Hill, 168; Culp's Hill July 1, 173, 176; July 3, 193; Morrow returns, 197; departs

Gettysburg, 202, 204; Wilderness, battle of, 223; color guard for burial of Abraham Lincoln, 226; color guard, 229; mustered out, 229; Gettysburg's long shadow, 232; losses at Gettysburg, 234-235; escorts Lincoln burial, 243-244; veterans return to the battlefield, 243-244, 246; reunion, 247-249; 1903 Reunion, 250; 1910 reunion, 251-254; monument at Gettysburg, 256; organization, 261; 50 Year Gettysburg Celebration, 270

Mickey, G. T., 271

Military Order of the Loyal Legion, 234

Miller, Pvt. Andy, 113

Miller, Charles A., 273

The Milwaukee Journal, 257

The Milwaukee Sunday Telegraph, 122, 275(n)

Milwaukee Soldiers Home, 251

Mississippi Military Units, *2nd Infantry*, 69, 89, 94, 107, 116, 118-124, 156, 158, 191, 197, 199, 217, 260; *10th Infantry*, 90; *42nd Infantry*, 89, 107

Mitchell, Sgt. John, 149, *photo*, 189

Mitchell, William, 273

Moore, Benjamin F., 269

Moore, Pvt. Charles, 278(n)

Moran, E.E., 268

Morrow, Col. Henry, 40, 197, 204, 214, 301(n); Chancellorsville Campaign, 34, 37; first commander of the 24th Michigan, 52; McPherson's Ridge, 131, 135, 141; Lutheran Theological Seminary, 152; wounded, 152, 173, 176, 163; chaos in town, 163-164, 172; meets Gen. Ewell, 172; prisoner, 180, 182, 193; left in Gettysburg, 203; leads brigade in Grand Review, 228; death of, 256; *photo*, 181

Morse, Albert C., 269

Morse, Pvt. William L., 284(n)

Morton, C., 268

Morton, Gov. Oliver, 5, 26

Moscrip, Edward, 267

"Mule train Charge," 146

Murphy, W. A., 121

Murphy, Cpl. W. B., 94, 116-117

Murray, W. H., 270

Myers, William, 273

Nately, Henry, 272

National Tribune, 175

Neff, Pvt. George F., 173, 180, 188, 192, 196

New Jersey Military Units, *23rd Infantry*, 272; *24th Infantry*, 273

New York Military Units, *1st Sharpshooters*, 209, 262; *7th Infantry*, 273; *8th Infantry*, 130; *13th Infantry*, 3, 273; *14th Brooklyn*, 11, 27, 30, 31, 107, 117, 120, 124, 185, 232, 287(n)-288(n); *20th Cavalry*, 278(n); *22nd Infantry*, 11; *23rd Infantry*, 261; *24th Infantry*, 11, 29, 274(n); *26th Infantry*, 273; *30th Infantry*, 11; *35th Infantry*, 261; *47th Infantry*, 273; *67th Infantry*, 272; *69th Infantry*, 3; *76th Infantry*, 27, 90, 107, 262; *79th Infantry*, 3; *84th Infantry*, 27; *91st Infantry*, 228, 262; *95th Infantry*, 27, 107, 112, 120, 124, 232, 287(n), 288(n); *120th Infantry*, 273; *121st Infantry*, 273; *147th Infantry*, 27, 107-108

New York Times, 209
Newton, Maj. Gen. John, 182, 213
Nickols, S. A., 267
Niles, Walter, 271
Nobels, Pvt. Frank, 279(n)
Nolett, John, 271
North Anna River, 225
North Carolina Military Units, *1st Infantry*, 272; *2nd Infantry*, 272; *4th Infantry*, 272; *11th Infantry*, 132, 138, 272; *22nd Infantry*, 272; *24th Infantry*, 272; *26th Infantry*, 138, 204, 234, 246, 271, 291(n); McPherson's Ridge, 132-133, 135, 137; Pickett's Charge, 191; veterans return to the battlefield, 243; reunion, 247-249; 1903 Reunion, 250; 1910 reunion, 252-253; monu ment at Gettysburg, 256; *43rd Infantry*, 171; *47th Infantry*, 132, 272; *50th Infantry*, 272; *52nd Infantry*, 132, 272; *55th Infantry*, 89, 107, 288(n)
Northup, J. E., 268
O'Connor, Pvt. Albert, 290(n)
O'Connor, Bert, 133, 143, 145
O'Connor, Col. Edgar, 89
Ohio Military, *73rd Infantry*, 162
Okey, Cpl. Cornelius, 114-115, 156
O'Neal, Gen. Edward A., 131
Otis, Maj. Cornelius, 78
Otis, George H., 267
Packard, George L., 270, 273
Palmer, James O., 271
Palmer, Pvt. William, 35, 217
Parker, Edward W., 269
Patrick, Gen. Marsena, 11
Pattee, John A., 253, 256, 270
Paxton, Miss Sallie, 198
Peach Orchard, 183

Peck, Color Sgt. Abel G., 96, 137
Pender, Gen. William D. and his division, 132, 291(n) 294(n)
Pennsylvania Military Units, *1st Light Artillery*, 148; *11th Infantry*, 148; *13th Cavalry*, 272-273; *54th Infantry*, 273; *56th Infantry*, 27, 90, 107, 123; *67th Infantry*, 270; *121st Infantry*, 130; *137th Infantry*, 273; *142nd Infantry*, 130; *143rd Infantry*, 130, 262; *147th Infantry*, 272-273; *149th Infantry*, 130, 262; *150th Infantry*, 130, 141, 262; *151st Infantry*, 130; *167th Infantry*, 208-209, 262, 296(n)
Pennsylvania Reserve Division, 70
Perkins, H. C., 269
Perrin, Gen. Abner and his brigade, 132, 147, 291(n), 294(n)
Perry, Allen A., 272
Petersburg, battle of, 226
Pettigrew, Frederick, 267
Pettigrew, Brig. Gen. James J., 81
Pettigrew's Brigade, 81, 128, 132, 139, 191, 234, 252-253, 271-272, 294(n)
Phelps, Oscar S., 270
Phillips, Cpl. David, 92, 138-139
Pickett, Maj. Gen. George E., 82, 190
Pickett's Charge, 191, 193, 238
Pierin, Dr. J.A., 272
Pischel, Frederick J., 268
Pisiny, Dr. J.A., 272
Pixley, Milley, 217
Pointon, Pvt. Mais, *photo*, 106
Poland, John W., 270
Polleys, Sgt. Thomas, 76, 112, 286(n)
Pope, Gen. John, 10, 18, 78
Port Hudson, siege of, 17
Powers, George L., 267
Preston, Surgeon A.W., 123, 289(n)

Proctor, John, 270
Pruyn, Howard F., 295(n)
Pugh, Elllis, 273
Purnett, Thomas, 271
Pursley, Lafayette, 268, 270
railroad cut at Gettysburg, 22, 108-110, 112, 114-126, 145, 148, 158, *photo*, 115
Rand, J. B., 267
Rand, T. B., 267
Randall, Gov. Alexander, 77, 210
Ransom's Brigade, 272
Ray, Pvt. William, 48, 96, 150, 152, 173, 180, 194-195, 197-198, 226
Reed, Pvt. Elisha, 90, 92, 98-99, 157, 192-193, 283(n)
Reed, William, 272
Reid, Whitelaw, 292(n)
Remington, Capt. William, 114, 117, 157, 159, 173, 295(n)
Reunion (1903), 247-250
Reunion (1910), 253-256; *photo*, 251, 252
Reunion (1914), 256
"Reunion and Banquet of The Iron Brigade," 246
Reynolds, Gen. John, 42, 47, 50, 70, 85, 92, 124-125, 128, 165, 213, 284(n); Chancellorsville, 29-30; march to Pennsylvania, 39; arrives at Gettysburg, 62, 65, 71; biography, 69, 71; death of, 69, 84, 94, 105, 107, 127, 133, 233; decision to fight at Gettysburg, 69, 82-83, 234; declines command of the army, 70; offers congratulations to Meade, 70; orders for Wadsworth, 81; arrives at Gettysburg, 82; considers Meade slow and hesitant, 82-83; *photo*, 69

Richardson, Lt. Hollon, 67-69, 138-139, 141, 150, 196, 229, 242, 269, *photo*, 255
Riley, William, 256, 302(n)
Rills, Charles, 271
Ripley, Horace, 269
Robinson, Col. William, 152, 211, 229, 297(n); Son-in-law, 67-69; McPherson's Ridge, 94, 96; commands the brigade, 139, 147, 214; returns to the battlefield, 241-242; death of, 255-256; *photo*, 241
Rockwell, Eli, 268
Rockwood, Frank B., 273
Rodes, Gen. Robert and his brigade, 130-131, 171, 185
Rogers, Lt. Clayton, 14-15, 40, 70, 105, 125, 145, 249-150, 165-167, 256, 281(n)-282(n), 289(n), 293(n), 301(n)
Rogers, Capt. Earl, 34, 40, 105, 113, 150, 289(n), 298(n)
Rolfe, Albert H., 268
Rood, Lt. Amos D., 48, 96, 139, 161, 202, 206, 269, 278(n)
Roosevelt, Theodore, 225
Rose, J. H., 272
Rosengarten, Lt. James, 291(n)
Rowley, Gen. Thomas, 131, 164-166, 293(n), 301(n)
Ruby, Cpl. Gabriel, 34, 277(n)
Russell, Washington, 269
Sage, Pvt. Milo G., 286(n)
Salisbury Prison, North Carolina, 276(n), 294(n)
Scales, Gen. Alfred M. and his brigade, 132, 147, 291(n), 294(n)
Schaeffer, Rev. Charles F., 177, 239
Schildt, Sgt. Henry, 114, 287(n)
Schlosser, Christian, 268
Schreiber, Pvt. Gottlieb, 113

Schunall, Daniel, 267
Scofbonrow, William H., 267
Scott, Gen. Winfield, 3
Scriven, Gen. George P., 273
Sedgwick, Maj. Gen. John, 29, 202
Selleck, W. Yates, 210-211, 239
Seminary Ridge, 92, 120, 150, 161, 168, 175, 188-189, 233
Service with the 6th Wisconsin Volunteers, 121
Seward, William, 3
Sharp, George W., 272
Shepard, Pvt. Adolphus, 278(n)
Shepherd, Lt. Henry C., 171
Sheridan, Gen. Philip, 228, 296(n)
Sherman, Gen. William T., 3
Showalter, Pvt. Levi, 78, 104
Sickles, Maj. Gen. Dan, 29, 62, 82
Siles, J. Q., 272
Simkins, Isaac P., 273
Sisters of Charity Catholic Convent, 284(n)
Small, Augela F., 273
Smead, Capt., 279(n)
Smith, C. S., 272
Smith, Sgt. Erastus, 110
Smith, Drum Maj. R. N., 78
Smith, S. F., 271
Smith, Steven D., 270
Smith, T. S., 273
Soldiers' National Cemetery, 260
"The Song of the Iron Brigade," 246
South Mountain, Battle of, 10-11, 15, 23, 71
Spitler, John M.F., 269
Spooner, Cyrus, 268
Spotsylvania Court House, battle of, 224
Stanton, Edwin M., 293(n)
Stedman, Pvt. Levi, 34, 49, 113, 277(n)

Steinwehr, Gen. Adolph von, 128
Stevens, Congressman Thaddeus, 129
Stevens, Lt. Col. George H., 279(n)
Stewart, 188
Stewart, Lt. James, 52, 54, 125, 127, 148-150, 163, 168, 177, 233, 279(n), *photo*, 53
Stoll, Rudolf, 267
Stone, J. M., 272
Stone, Gen. Roy, 131
Street, S. R., 272
Strong, Andrew, 273
Stuart, Maj. Gen. James E.B., 87
Sullivan, Pvt. James, 21, 23, 30, 32, 37, 46, 48, 65, 117, 119-120, 124, 156-157, 173, 179-180, 185-186, 188, 190-192, 195, 197-198, 227-228, 232, 255, 301(n), *photo*, 22
Sullivan, Pvt. Mickey, 109
Sutton, Pvt. George, 113
Sweet, Pvt. William, 113
Talty, Hugh, 156
Tarbox, Sgt. Albert E., 119, *photo*, 117
Tennessee Military Units, *1st Infantry*, 101; *7th Infantry*, 101; *14th Infantry*, 101
Thomas, Gen. Edward and his brigade, 132, 291(n)
Thompson, Pvt. Alfred, 113
Ticknor, Capt. John, 110, 295(n)
Tiffany Co., 135, 209-210, 239
Tongue, Pvt. Levi, 116, 179, 253, 300(n)
Topping, Lt. William O., 35
Townsend, Aldrich, 271
Townsend, Adjutant General E.D., 235
Trente, C. A., 271
Trumbull, Hoel, 32, 277(n)
Tunte, C. A., 271

United States Military Units, *1st Sharpshooters*, 300(n); *4th Artillery, Battery B*, 48, 52-55, 125-126, 152, 163, 167, 178, 271, 278(n)-279(n), 297(n); Gibbon commands, 7; march from Marsh Creek, 76; nickname, 76; early history, 127; railroad cut, 148; last to leave the field, 150; retreat through Gettysburg, 162; arrives on Cemetery Hill, 165; moves to Culp's Hill, 168; Culp's Hill July 1, 177; July 3, 188-189; Grand Review, 229; total casualties, 229; organization, 261; *5th Artillery*, 279(n); *21st Infantry*, 301(n); *125th Colored Troops*, 260

Upham, William H., 301(n)

Van Streenbergh, Charles, 273

Vance, Zebulon B., 132, 249, 300(n)

Vermont Military, *7th Infantry*, 273

"veteran volunteers," 215

Veteran Reserve Corps, 2, 113

Vicksburg, Mississippi, 17, 203, 206, 213, 218

Virginia Military Unit, 21st Infantry, 272

Waddell, Col. A.M., 246

Waddell, D.C., 272

Wadsworth, Gen. James, 7, 14, 25-26, 29, 65, 105, 107, 145, 149, 165, 190, 213, 282(n), 289(n), 296(n); Chancellorsville Campaign, 31, 35; march to Pennsylvania, 44, 46-47; arrives at Gettysburg, 62, 66, 81-83; railroad cut, 120, 124-125; McPherson's Ridge, 133, 143-144; retreat through Gettysburg, 156; Culp's Hill, 168; July 3, 192; death of, 224; *photo*, 36

Wagner, Cpl. Andrew, 193

Wainwright, Col. Charles, 50, 52, 70, 124-125, 163-164, 233

Waldschmidt, Julius, 269

Walker, Charles, 215

Walker, Philip H., 269

Walker, Pvt. Charles, 48

Wallar, Cpl. Frank, 114, 116-117, 123, 288(n)

Waller, Pvt. Sam, 34, 116-117

Walrod, John, 269

Walsh, George R., 270

Ward, Dr. Andrew J., 158, 162

Warren, Gen. Gouverneur K., 218, 223

Waterman, S.C., 269

Watrous, Jerome, 122, 199, 268, 275(n), 281(n)-282(n), 291(n), 297(n); McClellan names the brigade, 11; Ordnance Sgt., march to Pennsylvania, 49; march to Pennsylvania, 50; McPherson's Ridge, 133-134, 143, 145; chaos in town, 145-146; July 4, 197; Spotsylvania Court House, battle of, 225; 1910 reunion, 251, 253; *photo*, 144, 251

Webster, Noah N., 273

Weed, M.S., 270

Weldon Railroad, battle of, 227

Wells, Sidney, 268

Wheatfield, 183

Wheeler, Cpl. Cornelius, 85, 94, 177, *photo*, 84

White, David, 269

White, Edward, 272

White, I. N., 272

White, Pvt. Lyman, 104, 119

Whitmore, E., 269

Wilcox, Franklin, 268
Wilderness, the battle of the, 214, 221, 223-224
Wilkins, Frank, 267
Wilkins, Lucien, 267
Williams, Albert O., 271, 283(n)
Williams, George, 267
Williams, Pvt. Jared, 227
Williams, John J., 273
Williams, Sgt. Joseph, 85, 177
Williams, Col. Samuel J., 139, 214, 224, 256, 290(n)
Windsor, Pvt. Arland F., 286(n)
Winslow, Loring B.T., 268
Wisconsin Military Units, *1st Infantry*, 73, 87; *2nd Infantry*, 2, 5, 7, 11, 26, 54, 71, 84, 88-89, 92, 104, 139, 158, 162-163, 175, 177, 204, 207-208, 211, 214, 228-229, 237, 279(n), 284(n)-285, 298(n)-301(n); 2nd arrives in Wash. D.C., 1, 3; Bull Run, First Battle of, 4, 274(n); Chancellorsville Campaign, 31, 32, 37; weapons, 65; arrives at Gettysburg, 66, 73, 90; death of Reynolds, 69; march from Marsh Creek, 76, 78; nickname, 76; plunges into the fight, 85; first volley at Gettysburg, 94; McPherson's Ridge, 96-98, 101, 130, 137, 147; capture of Archer, 102; railroad cut, 124-125; retreat through Gettysburg, 157; Culp's Hill, July 1, 168, 176-177; July 3, 192; departs Gettysburg, 203; does not Veteran Reserve Corps, 216; Wilderness, battle of, 223; Spotsylvania Court House, battle of, 224; mustered out, 226; Gettysburg's long shadow, 232; losses at Gettysburg, 234-235; 1910 reunion, 255; organization, 261-262; 50 Year Gettysburg Celebration, 267; *photo*, 74; *3rd Infantry*, 300(n); *4th Infantry*, 49; *5th Infantry*, 4-5, 77, 300(n); *6th Infantry*, 5, 7-9, 11, 14, 18, 23-27, 29, 42, 44, 48-49, 54, 58, 61, 106, 109, 113, 122, 144, 148, 173, 180, 182, 185-186, 188, 197-198, 209, 214, 217-218, 223, 226-228, 275(n), 277(n), 281(n)-282(n), 286(n)-287(n), 297(n)-301(n); arrives in Wash. D.C., 4; Chancellorsville Campaign, 21, 30-32, 35, 37, 59; railroad cut, 22, 108, 110, 112, 117, 119-121, 124; march to Pennsylvania, 43, 46; weapons, 64-65; arrives on field, 66, 102-105, 165, 167; early history, 73, 77; nickname, 74, 76; march from Marsh Creek, 76-78; Lysander Cutler commands, 90; Chambersburg Pike, 107; McPherson's Ridge, 149; last to leave the field, 150; retreat through Gettysburg, 156, 158, 161-162; moves to Culp's Hill, 167-168; July 1, 176; Culp's Hill, July 1, 179; July 4, 195; Veteran Reserve Corps, 216; Grant reviews, 219; members from Indian tribes, 221; Wilderness, battle of, 221; mustered out, 229; Gettysburg's long shadow, 232; losses at Gettysburg, 235; veterans return to the battlefield, 246; 1910 reunion, 251, 253, 255; last survivor, 256; organization, 261, 264; 50 Year Gettysburg Celebration, 268; *7th Infantry*, 8, 12, 26, 48, 54, 67-68,

94, 96, 104, 133, 139, 152, 163, 172, 196-197, 202, 208, 214, 218, 226-228, 256, 274(n)-275(n), 279(n), 281(n), 284(n), 291(n)-292(n), 295(n), 298(n)-300(n); assigned to the brigade, 5; Chancellorsville Campaign, 35, 37; weapons, 65; arrives at Gettysburg, 66; nickname, 74, 76; march from Marsh Creek, 76; McPherson's Ridge, 96, 130-131, 137, 141; Callis commands, 147; Lutheran Theological Seminary, 150; Culp's Hill, July 1, 153; retreat through Gettysburg, 161; moves to Culp's Hill, 168; July 1, 173; Culp's Hill, July 1, 176; July 3, 194; July 4, 195; departs Gettysburg, 206; Veteran Reserve Corps, 215-216; Wilderness, battle of, 221, 223; Spotsylvania Court House, battle of, 224; mustered out, 229; Gettysburg's long shadow, 232; losses at Gettysburg, 235; veterans return to the battlefield, 241-242; 1910 reunion, 253, 255; organization, 261, 265; 50 Year Gettysburg Celebration, 269; *photo*, 76; *26th Infantry*, 300(n); *29th Infantry*, 272; *36th Infantry*, 238, 240; *49th Infantry*, 300(n); *Anderson Guards*, 34, 264; *Badger Rifles*, 265; *Badger State Guards*, 265; *Belle City Rifles*, 263; *Beloit Star Rifles*, 264; *Bragg's Rifles*, 113, 264; *Buffalo County Rifles*, 264; *Citizen Guard*, 263; *Citizens' Corps*, 264; *Columbia County Cadets*, 265; *Grand Rapids Union Guards*, 265; *Grant County Grays*, 263; *Janesville Volunteers*, 263; *La Crosse Light Guard*, 263; *Lancaster Union Guards*, 265; *Lemonweir Minute Men*, 22-23, 30, 61, 109, 232, 264, 277(n); *Lodi Guards*, 68, 265; *Marquette County Sharp Shooters*, 265; *Miner's Guards*, 263; *Montgomery Guards*, 264; *Northwestern Tigers*, 265; *Oshkosh Volunteers*, 263; *Platteville Guards*, 265; *Portage City Guards*, 263; *Prairie du Chien Volunteers*, 264; *Prescott Guards*, 9, 264; *Randall Guards*, 263; *Sauk County Riflemen*, 106, 217, 264; *Stoughton Light Guard*, 265; *Wisconsin Independent Battalion*, 261; *Wisconsin Rifles*, 263

Wisconsin Veterans Museum, 210, 281(n), 286(n), 292(n), 296(n)

Withrow, Alfred R., 268

Wolfe, Esaac, 273

Wood, A. J., 269-270

Wood, Cpl Andrew, 96, 105

Woods, Pvt. James, 13-15, 273

Woodward, G. M., 268

Wooter, J. W., 272

Wright, Sgt. Philander, 97-98, 267, 284(n)

About the Author

Award-winning journalist Lance J. Herdegen is the former director of the Institute of Civil War Studies at Carroll University. He previously worked as a reporter and editor for United Press International (UPI) news service covering national politics and civil rights. He currently serves as the historical consultant for the Civil War Museum of the Upper Middle West.

Lance is widely regarded as the leading authority on the Iron Brigade. He is the author of many articles, and his books include *Four Years with the Iron Brigade: The Civil War Journal of William R. Ray, Seventh Wisconsin Volunteers*; *The Men Stood Like Iron: How the Iron Brigade Won its Name*, and *In the Bloody Railroad Cut at Gettysburg*.